Listen to Me

Novelist and short-story writer, Shashi Deshpande has eleven novels, two crime novellas, a number of short-story collections, a book of essays, and four children's books to her credit. Three of her novels have received awards, including the Sahitya Akademi award for *That Long Silence*. Her latest novels are *Shadow Play* and *Strangers to Ourselves*. She has translated works from Kannada and Marathi into English, and her own work has been translated into various Indian and European languages.

Shashi Deshpande has participated in literary conferences and festivals, as well as lectured in universities, both in India and abroad.

She was awarded the Padma Shri in 2009.

Listen to Me

Shashi Deshpande

cntxt

First published in hardback by Context, an imprint of Westland Publications Private Limited, in 2018

Published in paperback by Context, an imprint of Westland Books, a division of Nasadiya Technologies Private Limited, in 2023

No. 269/2B, First Floor, 'Irai Arul', Vimalraj Street, Nethaji Nagar, Alapakkam Main Road, Maduravoyal, Chennai 600095

Westland, the Westland logo, Context and the Context logo are the trademarks of Nasadiya Technologies Private Limited, or its affiliates.

Shashi Deshpande asserts the moral right to be identified as the author of this work.

Copyright © Shashi Deshpande, 2018

ISBN: 9789357764766

10 9 8 7 6 5 4 3 2 1

The views and opinions expressed in this work are the author's own and the facts are as reported by them, and the publisher is in no way liable for the same.

All rights reserved

Typeset by R. Ajith Kumar
Printed at Saurabh Printers Pvt. Ltd.

No part of this book may be reproduced, or stored in a retrieval system, or transmitted in any form or by any means, electronic, mechanical, photocopying, recording, or otherwise, without express written permission of the publisher.

For Nandu, our dear son,
who left us with the same haste with which he did everything in his life

From listening to the stories of others, we learn to tell our own.
Margaret Atwood, *Curious Pursuits – Occasional Writing*

Contents

Prelude	1
Childhood	11
Schooling	30
Growing Up	61
Those Were the Days …	88
Apprenticeship	118
A Balancing Act	139
Making Sense of Life	161
Where Do We Belong?	185
The Private and the Public	202
Learning to Be 'An Author'	219
'A Damned Mob of Scribbling Women'	245
Inter Alia	270
Confrontations	306
Being Part of a Community	320
The Requisite Ending	347

Prelude

The biography is a novel that dare not speak its name.
Roland Barthes

WRITING ABOUT ONESELF IS a disease of our times, rampant among politicians, retired bureaucrats and army officers, movie stars, and business magnates – in fact, anyone who has, at some time, felt the touch of fame, even if only for a short while. It doesn't really matter whether the person can write. All that publishers need is the name and the material; ghostwriters will write the book and editors will do the rest. There is nothing surprising about this. What is surprising is that writers, to whom writing comes with ease, do not seem eager to write about themselves. For obvious reasons, there are more biographies of authors than autobiographies. I sometimes think Jane Austen would be staggered to find the number of books written about her – and hers was, seemingly, such an uneventful life. She, like most women writers of the time, shunned the public gaze, and to make sure that her life remained protected from it, her sister Cassandra tore up a great many of her own letters to Jane after her death. In spite of this, books continue to be written about her. Elizabeth

Gaskell, another reclusive author, who wrote *The Life of Charlotte Brontë*, cannily left instructions for her own correspondence to be destroyed. Yet, there are biographies about her as well. The few autobiographies of writers I have recently read invariably carry a disclaimer. P.D. James, for example, calls her book, *Time to Be in Earnest,* 'a partial autobiography' – recording just one year of her life. Penelope Lively begins her book, *Dancing Fish and Ammonites*, with a statement that it is not an autobiography, but rather 'a view from old age'. The first sentence in Somerset Maugham's *The Summing Up* is: 'This is not an autobiography nor is it a book of recollections.' In *Over Seventy*, P. G. Wodehouse says, 'It would be laughable for me to attempt a formal biography,' and then goes on to write a delightfully informal one.

One of the reasons for the comparative paucity of autobiographies by authors may be that when they are young, there is not much to write about and when they are at the peak of their careers, there is no time to write about themselves. And later, the diffidence of age sets in, the problem of memory becomes acute. Will I be able to remember what I did and when I did it and why? I have never carried a notebook around like some writers do, never jotted down notes with the thought that I would use these some day when I would write about my life. An idea far from my mind for many reasons (and yet, here I am). Nor have I kept a diary. (P.D. James thinks 'a diary intended for publication the most egotistical form of writing'.)

I did keep a diary when I was a young girl, a book in which I poured out my feelings and emotions – all the exaggerated, almost hysterical emotions of an adolescent. It was discovered by my brother and, with the cruelty of brothers, he read it aloud. Even now I cringe when I think of that moment, of the sight of the tattered notebook in his hands, of how hideously foolish my outpourings sounded. With an adolescent's morbid sensitivity, I wanted to die then and there. I have never kept a personal diary since. Memory, however poor it is, has always been my only resource.

My father, a writer himself, in his curiously, and I think cunningly titled book, *A Writer's Self Analysis*, has written very little about his personal life, except for some delightful stuff about his childhood days. In fact, the epigraph to the book provides a very cynical view of an autobiography. It is a quote from an obscure writer, Nicolas Berdyaev, which says that, in an autobiography, 'beneath a crust of modesty and forthrightness, there is a thick layer of vainglory, even of sentimentality'. Writers of autobiographies are, in other words, incapable of being honest; they are neither modest nor forthright. As a matter of fact, fiction writers write fiction so that, like actors, they can wear masks and disguises, so that they can hide their own selves behind other people, behind the characters they invent.

In any case, it is risky to write about oneself. It is not as painless as lying on a psychiatrist's couch and talking about oneself. (Or, the way it is today, with the psychiatrist looking at her/his watch, making sure you get out at the end of your fifteen minutes.) There are innumerable hazards in writing about oneself. It is more like a mental and emotional striptease. Will we be able to admit to the demon of envy which haunts all writers; in fact, all artistes? Will we be able to admit to our unseemly desires which, often, we cannot admit even to ourselves? (And I am not talking of sex here.) Will we be able to speak of foolish ambitions, admit to moments of cravenness and hypocrisy? And is it courageous to talk about these things, or is it foolhardy? Above all, will anyone be interested? Camus is right when he says, 'We all carry within us our places of exile, our crimes and our ravages. But our task is not to unleash them on the world: it is to fight them in ourselves and the others.'

There's also the truth which writers know well: there can be no self-indulgence in writing. You have to be hard on yourself, harder than you would be on others. The discipline, the rigour, the integrity that writing demands, emphatically rejects self-indulgence. Just as there is no room for love of oneself, love of your own words is also taboo. Writing demands honesty, it asks for ruthless self-criticism. And yet, while it may be cathartic to be open about yourself, it is also dangerous, because we live by some of our beliefs about ourselves. One of my earliest literary memories is of a passage from the *Katha Upanishad*, part of our Sanskrit text in my last year of school. This is the story of Uddalaka Aruni and his son Svetaketu, an arrogant young man of twenty-four, who had read the Vedas and thought himself very learned. This is how the story goes:

Svetaketu's father said to him, 'Listen to me, I will give you that instruction by which the unheard becomes heard, the unseen becomes the seen and the unknown becomes known.'

'Please instruct me,' the chastened boy replied.

And so it begins, one of the most famous dialogues in the Upanishads.

'Get me the fruit of the nyagrodha tree,' the father tells the son.

'Here it is.'

'Cut it,' the father commands.

'I have cut it.'

'What do you see?'

'I see a seed.'

'Break the seed.'

'I have done it.'

'What do you see?'

'Nothing.'

'That which you cannot see, that is the essence of the nyagrodha tree. The essence you cannot see is the self. That is what you are, Svetaketu.'

And so it goes on, question and answer, with innumerable examples, each one ending with *Tat satyam, sa atma, tat tvam asi*

Svetaketu. That is the truth, that is the self, that is what you are, Svetaketu.

Indeed, a search for 'Who am I?' on a cosmic scale. But this kind of search for the self is not for us ordinary humans, it is only for philosophers. For most of us, it is simpler. There is the self we want to present to the world, the self we *knowingly* present to the world, and there is the self hiding inside. And there is the constant conflict between them. Which one will win, which one will emerge? Even if we decide on a policy of honesty, there is no doubt that we can't help but see our younger selves with a kind of tenderness which colours our vision of that self; we can't help but see the past through a haze of nostalgia, which covers the blots, the warts. And we approach our later years with caution, because we know we may stumble over things we would rather not remember. For who knows what we did in our years of struggle, during times of intense love and hate, in moments of rage and despair?

So, why write about oneself, why revisit the past? Why exhume memories we have laid to rest, specially since we have learnt to live comfortably with the fact that they lie underground in an unmarked grave? And don't we know that memory, the tool with which we hope to capture Time, is such a flawed tool? Memory is famously capricious, unreliable and selective. How is it that I can remember very little of that most momentous event in most human lives, my own wedding? There are no photographs to jog my memory, no, not a single one, not even an amateur's attempts. I know it was not a time of professional photographers and videographers, but what were my parents doing, what were friends there for, why did no one take even a single picture? Whatever the reason, the fact is that there is not one picture of the wedding.

Whereas, I have a very lucid memory of a time just before the wedding. I was in Pune where the wedding was to take place, sleeping on the balcony of my long-dead grandfather's room, two younger cousins sleeping on either side of me. A song floated in from somewhere, a popular film song of the time, a tender pleading song full of the poignance of love. The words were the usual clichéd ones of film songs, but they, and the tune, filled me with some emotion I could not identify, an emotion that had nothing to do with my soon-to-happen wedding, nor with the man I was going to marry. It was an emotion that was detached from me and my life, and yet entered into me and pierced me to the heart. Yes, I remember this so well, but very little remains of my wedding.

Memories are indeed unreliable, notoriously unreliable. An even earlier memory is of my sister and I being taken on a bicycle to school. Just before we got to our school, we were stopped by a policeman and I, convinced that we had done something wrong, that three on a bicycle was an offence, and that we would be punished, began to howl. There's something wrong with this memory. I must have been four or five then, having just started school. How did I know that three on a bicycle was an offence? Did I know what an offence meant at all? And why was there a policeman on the road, for, in our town, there was almost no traffic in those days? But if this memory is not true, how is it that it is so vivid in my mind?

Memories are even more tricky where writers are concerned. When asked by the editor of a magazine to write a story that centred around Independence Day, I wrote about the first Independence Day, of a family setting out at midnight to attend the flag hoisting, of the torrent of rain that poured down, and how the horse of their tonga was frightened and how desperate they were, because the child-narrator's father had to be on time to give a speech. This came from my own memory of the first Independence Day, of our going to the Collector's Bungalow at midnight to see the flag hoisting. But was it raining then? Was the horse really scared? And the tongue-clicking encouragement of the tongawala to the horse, the rattle of the wooden handle of his whip against the spokes of the wheel – were these real? Or had I created them? I cannot now disentangle the two – my memory and my creation. It is as if what I wrote took over the event and erased whatever memory there was. Memories are not always preserved with the same fidelity as a fly in amber; they are fluid, changeable, subject to various factors.

Nevertheless, to write about oneself is part of the human desire to surmount death, to go on surviving. It is to leave a kind of 'I was here' mark, like drawings in caves, writings on rocks, scrawls of hearts and arrows on trees drawn by lovers, scratched lines in prison cells etched by prisoners. Without these marks, without the writing, the past becomes a blank, our lives erased as if they have never been. Perhaps it is also an attempt to make sense of a life that eludes understanding while we are living it. I am amazed today when I look at the shelves earmarked for my own books, shelves from which books are now overflowing on to other shelves, into other cupboards. How did I – a lazy, ambitionless girl, content to drift, wanting nothing so much as to be left to myself – work so hard for the last forty and more years, and produce all these books?

And there's something more. I know that my life has been so uneventful that, even if I were to write of all the events in my life, a few pages would suffice. So, why does anyone need an account of such an uneventful life? Perhaps, because no story stands on its own, no more than the life of any individual, however solitary, can be separate and discrete from the lives of other human beings. My life began when the world was on the cusp of change, when it was on the brink of the Second World War. The end of the war signalled the end of colonisation, with colonies falling throughout the world like houses of cards, followed by the spread of democracy. India was a part of these great changes, in fact it led the world in the change from colonialism to democracy. Since then, the world has been changing so rapidly, it has left us breathless; globalisation and swift technological changes have revolutionised our lives. And these have been, too, years of great cruelty, of wars, of mass migrations, both for economic reasons and conflict, years of hatred and genocide. At the same time, it has been an era when suppressed people everywhere have risen up in protest, affirming their right to live as a free people, with dignity. The stories of our times have emerged from all of these events, as well as from other local and minor happenings. I have been a witness to some of these things, the events have been the background to my life.

However, there is one story of oppression which has not been taken note of, and which has been considered, when acknowledged, as insignificant, something happening on the sidelines. Any opposition to this oppression has been regarded as a joke, if not an irritant, never as a serious movement. Yet, it has been the most successful oppression in history, one which has endured through the ages, throughout the world, a story which is not yet over. It is one of the strangest stories of oppression, in which the oppressor and the oppressed have lived together in seeming amity, in which the oppressed have been wholly complicit in their own oppression, almost typifying the Stockholm syndrome.

It is an oppression sanctified by all religions, continued by tradition, perpetuated and blessed by myth and customs, justified by pseudo-scientific arguments and, finally, validated and enforced by the law. It is a story buried in darkness and cloaked in silence. Yet, like all suppressed human stories, it erupted into oral tales, songs, myths and legends. In my lifetime I have seen this story come out into the open, I have witnessed the slow awakening of one half of the human race, I have seen this struggle slowly achieve a legitimacy and get identified for what it is – the struggle of an oppressed people. This struggle, the struggle of women to be considered equal human beings, is a part of my story. Or rather, I am a part of it, as an insider, an observer and above all, as a raconteur.

There is another thing in my life that has lifted it out of the mundane and has illuminated it. 'There must be some passion in life; otherwise life becomes humdrum.' I think these are Max Müller's words, though I have never been able to verify this. It is just such a passion that made sure my life was never dull, at least not to me. It is a passion for words, for language, for stories, for reading and, much later, for writing, which transformed my life. It began very early in life; in fact, I cannot remember a time when it was not part of me. Once again I find a memory, a very clear and vivid memory. I am standing with one foot on a rickety wooden revolving gate, a moment that is, for some reason that I just cannot understand, entwined with what I think is the earliest book I read. I have no idea where I got the book from, but I remember its title, *The Rambles of Three Children*. (Another of the miracles of memory, for often I cannot remember the title of a book I read last week.) It was, as is obvious, a book about three children roaming in the English countryside. Why it has stayed with me over the years, I have no idea. But I can even remember the names of two of the children, Elsie and Toby. And the other girl… Was she Nell? Possibly she was. If my memory has not misled me, it was with this book that it began, my life among books, first as a reader, then as a reader and writer.

I believe that if stories are born from individual memories, collective memories create history. 'Narratives define civilisations.' Toni Morrison's words. Indeed they do. I was born before India's independence, I was a girl during the first decade of euphoria in our country after independence. I witnessed the Nehruvian years of socialism, of a struggle to create a country out of disparate elements. These were, nevertheless, years of optimism. Later, there came the beginning of corruption, the threat of tyranny, of war and times of hardship. And in recent times, there has been a fear of the failure of the kind of democracy our Constitution-makers had envisaged. All of these things have gone into my novels, not directly narrated, for I am a writer of fiction, but as the background to the lives of my characters. Or, rather, the times have emerged through the lives of my characters. Without the context of those times, my characters' lives would remain incomplete.

So, too, my journey as a writer is meaningless unless it is seen in the context of the literature of which my writing is a part. This literature is Indian Writing in English (IWE). We have travelled together, this literature and I, through the years, though its journey has been far more dramatic than mine. Something in the story of IWE appeals to my fondness for drama, for surprises, for sudden twists and turns. And there are similarities in our stories, too, because both of us fought battles for our existence, for legitimacy, both of us struggled to get an identity and to shake off one that was ill-fitting. But while the journey of IWE has been one of early mediocrity, of later success and achievement, mine has been one of discoveries and revelations of myself and my world.

I know I cannot tell the story of IWE as it deserves to be told; I am not learned or knowledgeable enough. I can only tell the story as far as it touched mine. I can speak of the problems I had accepting that I was part of this literature. Of the problems it had accepting me. Of my hurt when it seemed to exclude me. And of how, later, I found to my surprise that I was a part of it. Yet, even though an insider, I was still an alien. *An alien insider.* A phrase used by one of the founding fathers of IWE, Prof. P. Lal; one that fits me to a T. This, then, is the story of an alien insider. A story I never expected I would write, because I don't enjoy the thought of writing about my personal life, but one which for some reason, I seem impelled to write. Perhaps, like all my other books, the reason for the writing of it will emerge in the course of writing. And perhaps, it strikes me now, this book is being written for the same reason that all my other books were written: because it asks to be written.

Childhood

I have had playmates, I have had companions,
In my days of childhood, in my joyful school-days.
Charles Lamb, *The Old Familiar Faces*

There is a possibility, a very strong possibility, that this is an apocryphal story. Even if it is, it has, through the course of the years, acquired a veneer of the truth; to my mind, at least, it carries a ring of the truth. The story is about an Englishman laying the foundation stone for a college in a small town in what was then called Bombay Presidency. The date? I will leave it vague. A writer whom I much admire, and who at the age of thirteen wrote a history of England in five chapters, declared at the very start of her book, 'There shall be few dates in this history.' Like her, I will have very few dates in this account, mainly because I am in general very unclear about dates.

This incident that I am going to speak of, for example – could it have happened sometime during the early part of the twentieth century? Or earlier? Well, best to leave it alone and get on with the story. The Englishman was giving a speech before getting down to the business of laying the foundation stone, which is when it happened. The writer I earlier mentioned says in the course of her history of England that 'the recital of any Events (except what I make myself) is uninteresting to me'. Like Jane Austen (yes, she is the writer I am speaking of), I am very happy to invent events, specially when there is no record of what really happened. And, therefore, I imagine that the Englishman's speech was a song in praise of the English who brought education to India, or possibly it was in praise of certain specific educationists.

The site chosen for building this college was on top of a hill, giving a bird's eye view of the town which lay before it. A town of undulating land, with many dips and rises. Earlier, this region had been a thick jungle, populated, it was said, with tigers. I am sure there was still a dense coverage of trees at the time I am writing about, so that not much of the town was visible. There was, however, one building which rose high among the trees, a large building of red stone, with a clock tower which loomed majestically above the surrounding areas. It was this building which caught the Englishman's eye while he was speaking. A Eureka moment for him, I imagine. He stopped in mid-sentence (I am still inventing), the trowel with which he was going to spread the cement, or whatever they did to lay a stone in those days, falling out of his hands. And, turning to his audience, or perhaps to the dignitaries on the dais with him, he asked, 'Why don't you make *that* your college?'

The Englishman must have been an influential officer, a *bada sahib*, for it did happen the way he had suggested. And the headquarters of the railways (which is what the building with the clock tower was) became Karnatak College. The foundation stone laid by the Englishman was abandoned and soon covered with creepers and bushes, until many years later, when Dr Radhakrishnan, then President of India, laid the foundation stone for a university in the place where the college was to have been. I was there on that day, one of the volunteers who had built a road from the college to this university-to-be site, much before the university became a reality.

To go back – for decades, Karnatak College was the only college in the region, with students coming from all over Karnataka, even places as far away as Karwar, and Goa, which, then being a Portuguese colony, had no English education. The original building soon became a large sprawl, with different departments, laboratories, hostels for students and houses for the staff being added. All the land around the original building, and even some land at a distance which belonged to the railways, became part of the college. Acquiring land must have been easy then; nobody could put a spoke in the British royal wheel.

Adjacent to the original building were two large Colonial style bungalows with pillared porches, houses for the Principal and the Vice-Principal of the college. There were homes for the other teaching staff, a few just outside the back gate, others some way off, on the way to the railway station, next to which were the boys' and the girls' hostels. There was one more house standing a little apart, in solitary splendour, not with the imposing dignity of the Principal's, or the Vice Principal's bungalows, yet with a larger compound than many others. It had, what may be called, a homely charm. Or perhaps it seems so to me because it was where we lived for some years. My father taught Sanskrit in the college, he must have been senior enough then to merit getting this bungalow. In family parlance, this house was called the 'college bungla'.

Our stay in this house was not very long, four or five years perhaps, but for some reason it became a very important landmark of my childhood. We changed many houses in those early years, but this one house I can remember in minute and vivid detail. The covered porch, slightly elevated above the ground, as all houses built by the British were (fear of snakes, perhaps), the stone floor of which was cool in summer so that we spent much time there. The main door led to a long, narrow strip of a hall in which there was a hat stand, something that was common then, very obviously meant to hang hats on (not only our father's solar topi, but also ours, for we children too wore them in the monsoon), and to keep umbrellas; there was a removable metal base to collect water from dripping umbrellas. The hall was divided by an asbestos partition, so that one-third of the hall became a study for my sister and me. It had a writing table, with chairs on either side; our school bags, our books, all the clutter that schoolchildren own and create, stayed in this room. An abiding memory of this room is not of studies, but of a day when my sister, hanging over the partition, which did not go up to the ceiling, silently watched me enact a role from a film we had seen just the day before. And when I slowly raised my head from the table, as the heroine had done, she burst into loud rude laughter. Why do we remember moments of embarrassment and foolishness so well, but forget better ones?

The hall led into the living room, chairs ranged along the wall as was the custom then. Also, perhaps, part of those times were the two large pictures of my parents on the wall, leaning towards each other, 'like two bulls getting ready to fight' – my father's words, which come back to me from some secret store as I write. On one side of the living room was the dining area, of which my most embarrassing memory is of having internal conversations, while I was eating, with a friend called (hold your breaths, you post-Colonials) Henry. Why Henry? Was I reading a book then with a character called Henry? Or maybe it came from our arithmetic lessons where we solved problems, like, John had ten apples, he gave two to David, three to Henry and so on. Wherever Henry came from, I am grateful that when I began writing, I left Henry where he belonged, in the books I read.

On the other side of the living room was the children's bedroom, our bedroom, our room, rather, for many other activities took place there, apart from sleeping. This was the largest room in the house, and very versatile too, for here my mother had her sewing machine, here we played cards and carom and other indoor games, and here, incredible memory, we performed plays, with a sari hung on a string, acting as a curtain. Our 'green room' was the store room, where we wet some red tissue paper and rubbed it on our lips and cheeks. I have a very clear memory of my sister, a friend and I acting a small bit about King Cophetua and the beggar-maid to an audience of three: my parents and a visiting friend of my father's. I remember that our friend, who played the role of the beggar-maid, kept forgetting her lines and I kept prompting her. And my father's friend exclaimed, 'It knows everything!' ('It' was me; in Kannada, children often had no gender.)

I can also remember we enacted a scene from *Pygmalion*. Those who don't believe me are free to be sceptical, for I am incredulous myself. *Pygmalion*? At that age? On the other hand, I can so clearly see the three of us, my sister, our friend and I, sitting on the broad window sill, acting the scene of the tea party in Mrs Higgins' house. Equally incredible is the memory of my sister, brother and I acting the grave-diggers' scene from *Hamlet*. A stronger memory, this one. And, a pleasing part of this memory is that while my sister and brother squabbled to be Hamlet, I was happy to take on any role. Even the grave-digger's role would do. Rare moments of altruism. And, perhaps, this entire memory is nothing but a chimera.

Our room led to my parents' room, which had a beautiful four-poster bed of ebony, with a matching dressing table. A writing table, part of the same set, was in my father's study next door. A small room, this study, with just enough space for the large baize-covered table, two chairs and a bookcase. All this furniture had been gifted to my father by his father-in-law, our grandfather. A small brass label declared that all of it came from the Army and

Navy Stores, Bombay. Bombay was only a name to us then, and we had no clue as to what the Army and Navy Stores was, but we were impressed by, and proud of these pieces. The study was perhaps the room where the 'thunder boxes' had been placed in the time of the sahibs; the lower level of the room, and the door leading outside, were strong pointers to such a possibility.

Someone, at some time, had planted a bed of mogras just outside the side door. I don't remember that we had such a thing as a proper garden, but there were these mogra bushes at the side of the house and some rose bushes in the front. My mother picked the petals of these fragrant roses and made what was called gulkand. One of the treasures in this garden were the two rows of nondescript bushes lining the pathway to the front door, which we discovered were – oh joy! – mehndi bushes.

Mehndi application became a regular feature of our life after that, as often as our mother would allow. We plucked as many leaves as we could, which were then ground to a fine paste, and after dinner, the paste was applied to our hands, rather, our fingernails and palms. A blob for each fingernail and a larger blob in the centre of the palm. We made a fist of our hands so that they could be tied up with a piece of cloth. We happily went to bed with these 'bandaged' hands, longing to wake up and see the effect in the morning. There they were, pale red nails and a squiggly untidy circle in the centre. But we were ecstatic. I see the intricate mehndi designs they now make with a pipette, so artistic and such varied and wonderful patterns. But I think our poor blobs gave us just as much pleasure as these professional mehndi designs give today, perhaps more.

I can remember taking a step from this towards sophistication, when we made our first acquaintance with nail polish, which was then known as Cutex. We'd been deposited in the home of a family friend, when we were to go on a school excursion. The train was at midnight and this house was next door to the railway station. When our parents left us with the family and went away, there was still much time before our train arrived. So, the daughter of our host offered to apply nail polish on our nails. I can remember our delight, our joy. I wouldn't be surprised if we felt suddenly beautiful. What is it with little girls?

This home, the college bungla, was the place where I began reading. I can remember a book, titled *The World's Greatest Books*, which was a treasure chest for me. The beautiful pictures in it dazzled me, they are still in my mind. A painting of the Blessed Damozel – I didn't know what these words meant, yet the line that accompanied the picture has not left me: 'The Blessed Damozel lean'd over the gold bar of Heaven.' A painting of Chatterton, the boy genius, dying in his attic, half fallen from the sofa, his body partly on the ground. Ophelia floating in the water, her face perfectly serene, her eyes unseeing, arms on both sides, palms open, her body surrounded by flowers. Another picture I remember is that of Rizzio, secretary to Mary, Queen of Scots, clinging to Mary's skirts, while he is being stabbed by a crowd of men.

I learnt later that Ophelia had been painted by John Everett Millais, and that his model, Elizabeth Siddal, later married Dante Gabriel Rossetti, the painter and the poet of *The Blessed Damozel*. All this fascinating information waiting for me, this world of writers and painters, waiting to be entered. At that time, as a child, I only knew that I loved the paintings, that they made a great impact on me, that nothing could equal the pleasure I had in that book. It was here, in this house, that I got my first book, a book I won as a prize for a competition held for children by the *Illustrated Weekly of India*. Titled *Pedro Picks Coffee in Brazil*, it too had wonderful pictures. I remember how I loved the deep brown of Pedro's face, the same colour as the coffee seeds. In this house I read *Arabian Nights*, *Alice in Wonderland* and yes, I think *Treasure Island* as well, all of which took me to distant lands, away from home.

All the books that made up my father's library, including *The World's Greatest Books*, were destroyed, eaten by white ants. The books, the entire cupboard in fact, had been left in a friend's house when my parents had to vacate the college bungla. The friend came home one day to convey the news that the books were all gone, eaten by white ants. Symbolic, I suppose, of what was happening to my father's life at the time. But the books remain with me, stored memories, like the beginning of a first love affair, nothing forgotten. And the house where this passion began, that too can never be forgotten. Nor the town where we lived an enchanted childhood in the college bungla, in the shadow of the college where our father was a teacher. The town was Dharwad.

The town you live in, as a child, the town you grow up in, becomes a part of you; it is like the skin you inhabit, something you are scarcely conscious of. The first time I learnt more about Dharwad was when I read a little about it for *In the Country of Deceit*, a novel I located in a Dharwad-like town, or rather, a Dharwad recreated. I read that it had been Maratha territory, ceded to an Englishman, Thomas Munro, in 1817. And that Thomas Munro, who brought peace and order into the region, was specially mentioned in the House of Commons as an accomplished statesman, a man who established 'an empire over the hearts and feelings of people'.

Even more fascinating was the story of a young English officer sent to help the Marathas find a way into a fort held by one of Tipu Sultan's men. This man, who skulked round the fort for a few days, was none other than Arthur Wellesley, the future Duke of Wellington, the long-nosed victor of Waterloo. I also read about a Walter Elliot, who was an assistant to the Collector at some time.

Walter Elliot? The name leapt out at me, for Walter Elliot is the man with whom Jane Austen opens *Persuasion*. Had Jane Austen taken the name from this man? No, such a theory was untenable; the dates didn't allow for it. In any case, the Walter Elliot of Dharwad was very different from the vain fop who was Anne Elliot's father. This Walter Elliot had the distinction of starting Kannada schools in the region, the first one with his own money. He was also an epigraphist and the man who wrote to his friend, Charles Darwin, about the flora and fauna of the region. Quite a distinguished man.

But the only name that remained in the Dharwad of our days was Thackeray. We walked past his tomb, the obelisk in the centre of a maidan, every day on our way to and from school. This was where Thackeray and two other soldiers were buried; it was called Thackeray's *gori*, locally. Thackeray's claim to fame was that he had died in the war against a rebel queen, Kittur Chennamma. St John Thackeray, to give him his full name, was, it was said, somehow related to the novelist William Thackeray, though there are different and confusing versions of the relationship. Clearly he had been a hero to the English; there had even been a village named Thackeraypura after him, but the name failed to catch on.

The one foreigner whose presence remains in Dharwad even today is Ferdinand Kittel, the German lexicographer who compiled the first Kannada dictionary. A college has been named after him; the Basel Mission Boys' School is now Kittel College. No, there was an Englishman who had been the Principal of Karnatak College. He did not leave after Independence like so many of his compatriots did. He stayed on, leading a very reclusive life. We used to see him at times, an elusive figure, always moving away so that one saw nothing but his back. He too left, finally.

What I learnt about Dharwad's past was fascinating; but for us children, Dharwad was nothing more than a place we lived in. It took middle age and nostalgia to bring the understanding that Dharwad was a beautiful place, to realise that we had had an enchanted childhood. Today, I think of the freedom which Dharwad allowed us with great gratitude; our parents never had to worry about us going out on our own, never had to escort us anywhere, like parents have to do in cities these days. We were left free, so free that maybe we were a little wild. Perhaps we were lucky that we left Dharwad before we reached the age where girls had to live the kind of circumscribed life that was considered appropriate for females. Because, for all its air of culture, Dharwad, like all small towns, had many taboos and rules for females.

I remember my mother refusing to enter a small restaurant, famous for its dosas, in spite of my father's persuasions. Her refusal was so vehement; clearly she thought it was wrong for a woman to go into a restaurant. She sat outside on the steps of the next building and the dosa was brought to her there. Later, in Delhi and Bangalore, when we went out to eat in restaurants, my mother always joined us. Each time my sister and I went from Bombay to Delhi for our vacation, the family would visit Moti Mahal, famous for its chicken, and later, when in Bangalore, we went to MTR for its delectable dosas. These were joyous family outings. My mother had no objection then to eating out. It now seems to me that it was the close scrutiny of Dharwad that she feared.

Even in our college in Dharwad, there was a canteen for girls which was so small that the table and benches took up almost all the space; girls had to squeeze through the little space between the bench and the table. The Dharwad Restaurant, the most 'decent' restaurant in town, had family cabins as well. There was something slightly attractively dangerous about sitting in a closed cabin, which is why I guess respectable women never entered these cabins. A friend of ours was said to go there when we were in college, for which reason she was considered 'forward'. A bad thing for a girl to be in those days. Girls should rightly be 'backward', it seemed.

(Loose, fast, forward – so many words for women who flout the rules!)

My sister and I once entered Dharwad Restaurant, not to eat, but to buy some things. I don't know whose idea it was; I am quite happy to give my sister the credit, for she was, after all, older than me, though both us were not even ten. We took a ten-rupee note from our father's drawer and went to the restaurant to buy – what? Pencils, I think. And some sweets. We were so little that we could scarcely look over the counter. I can still remember the man to whom we offered the money, looking down at us, partners in crime, with a kindly smile. He gave us what we wanted, but didn't take our money. And then, I guess, he told our father. Or, perhaps, the news travelled swiftly, as news always does in small places. We were called up before our father, who asked us where we had got the money from. From your drawer, I blurted out. Perhaps he was relieved to hear the truth, for he let us off without any kind of punishment.

We never lived in the heart of town, the '*ooru*', as the crowded inner cluster of shops and houses was called; we always lived on the outskirts of town. The last house we lived in before we left Dharwad, the house my father built for us, was on the edge of the town, with only mango and guava orchards beyond us. At night we could hear the halloing of the watchmen in these orchards; Dharwad was famous for its guavas and mangoes. We changed houses a number of times in Dharwad, but the two that linger in my memory are the college bungla, and the house my father built, in which we stayed perhaps four or five years at the most.

The road we took from our own house to go to school and later on to college, was the same one we had taken from the college bungla. This road, in a sense, emphasised the fact that Dharwad was an educational centre. First, there was the college and all its adjunct buildings, and a little later a government training college. After this came the government primary school, where, one presumes, the poor novice teachers were left to the mercies of little boys who, from what we saw of them playing on the roads, were actually little savages. Slightly ahead was the government girls' school and then, after a large tonga (where Thackeray's *gori* was situated), came our first school, St Joseph's School, also known as the convent, or the padre school. The centre for all Roman Catholics in town, the church, to which the faithful flocked on Sundays, dominated the school. We, too, entered the church without any hesitation, it was a part of our lives as well. Yet, for some reason, when the Angelus rang at noon, we did not, like the Christian students, cross ourselves, as if this were a line we could not cross. Since St Joseph's was not a high school, we had to move out after the fourth standard – the girls to Basel Mission Girls' High School and the boys to the corresponding boys' school.

Dharwad, as a district town, had good, tarred roads, but for us, it was always shortcuts, and shortcuts within shortcuts. We cut across grounds, at times even through fenced in areas. Trees flourished in Dharwad. Tamarind trees lined some of the roads we walked along and we saw the entire cycle of growth: tender leaves, flowers, little fruits, just like a new-born baby's fingers, then the semi-ripened fruit which was delicious to eat, and finally the ripe tamarinds, which were plucked with what I always felt to be a ruthlessness, the branches being savagely beaten, leaving behind a scene of utter devastation, the sad debris of injured branches and leaves left lying under the tree. The trees, however, remained unscathed, ready to flower and fruit the next year.

Throughout the year, they were used to advertise the films running in town, posters stuck to the trunks. I remember the three of us, my sister, our friend and I, staring up at a poster of a couple kissing. We looked at it in silence, none of us had any comment to make, and then we walked on, still silent. There were many distractions on the way, which made our walk to school interesting. In summer, St Joseph's had half-day school and going back home just after midday, we saw a shimmer on the road which looked like water, but which mysteriously disappeared as we got closer. A mirage, our Physics lessons were to tell us later. Did it rain more in those days? Statistics may prove otherwise, but I remember months of rain, of a steady drizzle, which never stopped during the monsoon months. Summer had its thunderstorms, as well, and in the evenings, hailstones accompanied the rain, filling us with delight. Monsoons turned the whole world green (and the backs of pyjamas, trousers and saris into a polka-dotted pattern as the red mud was spattered up by chappals), creepers and moss grew everywhere and water ran in the shallow gutters by the sides of the road. These were ideal for wading and someone once asked our father, 'Why do your children walk in the gutter?' I don't know what his reply was, but in our defence I can say that the gutters were clean, nothing in them except leaves and other detritus of the trees above, perhaps rarely, occasionally, bits of paper.

Everybody walked in Dharwad. There were no buses, almost no one had a car, and I have no memory of ever seeing a motorbike on the roads. The only motorbike we saw was in the circus, which a man rode inside a globular cage, which was called the 'something' (Globe?) of Death. It was scary. Men and boys cycled about town; I remember only one woman who cycled, our friend's mother, and she was Christian. My father had a bike and he went everywhere on it, trouser legs clipped at the ankles, giving him what I thought was a dashing air. We learnt cycling on his large bike, and since our legs would not reach the pedals if we sat on the seat, we put our legs through the bar and did what was called half-pedalling. Learning to ride a bike meant that our knees were forever bandaged, the red of something called Mercurochrome scarcely fading before another injury and a fresh application of Mercurochrome appeared.

People going out of town with luggage took a tonga, a long row of which stood outside the railway station. The smell of hay and dung and the sounds of the horses (ponies?) snuffling, are to me, an intrinsic part of the memory of that railway station.

This was our town. A provincial town. As we grew into adolescence, we felt slightly ashamed of living in such a small town. We felt inferior to those who lived in cities and we became much more conscious of our inferiority when we went to our mother's family home in Pune for our summer vacation. Here, we were made very conscious that we were small-towners; the very way we dressed marked us out as inferior creatures. It never occurred to us that our bungalow in Dharwad, set picturesquely among trees, with its large garden, was far superior to the Pune family home, which, though it was a large *wada*, was situated on a narrow crowded street in the midst of sagging old buildings. Nor did we know then, something that would become a matter of pride later, that Dharwad was famous for its writers and musicians. And though we knew nothing of its history, it was all around us.

The house which my father built was on a road on which some government bungalows were situated. I remember them, the pillared porches, the driveways lined by beds of seasonal flowers, everything about the houses crying out 'British-built' and 'Colonial'. We visited one of these houses when a Tamil family came to live in the District Judge's bungalow at the end of our road. The wife and children were, I imagine, bewildered by this strange place and the unknown language they heard around them. The two girls were in our school, which is why, perhaps, their mother brought them to our house once (in a car! Our mouths popped open when we saw that) and asked our mother whether we would occasionally go and play with them. It was not a very successful experiment. Their house overwhelmed us, with its many large rooms and passages. It was a gloomy house. We were expected to play board games with them, most of which we had never seen. The mother sat and smiled happily at the sight of her children playing with friends, but my sister and I were bored to death. We were not used to indoor games, nor to playing so politely. The only such games we played were carom (noisily, and with constant loud cries of 'cheating', 'it's not in', 'it's in') and cards, a game called five-three-two, which we played endlessly, passionately, during the holidays. We kept a careful watch on one another to see that there was no cheating. There was no such thing as being a good sport; whoever lost, threw down her cards and walked away. Which is why we devised an oath which we swore before we began playing, promising not to cheat and not to throw down our cards before the game ended. I doubt the oath helped.

Tuesday was market day in Dharwad. Since our home was on the road which led from the villages to the market, all morning we could see a steady stream of villagers going to the market to sell their stuff. A woman used to come home to sell butter. She brought out pats of butter from an earthen pot, and shaped them into round balls before piling them on the iron weighing scales, wiping her hand after each operation on a greasy rag. This was our weekly supply of butter. Market day was when our home was redolent with the incomparable aroma of fresh ghee. No one knew about cholesterol then, nor did one worry about putting on weight, and so the consumption of ghee was guilt-free and joyful. Hot, soft rice, plain dal, with only salt and lime and a spoon of ghee on top – what bliss! What I remember distinctly is the villagers coming home to ask for water. Knowing this would happen, extra water was stored on the day and any one of us who was around would pour water into the person's cupped hands. I was fascinated by the way they drank from their cupped palms, neatly, without spilling a drop, their throats moving up and down as they swallowed, ending with an 'aah' of satisfaction. Years later, I read Purandaradasa's poem about how one should live in this world:

'... like a bird that perches in the courtyard
and flies away on the very instant,
like the market which comes together from different paths
and when the day is done disperses in different directions
... So should one live this life.'

When I read these lines of the sixteenth-century saint-poet of Karnataka, I thought of the villagers going in a steady stream to the market in the morning and returning in the evening, leaving the market deserted, and I knew what Purandaradasa had meant.

'Throw a stone in Dharwad and you will hit either a writer or a musician,' was a much-quoted saying. Gangubai Hangal, Mallikarjun Mansur, Basavraj Rajguru lived in Dharwad, and Bhimsen Joshi had a connection with the town, though he never lived there. But surprisingly, none of the musicians were a part of my father's world. His connection to music was minimal. He confessed he had no ear for music and when he was translating the Natya Shastra at the end of his life, he left the music chapters alone, hoping for help from someone who knew and understood music.

In spite of this non-musicality, he engaged a music teacher for my sister and me, and this at a time when he was struggling with money problems. Earlier, we had learnt dancing which we had enjoyed. But music! And Hindustani classical music at that! One of the first things our teacher taught us was how to sit holding the taanpura – 'Just like the women you see in the pictures in the All India Radio magazine,' he said. He seemed to forget that the taanpura was almost as tall as we were, and heavy and unwieldy to manage. After a few months of reluctant learning, there came a time when my sister was out of town and I had to have lessons all by myself. I refused and burst into tears when gentle, and then angry persuasion failed. Our guruji, highly insulted, stalked out and never returned.

Then there was the time I was included in a children's programme on All India Radio – this, only because the Station Director knew my father. I was thrust into the studio among a group, which looked at me with hostility, while the group leader ignored me completely. I was so uncomfortable, knowing I was not welcome, that when the time came for me to sing, I only recited the lines! I had to hear a lot of criticism and meet a lot of hateful laughter when I came home. I never sang a line after that. Much later, I began listening to classical music and learnt to love it.

Yet the music of Dharwad came to me in other ways. Early mornings, when I lay in bed, I heard a young male voice singing. He was a student in the college, we learnt later, who admired K.L. Saigal and hoped to sing like him. He chose the quiet of morning hours to practice, and to throw his voice out into the open air and the silence. I listened with pleasure to the full-throated voice, the song coming closer and then fading away. It stirred me deeply. And left me with a glimpse of another world, a world of beauty and enchantment.

Another 'musical' experience, from a time when I was even younger: we had been playing on the college grounds and were sitting, exhausted after our games, trying to catch our breaths before going home. And then, one of the two students sitting near us began singing. A Marathi song. It was the magical time of twilight, a time when things slow down, voices are hushed and the senses are acutely awakened to everything around. A silence seemed to have fallen on everyone and the song came to me, framed in this silence, with such distinctness that it stayed with me for years. The words are still with me: '*Sakhey mee kaajal ghalu kashaalaa, ghanashyam nayani aalaa …*'

On the other hand, though I remember being present at the performance of one of the greats of Indian music, Bismillah Khan, the shehnai maestro, who came to Dharwad for the inauguration of the Dharwad Radio Station, I have absolutely no memory of his music. But the memory of a voice coming out of a house, a small and shabby house which we passed every day when going to school, is very clear. I knew in a vague way even then that there was something odd in the manner in which people spoke of the woman who lived in that house. And I now know that, when we heard her, she must have been doing her *riaz*. These two bits of knowledge came together and alchemised in the mysterious way memories do, creating Savitribai Indorekar, who was the starting point of *Small Remedies*.

Students, writers and theatre people were always a part of our lives. But the writers were Kannada writers, the discussions were in Kannada and about Kannada literature. Very few people had English books at home. There were no bookshops that sold English books in Dharwad, except perhaps textbooks. We were surrounded by a literary atmosphere, but it was all Kannada. The only writer in town, who wrote in English, was, perhaps, Prof. Armando Menezes, who taught English in college and wrote poetry. Even the other English professor, Prof. Inamdar, our father's ex-student and friend, wrote in Kannada.

So where did I get the books I read? Anywhere and everywhere. I remember reading *Pride and Prejudice* in the loft of a family friend's home on a visit. Reading cowboy books, Zane Grey, I think, which I found in a small cupboard in another house we visited. I read *Frenchman's Creek,* which I found in an uncle's room in Pune during a visit. I read the books in my grandfather's study in Pune during vacations, sneaking in fearfully, because the room was out of bounds to children. It was only when I joined Basel Mission school that I got books on a regular basis, because the school had a library – a grand name for what was just one locked cupboard in a senior classroom, opened by the teacher in charge during lunch hour on library day.

Almost at the same time, a library came into town, the Karnatak Granthalaya. My father had taken a leading role in getting this library for the town; I remember my sister and I going round collecting money for it. One day, when we were on our collection rounds, a woman who opened the door of a home we knocked on, told us, 'Go home, Gandhiji has been shot dead, there could be trouble.' The library and Gandhi's death are inextricably connected for me. I can remember how we raced home, breathless, panting and found a crowd of students who had come to listen to the announcement on the radio. My father was sitting in a chair, a handkerchief covering his wet face. The whole of the next day our house was crowded with students who came to hear the commentary on the funeral. I can still remember Melville de Mellow's rich baritone laden with grief and the utter silence in the room.

The Granthalaya was one of the most wonderful things that happened in Dharwad, at least as far as I was concerned. It was a proper library, a large room full of shelves, books arranged according to a system. As our father's children, we must have got membership right away (there was a children's section), and I became one of the most zealous and regular visitors to the library, though going to it meant a long walk of nearly three miles each way. The first day I went there, the librarian, who knew me – she was the daughter of a professor of Mathematics – gave me what I thought was a 'baby book'. I read it in ten minutes and returned it. She was convinced I had cheated, that I had not read the book at all; but she allowed me to choose a book myself this time. *Treasure Island* and *Alice in Wonderland* both came from this library, as also *The Arabian Nights, Black Beauty, Heidi* and so many more I can't recollect. And so it began, the passion that would be with me all my life, one which is still with me.

Schooling

> ... *my early and invincible love of reading, which I would not exchange for the treasures of India.*
>
> Edward Gibbon, *Autobiography*

Sт Joseph's, where we began our education, was a Roman Catholic school, the church a large presence in the compound, dominating everything else. The Principal of this school was a German (Father Cotta?) who smoked foul-smelling cigars (or were they cheroots? Or are they both the same thing?) and set children who came early to school the task of picking up cigar stubs from his garden. He left immediately after Independence, shedding tears, it was rumoured, because the British had gone. Though why a German should cry over the British departure was something that never occurred, either to those who spread the story, or to those of us who heard it. A new Principal came in his place; an Indian priest, Father Soares, who was young, dynamic, enthusiastic and revolutionised the school, making it into something totally different, totally Indian.

Unfortunately, I left school just a year after he came, though I remember he tried to persuade my father to let me stay on for a year more. We want good students, he said. But my father wanted me to join high school right away, possibly because my sister was already there and he wanted us to be together. This meant I skipped a class, which was back then called a double promotion. It resulted in my passing out of school when I was only thirteen and graduating when I was seventeen. My mother was proud of the fact, but I don't think it did me any good. I remember how much better I coped with studies at a mature age, even though I had a home and family to look after at the time.

The school which we girls went to after St Joseph's was Basel Mission Girls' High School (shortened to BMGHS), where we stayed until we passed our school-leaving examination. This too was a Christian school, started by the Basel Mission, in Switzerland. The Basel Mission Boys' School was much older than the girls' school, founded sometime in the nineteenth century. (No dates, remember?) Starting a girls' school must have been a sudden and hasty decision, because it was located in what had, perhaps, been the priest's home. Housing the school in this bungalow had possibly been a temporary measure; but there it remained all the years we lived in Dharwad and even for some years afterwards.

A foundation for a new school was laid sometime when I was still there. The foundation stone was laid, but nothing more happened. If the school building had a makeshift air, it was also homely. The classes were small, just about twenty students in a class, perhaps a little more or a little less. It could be that this was because the teaching in this school was in English. For us, who came from the convent, it was ideal, but unlike now, not many parents then wanted their children to have an English education.

The trellised porch at the entrance sufficed as an assembly point for the junior school. But the largest classroom, where the senior students assembled for morning prayers, was a tight fit. It was only during prayers that the fact that this was a Christian school was evident, for unlike in St Joseph's, the church was at some distance from the school, and fenced off, so that it never seemed to have anything to do with the school, or students. But for morning prayers we sang 'Lead kindly light', or 'Oh God our help in ages past', or 'Nearer my God to thee …' Prayers were often interrupted by a moment of drama, as a girl fainted. Lack of air, clearly, but the teachers who would delicately loosen the girl's bra, or whatever she wore under her blouse, thought otherwise. Whatever it was, the girl who had so distinguished herself moved around with a halo of martyrdom around her the entire day. I too fainted once, but not during prayers. Sadly, I remember nothing of that moment of glory, except that a teacher who lived nearby took me home, gave me idlis to eat and then brought me back to school. It was that kind of a school.

Since it had once been a home, the school had a kitchen, where we had, what was called, the domestic science class. We had sewing classes as well. It seemed that the school was trying to turn us into good wives and homemakers. I never took to cooking, though I learnt to hem, to stitch buttons and make buttonholes, to fix hooks and hook's eyes – skills which came in handy in later years. (I gave up on sewing and mending sometime after I started writing seriously. I learnt to use safety pins instead of re-fixing buttons or hooks. My younger son went even further, stapling anything that had come apart. A testimony to my abdication from these tasks!) But I enjoyed embroidery and did it for many years.

Happily, the rest of our studies had nothing to do with making good little women of us. Our classes were just as rigorous as they were for all students. We had reasonably well-equipped science laboratories which were in another building, a little distance from the main school, which meant we could enjoy a small walk before we got there. There were large grounds for us to play in, though not many girls played games. A few played 'ring', or, as it was officially called, tenniquoit (though I don't find the word in the dictionary); the play involved sedately throwing a rubber ring at one another over the net. Some girls played the slightly more energetic throw ball. We, the girls who came from the convent, were more active. We played a game called 'seven tiles' during lunch hour, which involved much running and shouting and the teachers didn't approve. They once took our ball away from us and I remember one of the teachers calling us '*junglees*'. I wonder now, why it didn't occur to us to question the playing of kabaddi, or hututu as we called it, during which even the quietest girl became a savage, pulling, pushing, dragging the enemy who came into her side of the court. Physical violence is something I abhor, I cannot bear even to look at it, not even on the screen. My size, too, made me an easy 'victim', so I would just let myself be captured the moment I crossed the line between the two teams. Not surprising that I was always the last to be chosen by a team leader. Kho-kho was another often-played game. I didn't mind it. What it required was speed and skilful dodging, both of which I had. None of these games cost the school much. They were country games which needed no equipment.

    What the school lacked – something I have begun to realise afresh, now that the campaign for toilets for girls is at its peak (there is even a movie based on the issue of toilets for women!) was proper toilets. There were three hole-in-the-ground toilets, open to the skies, with no water and with wicker doors that could never be closed. Someone had to stand outside on guard when you were using these. If you were on your own, you coughed or sang. These toilets were clearly only for an emergency, no one would otherwise go near these smelly holes. I wonder now how we managed, adolescent girls all of us, specially those of us, who, since we came from a long distance, left home early and got back late. What did we do? Mercifully, I can't remember. But I do remember that, occasionally, if a girl had a spot on the back of her dress, she was sent home, the offending red spot pinned in with a safety pin. The teachers dealt with this, the girls said nothing. It was a kind of 'there but for the grace of God go I' kind of feeling among the girls, I imagine.

What I remember of the school is how harmoniously all of us existed together. And I am not speaking of religion, which was never taken into account. In St Joseph's, of course, the Christians were marked out because of their connection with the church. But in Basel Mission, though we had Christians, Muslims and Hindus, no one ever took note of the girls' religion. There were no burqas or hijaabs then, and some of the Muslim last names, like Desai or Jagirdar, made religious identification difficult. What I am speaking of here is language. Though the teaching was in English, three languages were used in each class: Kannada, Marathi and English. We 'convent girls' spoke English among ourselves, but we spoke to the others in Kannada or Marathi. One or two of the girls, intent on improving their English, insisted on speaking the language with us. I remember a girl who courted me assiduously to learn English from me. In spite of the fact that she was two or three years older than me, she gave me much respect, calling me, only half jokingly, her guruji.

Years later, after I had become a writer and came to know the background of some other Indian English writers, I had a thought: what if, instead of going to a small, nondescript, poorly equipped, very ordinary school in a small town, I had gone to a noted school in a big city, a school with a distinguished faculty? What if I had gone abroad for further studies? Would it have made me a different writer? A better writer? I would have been a different person certainly, with greater confidence, and perhaps better equipped to deal with people and the world. But as a writer? I might have had better connections, a good network, and – something that always helps – friends in high places. But would that have made any difference to my writing?

My experiences would have been different, certainly, but for a writer it is what you make of your experiences that matters, not what those experiences are. Yet another day, I thought of my school in a different way; I thought of something I had not realised until then. We were a class of twenty-two girls. Two girls died, one while still in school, another in her first year of college. Two got married soon after passing out of school. One of them was a very clever girl who used to top the class, the other, a good friend of mine, was not very clever, but a witty and lively girl. We completely lost touch with both of them after their marriages; it was as if they vanished into another world altogether. Another girl was the daughter of a domestic servant. I remember she didn't have the money to pay her final examination fees. The teachers contributed and made it up between them. I never learned what happened to her after she left school. I truly hope hers was a story with a happy ending. Of the rest of us, one became a college teacher, one a mathematician, who later first became the Director of a major management institute and then the Director of a bank. And I became a writer. And seven of the remaining girls became doctors – yes, seven. Which means nearly 50 per cent of the girls in my class had careers.

Amazing statistics, these. Almost a miracle for those times. Or was it *because* of the times? This was in the fifties, when the country was on the cusp of change. It was a time of optimism, of excitement, of changes happening all around us. There was a burst of energy in the country; the trauma of Partition had been left behind, except by those who had suffered. We in the South had not suffered at all; we knew about Partition, but it was never real to us. Even the sudden influx of refugees from Sind, who came to the one Sindhi family in town for refuge, were more objects of curiosity for us than of tragedy.

One of the girls in the local Sindhi family was a classmate of mine and when we went to her house, we looked in amazement at the men and women sitting about on charpoys outside. They seemed to do nothing all day, except sit and talk in Sindhi, which sounded like gibberish to us, ignorant idiots that we were. Even their clothes seemed strange, because the women wore, not saris, but baggy salwars and kameezes. As far as we knew, women never wore anything but saris. The huge tragedy of their lives, the loss of home, the sudden and savage displacement – all these lay hidden under their strangeness.

Going back to the revelation I had of my class in school, perhaps it helped that Dharwad had always been an educational centre, that girls' education was not unknown. Or perhaps this incredible story of ambitious girls who went on to make careers for themselves was unique. I don't know whether other classes had this kind of a profile. My sister became a doctor and one of her classmates joined a just-started engineering college, the first girl to do so. The college was in the next town, Hubli, and she travelled by bus. Anyone who knows what buses were like then, will be able to imagine the hardship of going up and down every day. (And yes, no toilets for girls in the college.) Only her ambition must have kept her going.

I was not an ambitious girl. My sister decided, at a very early age, that she would become a doctor. I remember she wrote out a promise from my father to her in a book, in which he wrote, or rather, she wrote for him, that he would send her to medical college, a promise she made him sign. I had no ambitions at all, except to be left to myself. Later, I thought I would have been very well fitted for the role of the village scholar (a.k.a. the village idiot) in Pearl Buck's Chinese novels. He did nothing but pore over his books all day, leaving the entire responsibility of his family to his unfortunate wife and to those in the village who supported him, because they were proud of having a scholar in their midst. (It seems to me now that I never realised that this retreat from responsibilities was available only to men.) One ambition I did have in early childhood, however, was of becoming a railway guard. Going to the railway station was one of our pastimes as children. To watch a train come puffing in and to watch it steam out of the station was a great pleasure, almost the highlight of our lives. I found the guard, standing on the open deck of his little cabin as the train steamed out, a solitary figure of dignity and power (those flags tucked under his arms were what controlled the train) most fascinating. So did the idea of his little moving home in the cabin behind the deck enchant me. But this ambition didn't last beyond early childhood.

It was in high school that I became conscious of my love of language, love of words and of stories. I had always loved reading, but in this school I found myself responding even to my school texts, yes, even my Sanskrit text. I had not wanted to choose Sanskrit as my second language, mainly because all my friends had opted for French. I had been forced to choose Sanskrit by my father, because, he said, how could I not when he was a Sanskrit teacher. Strange logic, I thought it. This was one of my earliest conflicts with authority, which I, of course, lost! Perhaps my resentment at this coloured my vision of the subject, for I never liked Sanskrit. I hated the grammar with its millions of rigid rules. But in our final year we had, for the first time, some extracts from literature.

There was one piece from the Mahabharata, in which Draupadi was dragged into the court by Duryodhana's brother, Dushasana, after her husband Yudhishtira had lost everything, even her, while gambling with the wily Shakuni. There was something about that passage that fired all of us, something about Draupadi's arguments filled us with excitement. We loved it. I remember one of the girls asking for the meaning of '*rajasvala*'. In the passage, Draupadi says, '*Aham rajasvala asmi*'. What did she mean? Our teacher, a man who did not even raise his eyes to look at us, hemmed and hawed, and finally said, using a euphemism, that it meant 'I am menstruating'. What an instant connection this made between us and that heroine of ancient times! And the piece from the Upanishad, the dialogue between Svetaketu and his father about the soul – the fact that it has stayed with me through the years is an indication of how strongly I responded to it.

And, of course, there was English, my favourite subject. Apart from the prose, poetry and grammar, we, girls who had come from the convent, were allowed to take another English paper, instead of Kannada or Marathi; this was called Additional English. We were just about eight or ten of us in this class. If the entire school had a makeshift air, the room where we had our Additional English classes was the most informal of all. It wasn't even a room, just the space that connected the main building to the back of the house, where the kitchen and other utility spaces were located. There was a large rectangular table here, with benches on two sides and a chair at the head where our teacher sat facing a blank wall. We had to squeeze between the table and the bench to seat ourselves, but it was in this cramped space that I discovered the great joys of poetry.

Our teacher, Mr Ezra, who was stern when he taught us Maths, was a genial and easy man here. He allowed us to ask questions even outside the texts. I still remember the little poetry book (more precious because it had to be ordered from Bombay, it was not available in Dharwad), with an amazing collection of poems. The inside of the front cover had a picture of Rupert Brooke, a handsome young poet who died young, and, what seemed even more romantic, died in a war. All of us were a little in love with him, or rather, with that picture of his. Mr Ezra allowed us a few 'oohs' and 'aahs' over him before going on to his poem *The Soldier*, which moved us to tears. I can quote most of it even today. I now think that Mr Ezra loved poetry himself, which is why the class and the poems came alive and which is also why I have never forgotten the poems even after all the years.

We read Yeats' *The Lake Isle of Innisfree*, and when we were told the poem came to him when he was standing on a crowded pavement in London, near Charing Cross, we were thrilled that the poem connected us to London. And there was Wordsworth's *Daffodils*, which, in those pre-post-Colonial days, was only a poem. I never imagined that one day it would become a stick to beat English education and colonialism with. Since everything we read was strange to us, did it matter not knowing what daffodils were? The poetry was the thing. (Though *Daffodils* was never a favourite of mine!)

In college, Prof. Menezes taught us poetry and I can remember him walking up and down the narrow space between the benches and the dais, as he read the poems. He read with such feeling, that the first two lines of Keats' *The Eve of St Agnes* brought on goosebumps; I could almost feel the cold. *'Ah, bitter chill it was! The owl, for all his feathers, was a-cold.'* He also brought in the spooky element in *La Belle Dame Sans Merci* and in *Isabella and the Pot of Basil*. My brother's school texts, which I also read, gave me poems like *The Burial of Sir John Moore after Corunna* with its magnificent lines, 'Not a drum was heard, not a funeral note/ as his corse to the ramparts we hurried' – lines that carried the muffled beat of fear and grief. When, many years later, I came to know the context of this poem, I realised it was a doleful dirge on the defeat of the British, converted – as the English always seemed to be able to do – into something glorious. (A great example is *The Charge of the Light Brigade*!)

My brother's favourite poem, Coleridge's *Kubla Khan*, fascinated me as well. What glorious lines it had: 'In Xanadu did Kubla Khan a stately pleasure dome decree.' And those last lines: 'And all who heard should see them there/ And all should cry,

Beware Beware!/ His flashing eyes, his floating hair!' Magnificent. Truly magical, the way poets used words, what they made them do. There's no better way to learn about a language than to read the best poets. I am grateful to my school and my teacher for giving me the foundation on which I would build my writing.

It was in this school, too, that I learnt the vagaries of English grammar. Our Principal, Mr Ammanna, taught us this subject. He was a busy man and taught only two subjects, Chemistry and English grammar – and that too, only to the senior-most class. But he seemed to have no time even for that, for in the early part of the year, he rarely took any classes. I wonder now what kept him so busy in such a small school. But there he was, always in his office, poring over some papers on his table, the school peon jealously guarding his privacy. He would suddenly remember his classes when it was nearing the final exams, and when he taught us he was a glorious teacher. I found English grammar as fascinating as I had found Sanskrit grammar dry and boring. Mr Ammanna was everything a good teacher should be – enthusiastic, full of examples and anecdotes and interacting with students all the time. *Mum's the word*, he would say to me, finger on lips, when he asked a question of the class, *mum's the word*. Was I such a little show off then? But it is true that it was the one class I was confident about and comfortable in.

Fiction was, however, my first and lasting love. The school library was a godsend. The books must have been bought when the school was started, obviously nothing was added after that, for the books belonged to a distant past. William Harrison Ainsworth (anyone heard of him?), whose historical novels were spell-binding, Sir Walter Scott, whose books I devoured in those days, even if I skipped over a great number of pages, but whom I have never been able to look at again. There were sentimental novels like *The Rosary* and *East Lynne*. Even girls who didn't normally read books read *East Lynne*. We sobbed buckets over the tragedy of Isabel, we hated the other woman, Barbara, with great gusto. Years later, in one of O. Henry's brilliant stories, I read a delightful conversation between a burglar and the man being burgled, in which the two discuss their rheumatism and strike a bond when they speak of how passing a theatre playing *East Lynne*, brought on an attack of arthritis for both of them! There was a quaint novel called *John Halifax, Gentleman*, which I loved. Full of Victorian values, I wonder now what it meant to me, a girl in small-town India. And there was Marie Corelli whose *Thelma* and *Vendetta* were great favourites. In this library, I got the books of Angela Brazil, schoolgirl stories of midnight feasts and drama in schoolrooms. I still think they were wonderful books, better than Enid Blyton, but sadly they are forgotten. The fate of all books, except a few.

Reading became an obsession, an addiction. I read everything, not only books and magazines and the little booklets, leaflets and journals my father received as a writer, but also labels on bottles, signs on shop boards, ads in papers, movie posters. (Even today, I can't throw out any piece of paper without reading what's on it.) Like an alcoholic who swears off drinking on occasions, there were times, like before examinations, when I would make myself give up reading. I thought that this 'sacrifice' would give me some brownie points. But abstaining was hard, very hard; there is no doubt, I was an addict.

In time, reading also became, I suspect, an escape, for I remember some bad times in school, which came after I had typhoid. Typhoid was endemic in Dharwad (because of contaminated wells) and I had my stint of it like many others. Since the treatment then consisted of starving the patient, it meant a long convalescence (if you didn't die, that is, and I know at least half-a-dozen who did) and I had to stay away from school for nearly two months. Even after my recovery, I was very weak and walking three miles to school and back must have been exhausting. Worse, to make up for the time I'd lost, I also had to go for tuitions in Maths and Sanskrit, which meant I made four trips each day. I must have found myself physically unable to cope, and did badly in school. I put on a 'I don't care' attitude, I flouted rules, which didn't help. I was once sent out of class for reading a novel, holding it under my text, and I had to stand outside, in the passage, for the entire period, my disgrace open and loud. The teachers were puzzled because I had been a sincere student until then, doing my homework regularly, getting fairly good marks in all subjects, except Sanskrit.

In fact, I gained such a poor reputation that a new teacher, who taught us English composition, surprised by the story I had written, developing it from the few sketchy clues we were given, asked me, 'Did you write this yourself?' My story was full of conversation – I was influenced by Wodehouse, I think, whom I had just discovered through *Sam the Sudden*. I suspect there were a few 'good egg's in it and some 'what ho's as well. I also remember narrating the entire story of *Sam the Sudden* to my brother, wanting to share my joy with him. But my future as a story-teller was nowhere on the cards at that time.

My father connected my poor showing in studies and examinations to my fiction reading and sent a note to my class teacher saying I was not to be allowed to borrow any books from the library. I got around this blatantly unfair restriction by asking my friends to borrow the books I wanted and then surreptitiously taking them home to read. To escape my father's notice, I read in the early hours. My bed was next to a window that gave me sufficient light and, with the mosquito curtain snugly tucked in, I thought myself fairly safe. But one morning the curtain was flung open and I was caught. Apart from reprimanding me for flouting his rules, he also warned me that I would ruin my eyes by reading in such bad light. I think of this now, when my eyesight has become suspect, because of glaucoma and other eye problems.

Perhaps it was around this time that my father threatened that he would make me a clerk in the local Collector's office. For him, to work in a government office was the worst punishment possible for anyone. I don't think he said it often, he was not the kind to harp on anything. But his threat has stuck like a burr to my mind. I once spoke of it to a friend, lightly, joking, and he said, 'Obviously you were very hurt by the threat. Why else would you remember it so clearly?' I have no idea what impact it made on me then, whether I responded angrily, brazened it out, or just ignored it. Yet the fact remains that the words have stayed with me through the years.

Actually, I think I never took his threat seriously. Nor did comparisons with my sister, who always did well in school, faze me; she was either first or second in class, while my rank veered between fourth (my best rank) and seventh (my worst). I didn't mind this at all. The first time I was worried about my performance was after my school-leaving examinations, when I was afraid I would fail in Sanskrit and would therefore fail the entire examination. I had nightmares in the time between the examinations and the results. If I failed, apart from what my father would say, or my teachers think, what about my own self-esteem? In spite of my average performance in class, I never doubted my own intelligence. But what if I didn't clear this hurdle? Fortunately, I passed. That I got a first class (only 60 per cent, just scraped through, as my brother, in the nasty way of brothers, sneeringly said) mattered less to me than that I passed the examinations. Now on to college and, oh joy! No Maths, though Sanskrit would still be with me.

In time, I left all those fears behind; my anger and resentment against my father also vanished. But occasionally, his exaggerated reaction to my poor, or rather, not-so-good academic performance, made me wonder, that a man, who was so careful not to interfere in his children's lives, could go to the extent of making sure that

I was not allowed to use the school library. I know that it was academic excellence, rather than success, which mattered to him; he was proud, too, of his children's intelligence. And yet how could he, a writer himself, think that reading was wrong, how could he look at my reading as a waste of time?

When parents of child prodigies come to me now – prodigies who have written a novel, a poem or a story at a very young age – and ask me how best they can nurture the child's talent, when parents come to invite me to launch the book written by their teenaged, or even younger child, I remember how different it was for me. At the same time, I know that it did me good not to be burdened by my parents' attention, it was an advantage that I did not have to bear the weight of their expectations; I was free to grow, or not grow, in my own way. In any case, how could even my writer-father have imagined that the reading I was doing was a kind of apprenticeship which would lead to writing? I'm sure he never thought his day-dreaming, stubborn, argumentative daughter would one day become a writer, not until he actually read what I wrote. As for me, I often remember J.K. Rowling's advice, which I read somewhere, that there should be an 'expiry date' on resentment against parents. Yes, I did give up on my resentment at some time. But my curiosity, my surprise at my father's act of depriving me of books, remained with me. It was only after his death that I made a serendipitous discovery, which gave me a clue to his behaviour.

It must have been a few days after my father's death when, going through his papers, I came across an old diary. He was a meticulous diary-keeper, noting down events, commitments, meetings and lectures, as also the expenses of each day. This particular diary belonged to the fifties, and I wondered why he had kept it for so long. It fell open to a page where two pages had been glued together with the words, 'To be opened after my death', written on top. I showed it to my mother and, with her permission, unglued the pages. Inside, I found a statement, which was a will of sorts. Written, obviously, during the darkest days of his life, when he was unemployed, during a particularly low moment, perhaps, he had written that in case of his death, he wanted his friends to perform his plays and give the royalty to his children. And, to continue to help them in this manner 'until my children are able to stand on their own feet'. This was a revelation to me. I knew he was a positive-thinking man, but to put so much faith in his work and in his friends seemed overly optimistic to me. Or perhaps it was the optimism of desperation: he *had* to believe that his plays would be staged and earn money, that his friends would perform them regularly enough to provide a living for his children. If he didn't believe in these things, he was sunk.

However, what moved me deeply were the words 'until my children are able to stand on their own feet'. Most parents of the time would have written, 'until my daughters are married'. But he put his three children, his two daughters, as well as his son, in the same category. He thought of his daughters in the same way as he thought of his son. We always knew our father was different from most fathers; this convinced me he was almost unique.

This note also brought home to me his state of mind at the time. Some years after his death, I read his autobiography (only in bits and pieces) and came across a passage written about the time he was working in All India Radio, Bangalore. When in this job, he was the subject of much harassment and insidious persecution by a few local people for reasons too complicated to go into here. In his autobiography, he wrote that he was very tempted to give up his job and concentrate on his writing, which he was yearning to do. After years, a new play was simmering in his mind, plaguing him so much that one day he passed on the job of a recording to be done to his assistant, took the day off and wrote the play in one long stretch. He then went back to work. *I could not give up my job*, he wrote in his autobiography, *I had made my family suffer once and I would not do it again.* He didn't give up his job. He worked through the entire period of his contract and then, thankfully, I am certain, retired from all jobs.

This is the only reference to his family in his three- or four-hundred-page biography. Obviously, what his family had to go through during his years of unemployment hurt him greatly, it left a deep scar. From these few lines I came to know, for the first time, how much he had suffered in his years of joblessness, how he was haunted by the spectre of being without a job, without money, of suffering the humiliation of asking for favours and of borrowing money. Even as children we knew that there were problems at home. Some of the hardships touched us as well, though I am sure we were protected, to a great extent, by our parents, and by our age, from understanding the extent of the disaster. For us, the greatest change was that we had to quit our dear college bungla and move into a house different from it in every way. One of my father's students offered us a home to live in, a tiny doll's house in a large compound, which had three other houses in it. This was in Sadhankeri, a suburb on the extreme outskirts of town.

When I look back to the time, I wonder how my father, who confesses in his autobiography to being used to living in a large house, managed to stay all day in the very confined space of this home. Equally oddly, I have no memory of him in this house at all. But he was very much there, he *had* to be there, for, soon after we moved in, my mother was diagnosed as having TB and had to stay in Pune to be treated by her brother, a doctor. My father became, in effect, a single parent. A woman came from Pune to cook for us and to look after us. But poor thing, she was all at sea in alien surroundings, living in the midst of an unknown language, with the added baggage of the three of us behaving badly to her – well, two of us; my sister was always a good girl.

My worst memories of the time are of her plaiting my hair, of my constant complaints while she did it and of my dissatisfaction at what she had finally done. I had very long and thick hair and was very fussy about my plaits. I am sure the poor woman had very bad memories of putting up with my tantrums as well! An older girl from a neighbouring family took over this job of plaiting our hair; my sister's and mine. Maybe, I think charitably now, we were so upset by our mother's absence, we could not bear to see anyone else in her place. I don't remember pining for her, though. There was no time to think of her, because we left early for school and came back late. After an early dinner we sat down to do our homework.

The most dreadful I remember from then is the shark liver oil we had to swallow morning and evening. It was supposed to prevent us having TB, I think. Nauseating stuff. But our father would not relent; we had to have our daily dose of the evil-smelling oil. Though it was our father who kept our lives going, things slowly deteriorated, and money troubles began swamping him. My father had always been a proud man, he would never bend before anyone. Now he had become a supplicant for a job, for money.

Even we children faced some bad moments. I remember my class teacher once announcing loudly in class that my fees had been unpaid for some months. It was a humiliating experience. And there was a time when my mother 'stitched' notebooks for us from the papers given to my father by a sympathetic newspaper for translating the new Constitution of India into Kannada. (Now I can imagine what a tedious job the translation must have been. But he needed the money.) The teacher said I could not bring such books to school, I had to have the standard notebooks. My father sent back a note asking why these notebooks wouldn't do. I felt like crawling under the bench when the teacher read this out aloud.

We soon ran out of clothes and had to make do with the hand-me-downs we got from a cousin in Pune. I was very proud of these frocks, they were so obviously not-stitched-in-Dharwad. But I am sure seeing her daughters wear second-hand clothes must have hurt my mother, a proud and extremely sensitive woman, greatly. There came a time when my sister and I had no footwear. Sadhankeri was nearly four miles from school, and walking up and down had worn out our footwear. One evening, Shivaram Karanth, the writer, returning from our house, saw us walking home in our bare feet. He made the tonga turn around, went back home, taking us with him, and tore into my father, berating him for making his children suffer. The very next day, my father took us to the only footwear shop in Dharwad and had us measured for chappals. A far cry from the time he had brought us shoes from Bombay.

As a matter of fact, we didn't mind the long walk to and from school. We enjoyed dawdling on the road, picking up friends on the way, dropping them one by one on the way back and, when just the two of us were left, racing down the slope that took us home. Sadhankeri was a good place to live in. It was famous for having intellectuals and writers living in it. Besides, there were many children of our age to play with. It was a close-knit community; there were picnics and a concert every year, when everyone who wanted to, could exhibit her/his histrionic, musical or dancing talents.

When we moved out of Sadhankeri, the place we went to made Sadhankeri seem a paradise. This was a largish gloomy house, without electricity. I remember my sister and I doing our homework by the light of oil lamps, constantly squabbling over the lamp, each pulling it closer to herself. The families we lived amongst here were no company either, being very traditional orthodox Brahmins. My father must have been acutely uncomfortable among them. Or perhaps he was, fortunately, too busy to look around, for, in addition to all else, I came down with typhoid, which meant he had two patients to look after at home, since my mother was still convalescing. My father even had to cook (thank God I was too ill to eat, he was a terrible cook) until his brother sent a boy to help him. Yet, I remember vividly how patiently he nursed me and how cheerful he was when he opened the mosquito curtains of my bed in the morning to wake me up.

One of the major decisions anyone who writes an autobiography or a biography has to take, is how much to reveal and how much to elide over in silence. An even more knotty dilemma is: do we have any right to write about others? Is it right to reveal the things you know they would have concealed? And does the fact that they are no longer alive give us the right to ignore their wishes and, possibly, their dignity? I thought a great deal about these things and finally decided that I would go with the flow. I would write the way it came to me, and when it was done, I would look it over and if I found something that I thought would hurt a person, I would think about it. This part of my father's life, of our family life, of the time when we suffered acutely for lack of money, when he had to put up with humiliation, some of which overflowed on to us, was something we never spoke of in later years. But it is a very important part of my father's life, of our family life and therefore of my life. And, what I now see when I look back is not the poverty and the humiliation, but the fortitude and dignity with which my parents met their hardships, and the way they protected us, so that today my sister and I have more happy memories of the time than bitter ones. So I have let it be.

Besides, I have another reason, a selfish reason, for speaking of these times. There was an early review of my novel *That Long Silence*, a review which clubbed it with two other novels by women and gave it the heading of, 'An exclusive ladies club'. It made the writers of the novels seem ladies of leisure, people who lived a life of ease and comfort and wrote in their free time. If only they knew! I'd worked on my novel for six years, struggling to find time, coping with children's needs, with parents' problems, with major changes in our lives... I'd shopped, cooked, cleaned and ironed. How dared they belittle my work! I am sure the other two writers were as serious about their writing and had worked as hard as I had. But because we were women, women who wrote in *English*, a certain presumption was made about us. Actually, I now know that what the writer's life is like does not matter; only the book matters. But the words used here seemed to me to prejudice the reader even before she/he read the book. It made me very angry. I have met much worse responses since then, but this one, the first one, still remains a canker within me.

Apart from this, there is another family ghost that keeps peeping out, one more ghost I had thought I would keep out of this narrative. It is my brother's illness, a psychiatric problem that appeared when he was in his early twenties. This problem was buried in silence. I remember the first time my father spoke to my husband about what was happening to my brother, he finally said, 'Don't tell your wife.' The wife was me, his daughter! How could he say such a thing! But, for him, and even more for my mother, the necessity to conceal what was happening to my brother was as great as the grief of the illness itself. I think that the burden of keeping it a secret added to the huge weight of grief they were carrying.

Fortunately, my father shared his feelings with a doctor friend, and with my sister, both because she was a doctor (and the one who was struggling to make my brother accept treatment), and because he was always very close to her. But my mother never spoke of it, and she turned angry and aggressive if anyone did. Mental illness was a disgrace; it could not be disclosed.

Even at that time, this attitude seemed wrong to me. If a

fractured leg was no disgrace, why should a broken mind be one? And my brother's was a brilliant mind, a beautiful mind. He was a genius, with an IQ very few people have. He was not only brilliant academically – he completed his Ph.D in Physics in the shortest time of anyone in his university in Philadelphia – his literary taste was excellent, his language impeccable; he took pleasure in the exactitude both of words and figures, and his sense of humour was amazing. I spent some time with him when he was undergoing treatment. We had shared much as children. And for all his gravitas, he loved playing practical jokes on my sister and me. Childish pranks which he enjoyed hugely. He was also the only person who could say anything to our mother and get away with it. Himmler, he used to call her, I remember.

When he was admitted to NIMHANS (the institute where my husband worked) for psychiatric treatment, I had been frightened of who I would find in place of this brother I knew. I was reluctant to meet him. His psychiatrist, a friend and neighbour, pushed me into it. 'You have to meet him,' he said. 'He needs you.' I needn't have worried. My brother seemed exactly the same person he had always been; in fact, he seemed calm and at peace, all the resistance to treatment behind him. And his sense of humour was still intact, his affections still in place – he remembered my birthday, he spoke of my sons with fondness.

One evening, we sat and watched a patient, a young man, an adolescent really, horsing around, making people laugh. My brother told me he had just been brought in from some village. I wondered what was wrong with the boy, happy as he seemed to be. And innocent, taking joy in making others laugh. My brother too laughed heartily at his antics, and for a few moments, we were on the same side, my brother and I, while the boy was on the other. Then visitors' hour was over, it was time for me to go. I knew that my brother belonged to the same world the boy did and I was the outsider.

To lose such a son to a disease, a disease that made them, his parents, strangers to him, strangers he was hostile to, is a tragedy that is hard to imagine. The disease was not as well understood then as it is now, the drugs not so potent. And so we lost him. In the years since then, the wound has healed, perhaps, but the scar has not closed over it completely. At times, it suddenly opens. My parents were devastated by their loss, they were never the same again. My father tried hard to conceal his grief, but my mother's grief often burst out in terms of anger. My sister and I were not untouched, either; we still don't speak of him. Why then do I write of him now? I asked my sister's permission and she said she had no problems with my writing about him. Nevertheless, I do it with much hesitation, with many tremors, though I sincerely believe that openness is the most healing. I believe that by speaking of something, by writing about it, you are exorcising the ghost. I certainly hope so. I also hope that it helps in the fight against remembering. As long as there is memory, says Madhu at the end of *Small Remedies*, there's always the possibility of retrieval; as long as there is memory, loss is never total. Madhu's revelation and, at the same time, mine as well.

Returning to my narrative, it was at this most desperate time when he had no job and no money that my father decided he would build a home for us. He bought a piece of land in a very picturesque area, surrounded by trees and with no houses around. Convenient, too, for it was close to the college where both my sister and I were now studying and, though out of town, not too far off either. For the first time after we left the college bungla, we were comfortable and happy.

It was an oddly designed house, a skeleton, really, of the house that would eventually be built. Therefore, there was more room for future building and improvement, than space for the present. For living space we had two long halls, one only a narrow strip actually, and a kitchen with an open space and a dining room, the two connected by a passage, roofed, but otherwise open. When it rained, we had to stay in whichever part of the house we were in, or dash through the passage, braving the rain. But there was enough space all around, we had three large mango trees, the mangoes of a good quality, and a well which supplied drinking water. There was a Persian wheel attached to the well, which made us enthusiastic about drawing water out of it. I remember this time as one of happiness; I had joined college and the free and easy ways it offered, with the lack of constant supervision, suited me very well. I enjoyed not having to study Maths, and in English, I had *Pride and Prejudice* as a text in the first year and *The Mayor of Casterbridge* in the next year. My father's friend, Prof. Inamdar, taught us this text and I can still remember how his voice broke when he came to the end, as he read out Michael Henchard's will. His emotion awed the class into silence. I had never liked Hardy much, I felt he kind of squeezed tragedy out of life, but this passage still brings tears to my eyes. In college, I was also introduced to Shakespeare for the first time.

But for my parents, the bad days were still not over. There was a time when I found out that I had been given a scholarship – I came to know about it only when I saw it on the notice board – and I was asked to collect the entire year's sum from the office. I did, went home and gave the money to my father. He took it without a word. But he told the friend who was with him at the time that all the money he had with him at that moment was a single paisa coin, a large round coin, with which he used to tuck in his dhoti. (After he resigned from his college job, he gave up on Western dress and wore a dhoti and kurta for the rest of his life. He also changed his name from R.V. Jagirdar to Adya Rangacharya. And I became Shashi Adya instead of Shashi Jagirdar. Took a long time getting used to.) 'Now I can buy some provisions,' he said. I guess I can feel proud and pleased that I fed the family for a while, but at the time I only thought of my father's plight. My father still didn't have a job and worse, a job offer, on the strength of which he had spent money for some badly needed things, was withdrawn. There was a lot of politics involved in all this, for my father's caste was against him, though he had never counted himself as a Brahmin. In fact, when we applied for admission to college, he made us leave the caste column blank. (Though the clerk, to whom I submitted the form, very nonchalantly filled in my caste himself when I refused to do so. He knew who I was, he knew my caste! No chance of anonymity in a small town!)

My father had borrowed money to construct our house and the man who had loaned him the money had begun pestering him to return it. I remember the day he came home and yelled at my father. It was a shocking experience for us to see our always-respected, and often-feared father being shouted at, to see him taking it quietly.

It was a measure of my father's desperation that he began to consult an astrologer. A fat man who came every day in a tonga (paid for by my father) and sat almost all day eating paan. Each time after applying lime on his paan, he wiped his lime-y fingers on the wall, leaving white stripes behind. He spent a great deal of time making calculations on pieces of paper. I ask myself now how my father, a rational thinking man, could have fallen for the astrologer's claptrap. The man was treated as if he could change my father's luck with his mumbo jumbo. Then I think of my father's plight – no money, no job, a sick wife, and three children to support and educate. Of course he needed something to believe in, to cling on to.

Later, in Bangalore, when my husband, too, had given up his job, though for different reasons, and we moved into a cockroach-infested small house in the suburbs, I heard an astrologer, who lived opposite us, tell her clients, 'Next year all will be well.' She had a loud voice and we heard her say the same thing to every client. I imagine this hope is what makes us go on; without it, we might just as well give up. I guess my father was looking for hope from the astrologer.

I also wondered what it was that made my father give up his job. He resigned on principle, we were told, but we never knew exactly what it was. We heard that he was punished by a transfer without promotion because of the activities he took part in, some of which were taboo for government servants. True, he was always an activist, he supported the struggle for a unified Karnataka, he sheltered a young Communist on the run after the Quit India movement, and he was anti-authority and so on. We also heard that there was much envy, because of his popularity among students. I saw it myself decades later when I met an over-seventy-year-old woman who had been his student. She told me how charismatic he was, how awed the girls were by him and how he made their hearts flutter when they saw him. She blushed as she spoke and I was both amused and touched by her words.

I still don't know what made him resign, and if it was on a matter of principle, had he thought of the price he would pay? Was it worth it? Some friends had tried to dissuade him, but he had an idea of himself as a man who defied authority, a man who would not yield. I often thought he enjoyed ruffling feathers and shocking people. Why else would he have had a Muslim boy working for him in conservative Dharwad? And it was said that during his own wedding he, a chain smoker, lit his cigarette in the holy fire.

My mother supported him in all that he did; her loyalty to him was rock-hard, absolute. I know he was traumatised by the experience of those few years of unemployment. He confessed in his autobiography that he regretted what he had done. He had experienced unemployment and poverty earlier once, soon after he returned from England. Moneyless, alienated from his orthodox family, his faith in himself destroyed, he had thought of committing suicide. Now, with a wife and three children to support, he did not have that option, either.

I know that all his life he was torn by guilt at what my mother had to undergo. 'I have wronged her,' he said to me once, years later. She came from a very wealthy family in Pune. They were not only large landowners, my mother's father and his three brothers were successful in their own professions. My grandfather, the eldest brother, was a very prominent, successful and prosperous lawyer in Pune. The family home, a three-storeyed Peshwa-style *wada* built around three courtyards, was symbolic of their status and their prosperity. (The house had been bought for 16,000 rupees, my mother told me once, the entire sum paid in silver coins.) The silverware and jewellery that came out of the little safe in the '*tijori* room' during weddings and on festival days, were an indication of their landed wealth. I can still remember one of my aunts dressed for a wedding she had to attend, and how queenly she looked to my child's admiring eyes in her Chanderi nine-yard sari and her pearls.

My father, on the other hand, started his married life with almost nothing. During his jobless days, my mother had had to sell her jewellery, all of it given to her by her father. They must have been desperate to resort to this measure and it must have humiliated my father enormously. In fact, for some time she did not even have any decent saris to wear. These things must have hurt my father, all the more because she never complained about any of it. Yet, he did his best; I remember he subscribed to a new magazine for children brought out by The Times Group. I am sure it was not easy for him to do this, for, however little it cost, it would mean that something else would have to be sacrificed. We never thought of this. How could we? We loved the magazine, we waited eagerly for it, hanging over the gate all afternoon on the days it was to come. It was our first introduction to comics – Billy Bunter, King of the Royal Mounted, Hopalong Cassidy, The Lone Ranger and so many more. We were heartbroken when the magazine folded up.

While we had been given the gift of the magazine, we were not allowed to watch films. I remember looking wistfully through the barbed wire fence of our school at the theatre across the road, the very posters spelling out temptation. And the memory of how, once, our friends coached us into pleading with my father to let us see a film, telling us what to say, is still fresh in my mind. Very reluctantly, he agreed. My sister and I were not allowed to listen to film music on Radio Ceylon, either. We waited for him to go out, as he did every evening, and the moment he was gone, we switched on the radio. He got to know of it somehow (of course, my mother must have snitched on us), and so, one day, when we made a dash for the radio as soon as he had wheeled his bike out of the gate, we found that there was no plug. He had removed it. It was a mean trick, I thought. (My sister didn't agree. Her admiration of our father was total, she never wavered in her devotion to him.) What made him forbid us these things? Was it Puritanism? Or was it that he could not afford to give us the money for movie tickets? Now I think that it was neither of these; it was a fear that these things would distract us from our studies. Doing well in school and college was the one way to independence, to a dignified and self-respecting life. Yes, we had to be able to stand on our own feet.

For my twenty-first birthday, he gave me a gift of two books. One was a Sahitya Akademi publication, an English translation of Tagore's *Choker Bali* (*Binodini* in English), the other was *Six Great Modern Short Novels*. We were not a family which celebrated birthdays with parties or gifts; very few people did it then. This was the first time I had got a gift; it was the last time as well. At the time, I'd just completed my Law; I'd done very well, topped the university and got a gold medal. Perhaps it was in appreciation of this achievement that he gave me the books. Or, perhaps it was an atonement for the way he had reacted against my reading as a girl. I never thought of all this when I got the gift; I stumble on these thoughts as I write.

As if living in his own house had released something he had suppressed for long, he wrote a novel soon after we moved into it. I remember him reading it out to my mother sometime at night; in fact, he read it to her through the night. He also wrote a play, *Shokachakra* (The Wheel of Sorrow), which must have been brewing inside him since Gandhiji's death. It was a prophetic play, eerily predicting, with a sibylline clairvoyance, what would soon happen to the Congress party, to the country. It foresaw the end of Gandhism, the defeat of all that Gandhi had stood for and propagated. Soon, the Congress party would make just such a breakaway in ideals and principles from the man it called the Father of the Nation. This play was first staged in a movie theatre in Dharwad. I remember being present among the audience. The large audience watched the play in pin-drop silence and many people were wiping their tears when it ended. It must have been the last play he directed and staged in Dharwad.

Finally, he got a job in the Information and Broadcasting Ministry in Delhi. We had to leave Dharwad. Was there any regret? I don't remember. Did we celebrate? I don't remember that, either. But I remember that a Kannada newspaper in Hubli, which had supported him through his bad years, invited the family for an official farewell. My father, when he had to speak, suddenly broke down and sobbed. It was terrible to watch him. I had seen him cry only once before – when Gandhiji died. And I would see him break down once again, years later, at the tragedy of his son's life. He went to Delhi and joined work, while we stayed back. We had to complete our examinations, my mother had to wind up the house. Did we realise, my sister and I, that the family was going to be split? That our parents and brother would go to Delhi, my sister and I to Bombay, she to join a medical college, I to go to Elphinstone College, since I was underage for Delhi University? Perhaps we did; but for us it was, above all, a new beginning. We little knew that it was also the end of something. We would never come back to Dharwad again.

Nor did I know that for me Dharwad was not over, that, even if I left Dharwad, it would never leave me. Through the years, suddenly and in the most unexpected places, I would come across someone who recognised me, a person who said she/he was from Dharwad, too. A man waiting at the bus stop, like I was, in Bangalore, who got talking to me during our long wait and told me he had lived in Dharwad for some years and how he had loved the place, how hospitable the people were, how welcoming they were of strangers. A gentleman at the airport in Tehran who turned out to be an old classmate from the boys' school, like another man at an official dinner in Melbourne. A girl who shouted at me across the road in Mysore in the midst of the Dasara Festival celebration crowd. And in Lille, France, during a literary festival. I was having lunch with other delegates when I heard a voice say, 'My grandfather was a college teacher in a place called Dharwad.' I don't normally talk to people I don't know, but I immediately asked the speaker who his grandfather was. 'Armando Menezes,' he said. Yes, my teacher. There was Girish Karnad, another Dharwad man, whom I met as a fellow writer in Bangalore. And in London, in the Virago office, a very elegant and beautiful woman turned up and gave me a big hug, making me forget that I was shivering in my inadequate clothes, and that it was January in London. She was Aurora Figuerado, now Maria Couto, an old friend from St Joseph's in Dharwad, who was living in London at the time.

Besides, Dharwad came back to me in my dreams. I dreamt often of the crossroad near our house; again and again in my dream I found myself standing at the junction from where the roads diverged, looking at it and wondering where the roads went, unable to get an answer and finally waking up holding on to the thought of my ignorance and uncertainty. Dharwad came back to me in my writing, over and over again, not as itself, but with different names and in different guises. It was Saptagiri in *That Long Silence*, the unnamed small town in *The Dark Holds No Terrors*, Bhavanipur in *Small Remedies*, it was recreated as Rajnur in *In the Country of Deceit*. Mark Twain is supposed to have said that he moved cities, counties, even states if his writing needed it. The point is that the need of the novel is paramount, even greater than the need for authenticity. And therefore the various Dharwads I created in my novels, even if very different from what the town actually was, were to me the Dharwad I was born and grew up in.

Growing Up

When I was a child, I spake as a child, I understood as a child, I thought as a child;
but when I became a (wo)man I put away childish things.
The Bible (1 Corinthians)

BOMBAY WAS THE MECCA for us Dharwad dwellers, as it was, perhaps, for all small-towners. It was a glittering city, a buzzing city, a city of wonders – of red double-decker buses, of trams and electric trains. For us three siblings, it held the additional charm of being the place from where our favourite magazine *Junior* came. When a friend of mine went to Bombay on a school trip, the first thing I asked her on her return was whether she had been to *The Times of India* office. Years later, when I went as a writer to the *Femina* office (a magazine which belonged to The Times Group), I remembered the magazine and what it had meant to us, children living in a small town. Many of the girls in Dharwad were enamoured of Bombay as the centre of the fashion world. I remember a neighbour's daughter, on her return from Bombay, telling an admiring and avidly-listening group around her, that 'sleeves come up to here now' – encircling her arm just below the elbow as she spoke. (Later I found this very scene in *Pride and Prejudice*: Elizabeth's Aunt Gardiner telling the Bennets and their friends about the fashions in London.) I have no doubt that Dharwad soon had girls with their sleeves 'up to here', and that they remained that way long after Bombay had abandoned the fashion. For many, it was the film world that made the place so fascinating. I know some who expected to see film stars whizzing about in their glamorous cars when they went to Bombay. But mainly it was the place where people found jobs — from work in the *girnis* (the mills) to big jobs in international firms, Bombay had jobs for everyone. Which is why almost everyone had family and/or friends in Bombay. We too had family there: my mother's brother, my mother's sister, my father's cousins and many others more distant.

My father was a frequent visitor to Bombay as an examiner for the university examinations. In those days, Bombay University stretched all the way from Sind to Dharwad, and all examination results finally came out of the university office in Bombay. We heard the story of how my father, once, when he had to stay two months in Bombay as an examiner, rented a house in Shivaji Park (a posh area then and even later) for a very low rent. This was during war time, after the dock explosions had shaken Bombay, in 1944. Many people left Bombay and went to safer places, renting out their houses. I don't think we ever went with my father to Bombay. My sister had been in Bombay for two months when she had had to stay home for a year, because she was underage for entrance to the medical college and she had come back very knowing and, I thought, sophisticated.

Now my sister and I were to live in this big and fascinating city. Her admission formalities had already been completed. My staying in Bombay was a last-minute decision when my father found out that I, too, was under the age of admission to the graduate course in Delhi University. My mother completed all my admission formalities for college, as well as the hostel. I would be living in the Government Women's Hostel on Marine Drive. Admission to both college and hostel had been no problem since I had obtained very good marks in my pre-degree examinations. I had got the second rank in the university, something which surprised everyone, me most of all. For the first time, I had worked hard, getting up early every morning to study, and obviously my work had yielded results. My mother, after settling my sister and me in our hostels, and making sure that we were properly equipped, left for Delhi with my brother; his school would start soon. After they had gone, I was left, at the age of fifteen, to manage myself for the first time in my life.

Mine was a large hostel – five floors with thirty or more rooms on each floor. I didn't know a soul in the place. On my first day I saw groups of girls talking and laughing and it seemed to me that nobody cared whether I was alive or dead. I was on my own, of no account to anyone whatsoever. I knew then what loneliness was, I knew what being alone meant. I felt myself sinking into a deep dark pit of misery. (This is the language of the fifteen-year-old girl I was at the time.)

To make things worse, I was a small-town girl who had never used a phone, never seen a lift, never got into a bus, or – even more terrifying – the local electric trains. Everything intimidated me, everything conspired to make me feel an ignorant fool. Even going into a shop to purchase something was an ordeal; I had to nerve myself to tell the salesperson what I wanted. The first day of college, I had no clue about how to get there. I found another girl who, too, was going to Elphinstone and who, like me, was new to Bombay and didn't know the way, either. We joined forces, took a bus and found ourselves in Dhobi Talao, opposite St Xavier's College, instead. It was pouring, the roads flooded as they always were with the first rains. We were soon drenched in spite of our raincoats, and were unable to find our college, or the way to it. We went back to the hostel, miserable, feeling utter fools.

I had never seen rains like this before; the beginning of the monsoon is always dramatic in Bombay. Whereas Dharwad had gentle rains, which went on and on, all day and night. The word for this rain in Kannada was *jiti jiti* rain, a word that conveyed the sense of something annoying and nagging. Here, the rain poured out of the heavens, it pounded the streets and roofs of buildings with a ferocity I had never seen. The sea was just across the road from our hostel, and it was even more fearsome than the rain. It seemed to swallow the rain and send it back through waves that thundered and dashed against the sea wall, sending up sprays, which at times arched over the road and fell on the opposite pavement. It was an endless activity, the waves rolling back only to allow other waves to go through the same process. The rain and the sea appeared to form one unit and the flooded roads, which as I saw with amazement, seemed to create a watery world. The rooms in the hostel that faced the sea were blocked during the monsoon months, the balconies locked, so that we could not go on to them. My room faced the sea and, shuttered and closed, it was like a dark damp hole. One morning, overcome by misery, I began to cry. The *bai* who came to clean my room found me sobbing my heart out and, frightened by the intensity of my grief, brought a Marathi-speaking girl to comfort me. But neither she, nor the *bai*, could help and they finally left me alone.

I seemed to have lost my sense of myself; it was as if I had left the sharp, bright girl I had been, behind in Dharwad. College was no better. I had chosen Economics as my main subject, since I had been told that all intelligent students opted for Economics. Economics, I was told, gave you many opportunities for a good job. I had heard it said that, with an Economics degree, you could get a job in international banks, even perhaps abroad. However, I quickly realised this was not the right subject for me. I hated it; it was dry and drab, and worse, there were figures in it. I fell asleep during lectures, my pen trailing off and creating undecipherable scrawls. I often ask myself, why did I not change the subject when I realised how much I hated it? Perhaps because there was no one to tell me I could change my subject if I wanted to, that I did not have to go on struggling with Economics. To add to these woes, I felt a country bumpkin among the sophisticated students in college. I had to listen to comments on the way I dressed, the way I plaited my hair, comments which seemed to demolish me.

Luckily, as had to happen, things improved in a while. I had a few things on my side. I had two homes in Bombay, my mother's sister's and her brother's, both of whom lived just a few bus stops away, though in opposite directions, from my hostel. I visited them, alternately, every weekend. I am sure I was a nuisance at times, but they never let me feel it. I got both affection and good home-cooked food when I went to see them. And a shoulder to weep on in my aunt's house. The other asset was my knowledge of Marathi. It was my mother tongue in a literal sense, the first language I had spoken after birth. Knowing Marathi made me belong. If I had been identified as a Kannada girl (or a *Madrasi*, as all of us South Indians were called then) I would have been much more of an outsider.

I also, miraculously it seemed, came across a girl in the hostel who had been in our convent school in Dharwad. She recognised me and soon we, with some other girls, formed a group which remained intact my two years in the hostel. My age, too, helped. I was younger than all my classmates, younger than my friends in the hostel, which made them protective of me. I had lived a very sheltered life until then and I was very innocent. I remember my shock when I saw a girl shaving her legs in the hostel, quite openly, one leg on a stool, the tap in the wash basin running. I stood and stared. I'd never known anyone who shaved her legs. The girl looked at me and sang out, 'Hello,' in a very natural manner. She was not embarrassed at all. It was I, who rushed away from there.

This innocence got me into trouble when I gave my name and my hostel address in a newspaper column which promised penfriends. I got about a dozen letters the first day, a few more the next day. And on the third day, there was an avalanche of letters from men, both young and old, all of them panting to become penfriends with this fifteen-year-old who was living in a hostel and was, therefore, safely free of the supervision of parents. The hostel Superintendent, Mrs Maclean, called me to her office and showed me the letters. Accusingly, I thought. I burst into tears. What had I done? My friends came to plead my innocence, my father wrote from Delhi to apologise on my behalf. It was decided that Mrs Maclean would take charge of all the letters that came to me and give me only the ones from family and friends; she would deal with the rest. My friends were convinced that she was having a great time reading the letters herself, and kept telling me to get them back from her after she was done with reading them. I wouldn't have dared.

Mrs Maclean was a martinet, everyone was scared of her. There was a joke among the girls that she had a soft corner for only three people, three 'M's: Mr Maclean; Morarji Desai, then Chief Minister of Bombay and in a sense her boss; and Mr Manuel, our mess manager, the only young and fairly personable man around us. Mr Manuel was wildly popular among the girls, though I must say he kept his distance and dignity with them. It was said that a volatile girl once threw herself at him, crying out, 'Thank God for you, Mr Manuel.' She openly confessed she was sick of being surrounded by females all the time, since she was also studying in a girls' college. Mrs Maclean was kind to me during this penfriends episode; she was always protective of her girls. Once she called a special meeting when she got a letter from an unknown male, telling her that a girl in such and such a room had a mole on her breast. I think he even specified which breast. Without identifying the girl, Mrs Maclean gave us some advice – switch off the lights when undressing, she said, and when you come to the crucial stage, just duck. We had fits of giggles trying to figure out how to undress and duck at the same time.

I had also become, in my very early days, a regular visitor to my sister's hostel in the J.J. Hospital campus. It was a hostel for medical students and therefore had a very easy and casual atmosphere. The schedule of these students made strict rules impossible; girls went out and came in at all times, according to their duty hours. To be there, occasionally to have lunch with my sister – the food was better than in our hostel – somehow assuaged my homesickness. (It was here that it began, my habit of relying on my sister in times of trouble. I never went to my parents with any of my problems after that.) It was not very easy to get to her hostel from mine. I had to take a bus to a certain point, then a tram. Once, returning in the evening, for some reason no tram arrived. One did come after a while, but it was so full I could not get in. I was desperate. Eight o'clock was curfew hour in my hostel, at which time the gate would be locked. I began to walk along the tram tracks, and finally reached a place from where I could get a bus. Later, my sister rang me and asked what I had been doing in the red light area! A friend of hers had seen me walking there, and shocked, rushed to tell my sister about it. My sister had panicked. But I did not know it was a red light district. I must have seen women standing at the doors and windows, but I was so engrossed in getting back in time I took no note of them.

New experiences, new fears, new mistakes. The only thing that connected me to my old self was reading. As always, I managed to get books from somewhere. An uncle had, at some time, subscribed to a set of books and I devoured these. I remember *The Man in the Gray Flannel Suit, The Song of Bernadette, The Nun's Story, The Cruel Sea, Désirée* (how I loved that book!) – all the best sellers of the time. I read the entire collection in a very short time; a few weekend visits sufficed. Reasonably familiar with the streets around my college by now, I found old books being sold on the pavement and bought them for a few annas. (For the ignorant: sixteen annas made a rupee.) I soon had a small collection of Agatha Christie books. My greatest treat was buying a copy of *Woman & Home* at a bookstall near my college. It cost quite a lot, which meant that I got off the bus two stops earlier to save the money for it. I was completely fascinated by stories of quiet, brown-eyed, brown-haired girls, who triumphed over glamorous blondes, and finally got the dark handsome masterful men. Romance entered my life with these stories of men and women in distant lands, though it had nothing to do with me or with my life.

Two years of hostel life, two years of learning to live with others, of managing myself, of life in a big city. Bombay was the biggest, the richest city in India then; even Delhi, which we visited during vacations, though it had a royal touch, with its broad roads and stately houses, still had, in those days, a provincial feel. In Bombay, standing in the evenings on the balcony of the hostel, we watched cars going in a steady stream on Marine Drive, that beautiful sea-bordered road. Big American cars. Cadillacs, Chevrolets, Studebakers, Fords and many other models. The stylish, rakish convertibles were a great novelty, and to me they seemed the epitome of luxury and glamour. Especially when a young man, wearing dark glasses, one hand laid negligently and casually on the door, was driving it.

Our hostel also gave us the opportunity of seeing State guests go past. It was the time of Nehru's flirtation with Communism and

I remember seeing the Russian leaders, Bulganin and Khrushchev, driving on Marine Drive in an open car. (Innocent days indeed, without fears of bombs and terrorists.) I vaguely remember the cries of *Hindi Chini bhai bhai*, so perhaps we saw the Chinese premier, Chou En-lai, too. If so, I am quite sure we waved cheerfully at him as well. With the grandstand view we had, we could do no less. In any case, the Chinese betrayal was still some years away from us. And Nehru was still the blue-eyed boy of the people, though disillusionment was creeping in.

Nehru has become the villain of post-Independence India. People forget that freedom came with the violence and bloodshed of Partition; they forget that the leaders of that time made it possible for people to get over the frenzied hatred of Partition and to move on. In time, Nehru's foreign policy of Panchshila and non-alignment seemed to catapult us among the important nations of the world. But Nehru's mistakes seem to have overlaid these successes. Krishna Menon, that terrible man, whose greatest achievement is his marathon speech in the U.N. General Assembly, was involved in a scam, and Nehru supported him.

In fact, the father of one of the girls in our hostel had been in the Indian High Comission in London in some capacity at the time of the scam and it was said that he had some knowledge of the truth of what had happened. He was found dead on the road at the time when Menon was standing for elections to Parliament from Bombay and was taken to a public hospital as an unclaimed body. Obviously, there were whispers. But would anyone speak openly about Nehru's man? Later there was China – a disaster on a national scale, for which once again Krishna Menon was held responsible. But why would we young girls think about these things? For us, it was a good time. 'Bliss was it in that dawn to be alive/ but to be young was very heaven.'

All that my father could give my sister and me, in those days, was 100 rupees a month each. I am amazed now when I think of the number of things I managed to do with it. Food and transport took a major share of the money. I bought books (second-hand ones) and my copy of *Woman & Home* every month. Then there were infrequent visits to eating-places, the ones we could afford. Eating *bhel* at Nana Chowk was a great treat. And of course there were movies. I read J.B. Priestley's *Angel Pavement* some years later, which was about the entry of Hollywood films into England and the consequent slow death of the music halls. To attract customers to this new entertainment, movie theatres were made very plush; for young English boys and girls, the theatres spelt both glamour and luxury and brought the magic of Hollywood into their lives. Which was what spelt the death of the music halls. (All the magic and charm of the music hall era comes through in Priestley's *The Good Companions*, an amazingly good book.) The first time I entered a theatre in Bombay, I looked round with the same open-eyed wonder the English boys and girls must have done – the plush carpets, the comfortable padded push-back seats, the almost-royal scarlet curtain which went up slowly, creating beautiful semi-circular folds at the bottom. All these, and the soft music, transported me to another world. I had been used to the theatres in Dharwad, in which females, both young and old, paid five annas for a ticket in the 'zenana', with a real purdah, a musty, smelly one, which was opened only when the lights went off. The crackle of peanuts being shelled accompanied the conversation in the films, and the sickening smell of raw coconut hair oil and the even worse odour of the after-effects of all that peanut eating, floated around and above the spectators.

This was also the time of the linguistic reorganisation of states. A man fasted to death demanding the creation of a separate state for the Telugu-speaking people, and Nehru had to give in to the demand for creating states on the basis of language. Bombay posed a problem. A cosmopolitan city, with people from all over India living in it, it was proposed to become an independent city-state, at which the Maharashtrians protested. I remember the slogan, 'Maharashtra only with Mumbai', a cry which was taken up by all Maharashtrians. There were riots in the city. Finally, to put an end to the violence, the government gave in, and Bombay became the capital of the newly formed state of Maharashtra. It was the end of what Bombay had been and stood for; it lost its cosmopolitanism and its broad-minded acceptance of everyone. It also created the right atmosphere for a linguistic fanaticism, which culminated in the formation of a political party, the Shiv Sena. This party, entirely built on linguistic chauvinism and hatred of others, changed the character of the city forever.

The politics of this language frenzy reached our hostel, and Marathi girls, wearing black armbands, tried to force the Gujarati girls to do so as well. I, though identified as a Marathi person, had no such clear-cut loyalty, nor did I like the divisive frenzy. I refused to wear an armband. I lost a friend at the time, but I learnt my own strength, learnt that I could not be forced to do anything against my will. The Goa Liberation movement also came at this time. Fortunately, everyone was on the same side now, on the side of a liberated Goa and against the dictator Salazar. I remember marching on the streets crying out 'threatening' slogans like, '*Ek jelabi tel mein, Salazar jail mein!*'

At the end of the first year, I had a group of good friends in the hostel and I was a part of many activities. I learnt to roller-skate, went bicycling on Marine Drive (and went bang against a woman who was sweeping the road, my front wheel going right into the cleft in her backside!) and danced a fisherwoman's dance during a concert. I had got used to the hostel, to the routine, to the hostel food, and even to the clanging of the lift door all day, to the constant cries of 'Please close the lift door', which echoed through the hostel when someone left the door partially open and the lift was stalled. However, my academic life was not so happy. I had just two or three good friends in college and I was never happy or at home in Elphinstone. I felt that most of the students were snobs, though maybe it was my complex. But I do remember one of the girls speaking of me as 'these people' – by which she meant small-towners. What was worse was that I could never make friends with Economics. As the final examination came closer, I was terrified at my lack of preparation, and my inadequate understanding of some areas of Economics. In a way, I was lucky I fell ill during the preliminary examinations and was able to reach the final examination without doing this pre-exam test. My illness was also the excuse that saved me from the disgrace of my poor performance in the finals. Even my father had nothing to say except that I should stay at home for a year and recoup my health before going on to anything else. In any case, I was not even thinking of post-graduation; I would have nothing to do with Economics. At this time, too, my father's stay in Delhi came to an end and he had to go to Bangalore to join All India Radio. And so I went with my parents and brother to Bangalore and began family life all over again.

Going to Bombay from Dharwad had been a big step for me, almost the same as going to the USA is for the globe-trotting youngsters of today. Going to Bangalore from Bombay did not seem so momentous. It was more about being back with the family than going to Bangalore. I had no idea then that it was to be the place in which I would live the largest part of my life. The reorganisation of states, which had made Bombay go up in flames, had happily unified all the Kannada-speaking areas – which until then had been parts of different states – and had formed a composite state. Bangalore had the dignity of becoming the capital of this state. Compared to Bombay, however, Bangalore was still a small town. And slow and lethargic as well, no bustle in it at all. I remember I once got up from my seat in the bus well before my stop, preparing to get off, like I had always done in Bombay, when the conductor waved me back to my seat. 'What's the hurry?' he asked.

Shops opened late, closed for lunch and reopened only by about four in the evening. Buying anything was a patience-wearing exercise, the shop owners or salespersons were so slow. *Jhutkas* were still an accepted form of transport. For those who don't know what a *jhutka* is, it is a contraption without seats, unlike a tonga, driven by a tired and miserable looking pony. You sat with folded legs on the floor and continually moved up and down according to the driver's instructions – to keep the balance, as he said. *Move a little to the front*, he would say, or, *move back*. And you, sitting on your bottom, had to move in the most undignified way, according to his instructions. Bangalore was, then, really two cities; it was divided into the City and the Cantonment, a sharp line between the two. Almost an 'East is East and West is West' kind of thing. The Cantonment was the posh area. I remember a friend of mine once asking me in a kind of horrified disbelief, 'You live in the City?'

But compared to Bombay, it was a remarkably clean city. Clean streets, neat little houses with a sampige tree and a coconut palm in the front yard, where early mornings the housewife or the maid would draw a new rangoli design every day, after first washing the yard with a bucket of water. There were also older bungalows with huge compounds, gardens and trees. Roadside trees bloomed with flowers of different colours through the year. These flowering trees were my special delight. From February to May, various trees flowered with blooms of different colours, creating a kind of colourful canopy on many roads. The markets were fragrant with jasmine strings and rajnigandha garlands and the streets outside the market were piled with heaps of flowers during festivals. It was a city of flowers and gardens. Apart from the two big parks, Cubbon Park and Lal Bagh, you could suddenly come across a little garden tucked away in some corner, an island of greenery and colours. I remember a small garden at the entrance to Malleswaram where my parents lived, one of the most beautiful and well-designed gardens I have seen in Bangalore. There were flowering trees, flowering bushes and bowers over which creepers of fragrant white flowers climbed. It was situated in an area of dingy buildings with a cotton mill just opposite. Afternoons, you could see the workers sitting in the shade and eating their lunch, and men lying under the shade having a nap. I don't know if the garden still exists. The mill has certainly gone; it was demolished and a huge mall now stands in its place. I don't have the courage to go all the way and find that the garden, too, has disappeared.

At that time, because of the reorganisation of the state, there was an influx of people from different areas – lawyers, government officials, in fact, anyone who had to be closer to the centre of power for their work. But they were not very welcome. The locals were insular, suspicious of 'outsiders'. 'Outsiders' in turn scornfully said that 'these people' knew nothing of the country, nothing of the world beyond the Tungabhadra river. Bangalore had been part of Mysore State, a princely state and people still worshipped their portly Maharaja. When they spoke of him, they folded their hands, the way I would later see people in Shantiniketan do when they spoke of Tagore. Those like us who had lived in British India and had a healthy hostility to authority found this surprising. Everything was different here, as we saw from the moment my father received us at the station and deposited us at the hotel where we were to stay.

My father had come to Bangalore earlier than us. He had had a disastrous journey. He had been pickpocketed as he reached Delhi station and had lost all his money, as well as his ticket to Bangalore. He had this tendency to be pickpocketed; I used to imagine pickpockets cheering when they saw him coming. Later, my mother stitched inside pockets for him where he kept his money, always a bare minimum. Anyway, he was able to extricate himself from the catastrophe, which would have driven a lesser man to desperation. He met an M.P. from Karnataka who convinced the ticket checker to give him a fresh ticket; he also gave my father a loan of a small sum for his travelling expenses. By the time we got to Bangalore, this was an old forgotten story as far as my father was concerned; he was immediately absorbed in his work. And, typically, he had not thought of finding a home for his family. And therefore the hotel.

In the hotel, we were immediately exposed to the culture of the city, the food especially. Idlis and dosas for breakfast and mountains of rice and sambar for lunch, the smell of the food struggling with the equally strong smell of the agarbattis and the gentler perfume of the mogras which adorned the pictures of gods, for whom a puja was done every morning. We three siblings had a good time, as we always did when we were together, but I suppose our mother was acutely uncomfortable, caged into one room all day, since there was always a crowd of men outside. There was scarcely a woman to be seen in the place.

My father, or rather one of his assistants, found us a temporary accommodation in the house of a wealthy man. We were given rooms on the first floor. The railway line was just across the road and we could see the trains to Madras going past from the large balcony where we spent most of our time. We had no furniture at all, which made it a kind of camping life. So there we were, neither guests nor tenants, almost a part of the life of strangers we had never met and whom we scarcely spoke to in the few days we lived there. The smell of their food and their talk came clearly to us through the open courtyard in the centre and we soon came to know that it was an odd household. The man had two wives; he had remarried because he had no children from his first marriage. (It was only in British India that bigamy was a crime.) The second wife, a very young woman, had no children either, and ignorant of the possibility that it was the man's fault, they kept consulting astrologers, who announced that 'the child will come, the child will come'. If, as seemed very likely, no child 'came', I am sure both the women would be blamed. I wonder whether the man 'married' again, for a third time, in search of a son, like Henry VIII. We stayed here a very short while, and after a month or so in a terrible house with an aggressive landlady, we moved into a better place, where we lived for some time.

My father, anxious about my health — I'd never been the same after my pre-examination bout of fever — insisted I stay at home for a year and do nothing. I did stay home for a year, but looking back, it does not seem that I did nothing. I joined a typing class (something all students did in their free time then, boys to equip themselves for a job, girls to while their time until they got married) and learnt typing. I little knew, as I typed *asdfg asdfg, qwert, poiuy*, how important this was going to be, and how useful it would be to me later.

I also joined a dance class. An eminent dancing couple, U.S. Krishnarao and Chandrabhaga Devi took me in, mainly I think because they knew and respected my father. (There was a lot of nepotism going on in those early years of my life!) Since my father couldn't afford to pay the full fees, I was teamed with another newcomer, a young woman who had a job, and we shared the fees. I loved the beat, the rhythm and the precision of Bharat Natyam, but for the life of me, I couldn't produce the emotions, the *bhavas*, which we were supposed to bring out — all the emotions from happiness to anger. They were so predictably expressed, I thought of them the same way I later looked at clichés and stereotypes in language. I also had problems with my guru (his wife was a sweetie), who kept on at me because I did not wear bangles or a bindi. 'Do you know which Hindu women don't wear bangles and a bindi?' he asked me once in an ominous voice. I didn't defend myself. How could I tell him that these things – bangles, earrings, chains, etc. – weighed me down, they made me feel confined? I found it hard even to wear a watch. I remember that I removed the toe rings I'd had to wear during my wedding ceremonies immediately after the rituals were over. Even today, the moment I get home, I remove all these accessories. My dance guruji was also disapproving of my carrying a book all the time. 'A substitute for a baby,' he said. I didn't argue with that either, I just went on doing whatever I was doing.

    These, dancing and typing, were my only two obvious activities. Apart from this I did nothing, but I was, in fact, like a sponge, absorbing everything. We lived in a place that had three homes in one complex, our landlord living upstairs, and a family in a tiny little place at the back. Their front door and our back door aligned. Afternoons, the women, including my mother, sat and chatted. I listened to them, and got a glimpse of the way women were when they were on their own; I saw them easy, comfortable and relaxed. I was never to forget this and, when later I wrote about women's lives, these conversations and the atmosphere surrounding them, came back to me.

    I listened to my father conversing with friends and admirers. Back in Karnataka, he had a new lease of life. He did a great deal of writing in these years, he wrote plays, which were innovative and very different from what he had done in the first phase of his writing. He was a part of many theatre activities in the city and was associated with a number of institutions, both in Bangalore and Delhi. I was a silent listener and an invisible observer of many of the activities that took place at home. There were meetings, conversations, play-readings. I listened to my father reading out a play to a group of theatre enthusiasts. Later, I watched the rehearsals at home of his new and very revolutionary play (*Kelu Janmejaya* – Listen, Janmejaya) and attended its first performance. The atmosphere in the theatre was electric and the audience watched the play in total silence. There was a question/answer session afterwards and the questions poured in. My father, who had been chain-smoking, pacing restlessly outside, as he always did during a first performance, met the questions with aplomb. For the first time I saw the public side of a writer. During this time, my father, sorry for me perhaps at having to stay home, took me to a lecture by Toynbee, and to a performance of *The Tempest* by a group from England. I had studied Shakespeare in college, but watching the play brought Shakespeare close; these were real people, talking to one another as all humans did.

And, of course, I read. I read more during this time, I think, than at any other time in my life. I was a member of the British Council library, which had just opened in Bangalore. I must have been the most regular subscriber, bringing home four books each week and then promptly going back for more. I had begun reading Rumer Godden's *An Episode of Sparrows* when we were visiting a family friend in hospital. Sadly, I had read only a few pages when we had to leave. But I found this book in the British library and read all of Rumer Godden's books after that. I became a member of the USIS (United States Information Services) library as well, and for the first time got access to American literature. I even read dictionaries (words, their etymology, the various shades of their meanings fascinated me, still fascinate me) and self-help books like French, German and Hindi self-instructors, though I was never able to find my way into any of the languages through these books. In fact, Hindi came to me through films and film songs, They gave me a rich stock of words for love – *pyar, prem, mohabbat, ishq* and so on. Not something one can use in daily life! This was also the time when I read a great many plays. I had read Sanskrit plays when I was a girl in Dharwad and had been fascinated by them. We had a collection of Tolstoy's plays at home – a book in a very small format. Not many people know of his plays, but I devoured them with passion. I loved the sprightly lady's maid, Tanya, in *The Fruits of Enlightenment* (all the plays had titles like this), a play about the effete aristocracy and land-starved peasants (you could see the revolution coming), and shuddered at the terrible rural story of adultery, incest, murder and infanticide (you could see the revolution coming here as well). I must have read the plays so often that the book seemed to get the shape of my palm! I still have the book with me, it must be a rare copy today.

Bernard Shaw became a favourite, specially his *Arms and the Man*, the first play of his that I read; I was completely enchanted by it. It is amazing how I loved the romance (or rather, two romances) in a play that set out to destroy falsely romantic ideas. And there was *Saint Joan*, which begins so prosaically with, 'No eggs! No eggs!', and ends with the making of a saint. I have always identified Joan with Shaw's Joan since then. After going to Delhi, my father had acquired a small library, mostly plays, and I read Terence Rattigan (*The Browning Version* affected me deeply), John Synge, Eugene O'Neill, Sartre, Tennessee Williams, and so many others. Arthur Miller was a great discovery; *A View from the Bridge* and *The Crucible* made an impact I have never forgotten. However, it was long before I linked *The Crucible* and its theme of the Salem witch trials to the McCarthy era in the USA. Miller's *Death of a Salesman* seemed a bit tawdry to me. I had to become an adult to see the tragedy in it, the tragedy of the American dream and the price to be paid for achieving it.

Even though I loved plays, when I began writing I never thought of writing a play. I felt there was a complete disjunction between the people, Indian women and men, and the language, English, that they would have to speak on the stage. I have always thought that this is one of the reasons drama in English lags behind the other genres of literature in India. There is a definite change in the scene today, there are more plays in English. In Bangalore, we had Mahesh Dattani, and there's still Poile Sengupta. Even Girish Karnad, who is a Kannada dramatist, wrote an original play in English many years later. Now there are scores of young writers writing plays in English. This, perhaps, has become possible because of the increased use of English in urban Indian life. But these are subjects for critics to write about; I don't know enough to make any kind of a statement.

In spite of all these things, I was living in a kind of nothingness. I had no idea that this blankness, this silence, this non-action, was the starting block from where my writing would take off; the one thing I knew was that I was never bored. All the ideas, the emotions and the experiences of this time, the different kinds of languages that I heard, would come back to me later. When the year was over I joined a law college, which, back then, was a two-year course after graduation. I was a student again and a much happier student than I had been in Bombay. The classes were in the mornings since the course was meant mainly for working students. I can still remember my early morning walks to the bus stop. It seems to me that it was always pleasant; Bangalore was beautiful then. Every morning, I had to brave the comments of some boys who stayed in a 'lodge' near the bus stop. I walked past, pretending I didn't hear them. To be fair, I think they were innocent comments, mostly about my long hair and my two plaits. The bus stop had a small market behind it and a *jhutka* stand nearby; the smell of the mogra flowers and horse dung combined and even today when I think of those days the smell comes back to me.

The subject of Law, unlike Economics, was a pleasure. I found myself enjoying the subjects – Jurisprudence, Hindu and Muslim personal laws, Constitutional law, the Indian Penal Code. It was the time when the Hindu Code Bill, bringing about changes in Hindu personal laws, was being passed in Parliament. Today, when a uniform civil code is still being resisted, I remember Ambedkar (the man all political parties pay homage to, because they want to be sure of the votes of his followers). He was the Law Minister at the time and he resigned, because the Hindu Code Bill, which was introduced and debated in Parliament was dropped, because Nehru said there was too much opposition to it. Ambedkar's explanation of his resignation, a long and fascinating document, asks, 'How strong was the opposition?' But obviously there was a strong opposition to changes in the Hindu law which would benefit women. When the bill was finally passed, it was a much-diluted version of what it was initially supposed to be. A number of concessions had to be made to the older and more conventional beliefs and ways of thinking. Members of Parliament felt that their voters (male voters, of course) would not welcome any drastic changes. I'm sure they themselves were also against any changes that gave women more rights.

Things are changing today, but the opposition to reforms, which try to restore the balance between the two genders, is still strong. Even as I write this, the Supreme Court has ruled against the triple talaq, a result of the opposition and the activism, which has come from within the Muslim community, from the Muslim women themselves. This is how changes should come and will come. And, having the law to back any movement makes a great difference; legislation and activism have to go hand in hand. That the Bombay High Court allowed the entry of women into the inner sanctum of the Haji Ali dargah in Mumbai was the culmination of various factors: women's activism, the strength of our Constitution and the understanding of the judges that changes are inevitable. Though the failure of the Parliament to pass the Women's Reservation Bill, giving women 33 per cent of the seats in Parliament is depressing, it is expected. Why would men pass a Bill that would take away their comfortable seats in Parliament from under them? But I see some radical and very necessary judgements, specially concerning women, coming out of the Supreme Court; these changes give me hope.

Going back to my life as a law student, I made some good friends in my two years of college. Recently, I found some photographs we had taken soon after the final examinations, when we knew we would soon be parting ways. As always, at this stage in life, seeing old pictures filled me with nostalgia and brought back many memories. And seeing us friends posing in Lal Bagh (taking pictures was a serious business in those days, you didn't grin and/or make a kissy mouth), I realised that surprisingly, none of us became practising lawyers, nor did we have anything to do with the law after that. But studying law did a great deal for my self-morale, especially when I topped the university and got a gold medal. In later years, I found in myself an understanding of what the law was for, a respect for it and for the role it plays in society. Perhaps it is this understanding, this respect, which makes me so intolerant of law-breakers, whether they jump the red light, steal, murder or cheat. Or rob banks. (The words 'bank robber' have a new connotation now. You don't need to wave a gun at the cashier; you only need to have access to the top bosses and take loans you never return.)

I also think that a basic knowledge of the law should be part of everyone's education. And yet, after my results, when the question, 'Now what?' was asked, I knew I didn't want to become a lawyer; I was too shy, too frightened to open my mouth in public. Nevertheless, I joined a criminal lawyer's office for a year, once again getting in because the lawyer knew my father. While I had loved the abstract subject of Jurisprudence and the concept of personal laws, I just could not take to the way the law was practised.

There was a huge gap between the theory and the practice. The lawyer, my senior, as the terminology went, recognised my feelings, perhaps, for he gave me one brief (a case that was going in appeal) to study at the beginning. Apart from a desire to correct the execrable English, I didn't know what to do with it and gave it back wordlessly. He never involved me in anything after that.

I spent the rest of the year hanging around the courts. The High Court building is one of the most beautiful heritage buildings in Bangalore, set in the equally beautiful Cubbon Park. It was a pleasure to be in such surroundings. I listened to cases in the High Court, absorbed what I saw and heard, and once again found something that would come in handy years later. I did learn a bit about the law. And, more than that, I saw how the judges snubbed lawyers, even the most successful ones, and how humbly lawyers took the rebuke. I also saw how opposing lawyers walked off as friends after they came out of the court where they had been fighting each other. Nobody spoke to me in my whole year there. Or rather, I didn't speak to anyone. Only one lawyer, a woman, one of the very few in the High Court at the time, spoke to me. She was very kind and friendly. I never forgot her. And by a coincidence, I was sitting next to her years later in Rashtrapati Bhavan, where both of us were waiting to receive our Padma awards. A coincidence, but then life is full of them. Those who object to coincidences in novels ignore this truth.

The next year, I was invited by a classmate from law college to work for a new kind of law reporter. I had to edit important cases which had become precedents, condensing the judgement and keeping only the pertinent points. This was work I could do from home. I found myself very comfortable with the work. I was happy that I was being paid for it as well, earning money felt good. I gave the money to my mother; she saved it and made gold bangles for me, for my wedding. I gave up working with the law reporter when I got married, and forgot all about it. I missed the clue which my pleasure in writing, and the growing knowledge of my skill at it, had provided.

Decades later, I had to edit a translation of my father's two books on the Bhagvad Gita. I was reluctant to do it because I was in the midst of writing *The Binding Vine* then. But my mother, after my father's death, had contacted a publisher who was willing to publish the translation (it had been translated by a scholarly friend of my father's) if I edited it to a reasonable length. The book was very long, but I could not refuse my mother – the publisher was emphatic that I edit it – so I took it on. It was laborious and tedious work. I had to read the original Kannada book, which was hard for me, and I had to rewrite much of the translation. But when I think of it now, I am glad I did it, for I got something very valuable out of it. I got a very minute understanding of what the Gita was about. Until then, like it is for most people, my knowledge was confined to a few verses, specially the two verses which almost everyone, who wants to reveal a knowledge of the Gita, quotes. Even the TV serials use these *shlokas* as a kind of background to portentous events. In one *shloka*, Krishna promises he will come back to the earth again and again to punish evil-doers (*Sambhavami yuge yuge*, Chapter 4, *shlokas* 7 & 8). Another is about having a right to action, not to the fruits of the action (*Karmanyeva adhikar astu na phaleshu kadachana*, Chapter 2, *shloka* 47).

Wonderful though it sounds, I am very sceptical of Krishna, or any Messiah for that matter, coming to birth in this age. If he does come, I am afraid he will be helpless to combat the evil, there is so much of it, and there is such an easy acceptance of it. The second verse, about not having a right to the fruits of your action, was interpreted by my father as applying, not to an ordinary person, but only to a leader of men like Arjuna. Why, my father asked in his book, would any human undertake an activity unless she/he wanted to enjoy the fruits of it? I agree with him. It is not the ordinary man, but the leader who has to be selfless.

However, the verses which struck a chord within me were not these popular ones. There's a *shloka* that comes at the end of the Gita in which Krishna tells Arjuna, 'I have given you the knowledge, now do as you desire.' (*Yathecchasi tatha kuru*, Chapter 18, *shloka* 3). This seems to me such a momentous message, a statement that so clearly spells out human autonomy, that I am surprised not more note is taken of it. To have the knowledge and then to decide what to do – there is no greater wisdom than this.

In John Steinbeck's *East of Eden*, I came across a story, told by a Chinese man, Lee, which conveys the same message in another way. This story is about some verses from the Bible (sixteen verses of the fourth chapter of the Genesis), which narrate what happened after Cain killed his brother, Abel. In the King James version, Lee read that God tells Cain, '*Thou shalt rule over sin.*' Later, he finds that the words used in the American Standard translation of the Bible are, '*Do thou rule over sin.*' He is intrigued by the different words used in the two versions, words which convey very different meanings; for, if '*thou shalt*', is a promise, '*do thou*', is an order. And so, out of a curiosity to know what the original word, which had been translated so differently, was, he, along with four other Chinese scholars, started learning Hebrew. After two years of learning the language and after much reading and discussion with a Rabbi, they finally came to the sixteen verses and got 'the gold from our mining', as Lee calls it. They discovered that the original Hebrew word was '*timshel*' – which meant neither '*thou shalt*', nor '*do thou*', but '*thou mayst*'. '*Thou mayst rule over sin*': these words, unlike the words in the other two versions, give humanity the choice. For, if '*thou mayst*', it is also true that the option of '*thou mayst not*' exists. Lee's words about what this revelation did to him are worth quoting. 'I have a new love for that glittering instrument, the human soul,' he says. 'It is a lovely and unique thing in the universe. It is always attacked, but never destroyed, because *thou mayst*.' Lee is right. To know we have the choice is to change our whole idea of ourselves and our lives. It is as significant as Krishna's '*Yathecchasi tatha kuru*'. These are words, which, if understood by more humans, could make the world a different place. Specially at this moment, when the idea of a god telling people what to do (mostly cruel things), seems, in the most unlikely way, to have come back.

Another verse that has left a deep impression on me is the one in which Krishna tells Arjuna, 'Don't worry about killing your enemies, I have already killed them. You are only the instrument.' (*Nimitta matra bhava Savyasachin*, Chapter 11, *shloka* 33). As a writer I have taken this statement to heart. I understand it very well, because I have long since recognised that, when I write, I am different from the person I am. I have been given a gift and when I write, I am the instrument through which it is expressed. This thought takes away the ego so many artists have (or, it should), it takes away the burden of the ego, which can at times be so destructive. Not that understanding the truth that it is not me, I am only the instrument, makes the ego completely disappear! As I've learnt, it makes its presence felt more often than is ideal.

And there's the concept of *svakarma* and *parakarma*. Not once, but twice, Krishna speaks of *svakarma* and *parakarma* (Chapter 3, *shloka* 35 and Chapter 18, *shloka* 47). 'Better is doing one's work (*svakarma*), even if badly done, than the duty of others (*parakarma*).' Which means that you need to recognise what is your own work. To be able to do that, it seems to me, is the greatest achievement in life. And I was, I now realise, beginning to find my work through rejecting what was not mine. Nothing I had done was a waste. My father had hoped I would appear for the IAS (the Civil Services) examination. He got me reading material containing information about what subjects one could choose, an application form and a booklet on how to apply. I read all of it and knew I could manage the written examinations. But the viva? It was like the thought of speaking in the courtroom as a lawyer. I couldn't do it. I was too lacking in self-confidence. I let the opportunity go. If my father was disappointed, he said nothing. Sometimes I wonder how my life would have been if I had indeed joined the Civil Services. What if my father had insisted …? But no regrets. My recognition of what was to be my work was yet to come, but when it came, it was absolute. There was to be no more stumbling, no more fumbling, after that.

Those Were the Days ...

When you are a married man, Samivel, you'll understand a good many things as you don't understand now.
Charles Dickens, *The Pickwick Papers*

Before I could find my way to my work, there was marriage. Marriage had been looming on the horizon for some time. My mother, naturally I suppose, had been agitating for quite a while for her daughters to get married. Prodded by her, my father had moved from indifference to some action. According to my mother, the first time she spoke to him of it, he said, 'What am I supposed to do? They should fix up their own marriages. Didn't I arrange mine?' I imagine he hated the process of an arranged marriage, specially the kind of humbling the girl's parents had to put up with.

Though we ourselves have sons, not daughters, we had dreaded the thought of 'seeing girls', we'd told our sons we'd rather they found their own partners. Which, thankfully, they did. But my father, I'm sure, had no such hopes, not about me, anyway. My sister was a medical student; for five years young women and men worked together. Many marriages came out of this contiguity. My sister was also a very popular girl. But I? If they had not arranged my marriage, I am sure I would have remained a spinster. (Doesn't sound so dreadful when I think of the positives: no responsibilities, no cooking, being left to myself!)

In my own defence, I must say that in those days there were few places or occasions when the two sexes could meet. In Dharwad, no boy and girl, no young man and woman, could ever meet on their own. If they did, the boy got away with it, while the girl was branded 'fast' (which was as bad as being 'forward'). Nevertheless, there were couples who did manage to meet. What force is there in this world which can control the primal urge of male and female to come together? What inhibitor is there that can suppress raging hormones? Caught as we all are in the loop of continuing the human race, mating has to, and will, happen. But in those days, segregation was the motto and a meeting between male and female had to be clandestine.

The first time boys and girls shared space in Dharwad was in college. Even then, they were kept apart in one way or another. Our class in college had three rows of benches for the boys and one row for the girls. This row was next to three doors out of which we could make a discreet entrance and exit, without having to run the gauntlet of lecherous male eyes. When I think of it now, there was a very unhealthy atmosphere in college. Many of the boys had never mixed with girls, they had no idea how to behave with them. They never spoke directly to the girls; instead, oblique suggestive remarks were made as girls passed by. And there was paper arrow throwing.

I always felt a kind of hidden menace in the frenzy with which these innocuous objects were flung at girls. As if they were weapons of their libido! At times, they made a concerted target of a girl and I remember one girl putting her head down on the bench when this happened to her. Why were girls so meek? Bombay had a much better atmosphere, a healthy mixing of boys and girls. But I never made any male friends in Bombay either, nobody special. I was too young and looked even younger. Later, in law college, I could sense interest from some male students, but I never felt the desire to respond to anyone. And so arranged marriage it had to be.

As things happen in the course of arranging marriages, my father was told about a suitable young man by an old student of his who knew this man and his family very well. The man being proposed for me was a doctor doing his post-graduation in G.S. Medical College, Bombay, which was attached to K.E.M. Hospital. I remember we met in the home of a senior doctor, the young man's teacher, who was from Dharwad. He too was a Deshpande. And there were two other Deshpandes in the room that day. I wondered which Deshpande was the right one! I had a 'I don't care' attitude, which amazes me when I think of it now. My father, when he met the young man, was suitably impressed by him. Unlike my father, I was hesitant, not because of the man, but because of marriage itself. I was not sure I wanted to get married. My uncle, who had been delegated by my father to talk to me, bluntly asked me, 'What do you want to do then?' I had no idea. A college friend of mine, who had a job in Bombay, was staying in a paying guest place and was trying to persuade me to join her. I could share her room and look for a job, she had said. But what kind of a job would I get? I lacked the courage even to make the attempt to look for one, and finally decided marriage was the only option for me. I didn't realise it required more courage to marry a man I'd met only a few times, than to look for a job. I often joke that I married to get away from my mother. There is some truth in it, because I felt unwanted at home; my mother's constant harping on marriage made me feel I had over-stayed. So, I agreed.

We got married in Pune. An aunt, who was an authority on marriage rituals, saw to it that even the pre-marriage rituals were duly performed. I have little memory of these things, or of the rest of it. But I do remember that the black bead chain, which my husband-to-be would put around my neck was, I was told by my aunt, supposed to be threaded by a prostitute. These women were the ultimate *saubhagyas* (women who have husbands living); because they never had husbands, they would never become that inauspicious thing – widows. The strangest logic I had ever heard. I also remember that my mother-in-law changed my name, which was a done thing at the time. I was offended. Not that I liked my name. I was always a little resentful that my father, a Sanskrit scholar, could find no other names for us than the very common names, Usha and Shashi. But changing my name? No way! Happily, no one used this 'new name' of mine. If anyone had done, I would have just pretended to be deaf! Thankfully, I continued to be Shashi; however boring the name was, it was mine.

One thing I realised soon after marriage was that there were a great many differences between the man I married and me. Our marriage could have been a disaster. Having always lived among teachers, writers and professionals, his was a kind of family I had never known. They were a rural landed family – conservative, orthodox and traditional, his mother a shaven widow. Surprisingly, it was my mother who got cold feet, who worried about whether I would be able to become part of such a family, having been brought up, as I had been, in a very liberal and open atmosphere. My father, ever the optimist, was more sanguine. He is an independent young man, he told my mother. He will live the way *he* wants. Was this what he hoped? Or was this what he guessed from the fact that, unlike most men, the young man never spoke of 'asking' his mother or brothers; he said he would *tell* them that he had decided on the girl he would marry. And my father was right, for the man I married did tell me later that we would live our life the way we wanted. I took this for granted then, but find it remarkable now.

Moreover, in time I realised that the words 'rural', 'orthodox', 'traditional' could not contain the family. Generalisations, as I would learn later when I began to write, can be very misleading. This was not the usual kind of family. My husband said he wanted a simple wedding and the family went along with him. He decided that only twelve of them would come for the wedding and so it was. The most surprising thing was that, when it was time for the wedding rituals to begin, even as an envoy from our family was being despatched to escort them to the wedding place, as was traditionally done, the bridegroom and his brother walked in, casually and without any fuss. No band, no *baaja*, no *baraat*. 'Let's not keep them waiting,' his eldest brother, a very dignified man who had taken their father's place, said. I think now that this was in deference to my father, out of respect for him. My husband himself had moved away from the orthodoxy in which he had grown up. His medical education helped him to look at things rationally, made him reject unreasonable rules and taboos, specially all ideas about the impurities of the human body. For him, the human body was not a pain, as it was to me, not something which needed constant purifying, as it was to his mother; it was a marvel, a miracle, an immensely complex system put together with exquisite precision. (I gave this point of view to the Anatomy professor in my novel *Moving On*.)

Like most people who start their married life in Bombay, we had no home and lived for a short while in a room sublet to us by a family my husband knew. A horrid smelly little room, an even more vile-smelling bathroom, and a family in which the women were prone to prying. There was nothing for me to do all day once my husband went to the hospital; but, thankfully, I had a whole set of Dickens given to me as a wedding gift by a friend (God bless her) and I read, or rather re-read, all of them, one after another. We lived close to Shivaji Park, so evenings were spent by the sea which was just a street away. The sea never ceased to fascinate me – I, who had lived in a landlocked place all my life. Cooking was an ordeal. Even worse was the thought that if I wanted to eat I had to cook! Worse, the cooking had to be done on a stove that I found hard even to light. And once my husband had lit the stove for me, I didn't know where to begin. I realised why my father, of all people, had been so insistent that I learn some cooking before I got married. I was a complete novice, because I had never taken any interest in cooking and my mother, too, hated anyone else coming into her kitchen. Nor did she have the patience to teach me. I could only peel potatoes, peas, and roast groundnuts. And I could roast masalas, at which I was supposed to be very good. (Though I did not know the names of all the masalas I was roasting!) It could have been tragic and our marriage could have ended within a month, it could have foundered on this rock of my ignorance of cooking, of my disinterest in it, for my husband is a man who appreciates good food. The women in his family were excellent cooks, who could turn out an excellent meal for unexpected guests, at any time, even at midnight, without batting an eyelid. So I was told (I didn't want to hear these stories). In my own home, my father was indifferent to what he ate; he ate whatever was put before him. His only occasional complaint was about the tea; he hated it being too sweet. My mother, who was an enthusiastic cook, had to wait in vain for some words of praise.

It was this task of cooking that made me realise what all of us understand at some time or another: that freedom is an illusion. I learnt that life does not give anyone, man or woman, the luxury of doing only what you like to do, what you want to do. I can't believe now that I was so naïve as not to have thought of this earlier. I had imagined that marriage, having my own home, would make me independent, which I could not be in my parents' house. But I had other anxieties. I remember, with much embarrassment, that very early on, I spoke to my husband, bravely, but hesitantly, afraid of being laughed at, that I was not going to be treated the way I had seen most wives being treated. As subordinates. As inferiors. I had thought that even the language used by husbands to wives was wrong. Commanding. Authoritative. (I wonder now whether they used the language of love only in bed – or whether they used it at all.) I wanted an equal relationship. He didn't laugh, thank God! He agreed.

Now, I wonder whether he did so as the only way to respond to such a strange demand, or as the easiest way to end the matter. But no; fortunately for me, he was not the type to impose his will on others. Nevertheless, I guess I was very naïve to think that I could make such a demand. Or stupid. It seems strange that I had these thoughts, because all the women I saw around me seemed to be playing the role of wife almost effortlessly. There were enough role models around: mother, aunts, cousins, friends, who assumed the role of wife/housewife immediately after marriage, as if they were born to it.

A letter written to me by my father's friend, Dr Shivaram, a doctor and writer, and a brilliant man, remains to me the most visible and clear idea of what my role was to be. He wrote that I now held the honour and happiness of two families in my hands, that the happiness of my new family was in my hands and it was my duty never to forget it and so on. (Did he have some doubts about me, had my father said something about my wilfulness? Was this why Dr Shivaram wrote the letter to me?) I remember I was vaguely flattered at the importance this gave me. Much later it occurred to me that this was how women had been conned into doing all the things they had to do as wives and mothers, doing things they didn't really want to do. However, I didn't say this aloud. No one would have taken me seriously, especially not my own family. It would have been regarded as just one more of 'Shashi's queer ideas'.

Surprisingly, or maybe not so surprisingly, because it was my nature to do whatever I had to with my whole heart, I learnt the basics of cooking. I soon realised that cooking is an art I would never be skilled at. I remember the agony of those early days, agonising, as soon as I woke up, over what to cook, and how to do it. In time, with some long-distance help from my mother, and from my mother-in-law when she came to stay with us, I learnt some everyday cooking, though my food was never more than just edible. There were some occasional happy flukes, and I was lucky that chapattis, every bride's nightmare, never fazed me; I produced fairly good stuff, except for the odd shapes and sizes, even in the early days. It helped too that my husband knew something of cooking (actually, he knew more than I did) and I could fall back on his knowledge, both theoretical and practical, in times of crises. Years later, I found out the advantage of my indifferent cooking: neither of my daughters-in-law, I am sure, has had to put up with that maddening sentence uttered by many men, 'Why can't you cook like my mother?'

But marriage had made a welcome difference as well. I no longer saw life through a telescopic lens. I was close to it, inside it now. I gained confidence because I knew that I mattered to someone. What more do we as humans want but this feeling of being needed? What else do we struggle for in life but to know we have this? The fact that in time we learn that our importance in another's life is an illusion, does not matter. Ultimately, however, it was having children that changed, not only my life, but *me* completely. For most humans, having children is the real rite of passage to adulthood. Becoming a mother took me into a world of intense emotions. The years of nothingness, of blankness, which had come before marriage, made it possible for me to be filled with strong emotions of caring and protectiveness, almost a surrender of one's self. When the children came – I had two children within the first four years of marriage — they occupied the entire territory of my life. There was no space left for anything else, no question of freedom; life was dictated by the needs of the infants. Books, movies, outings, friends — all these disappeared from my life. I was cut off from everything. There is something almost frightening about the total surrender of self that comes when you have children. Fortunately, this intensity does not last forever, it settles down in time to a steady, constant bond. I knew, as the children grew out of infancy, that, deeply involved though I was in my family, home and children, this was not enough for me. I wanted something more.

Soon after our first son was born, we were allotted an apartment in the doctors' quarters in Parel, just behind the hospital. It was a shabby old building, unpainted for years. But we had an amazingly large apartment, our bedroom being as big as an entire normal home in Bombay. There was a lawn for the children to play in, as well as a garden. These were great luxuries in Bombay, specially in Parel, which was the heart of the working class and the mill areas. Living in Parel was a vitalising experience. This Bombay was very different from the Bombay of Marine Drive, where I had lived as a college girl. Here, there were endless rows of sooty grey buildings, all so alike that they merged into one another, with mossy walls that were always damp because of the sewage pipes that marked the rows of toilets. Clothes flapped outside windows on cleverly put-together contraptions of multiple ropes, and little tulsi plants in Dalda tins perched precariously on planks hung outside the window. Quite different from the rows of stately colonial buildings that surrounded my college, where, under pillared porticos, hawkers sold all kinds of things, mainly stuff smuggled from abroad — perfumes, sunglasses, manicure sets, little gadgets and so much more.

Marine Drive, where my hostel had been, had a long row of stately buildings where only the rich lived. In Parel, hawkers sold rejects from the mills, damaged cotton clothes, mainly. Vegetables and dried fish were not weighed, but sold in fistfuls. Jewellery shops were round every corner, but they were more for pawning stuff, than for buying gold or silver. The cotton mills dominated everything in this area; hooters, which indicated a change of shift, marked out the hours for us. Even at midnight, handcarts sold boiled eggs to workers coming off their shift. Lying in bed at night, unable to go back to sleep after I had been woken up by the baby, I heard the steady tramp-tramp of workers' shoes as they marched to work; there was something martial in the sound of the shoes, something eerie in the total silence in which they walked together. And there was the fluff, the soot, which floated out of the factory chimneys and covered everything – our floors and our furniture. Our baby's knees, when he began to crawl, were so deeply ingrained with the soot that no amount of scrubbing could wash it off, and when he cried, his tears created runnels through the black soot on his face. We looked at it as just a nuisance then. We were yet to become aware of pollution.

We were surrounded by hospitals. There was Haffkine Institute on one side (named after Waldemar Haffkine, who discovered the plague vaccine), the Wadia Children's and Maternity Hospitals and the Tata Cancer Hospital a little ahead, and the veterinary hospital on the other side of us. And, of course, just opposite was the hospital my husband worked in, the K.E.M. Hospital. Our building, the Assistant Dean's Bungalow, with eight apartments, was sandwiched between the Dean's Bungalow and the Nurses' Quarters. One of the great pleasures of our home was the row of broad seats in the long entrance hall, where you could sit all day watching the road and never get bored.

Early mornings, we would watch nurses going to work, one of whom was the girl who was to become news, and remain news, for the next almost fifty years – Aruna Shanbaug, the nurse who was raped. Patients came in all day and the dead exited through a scarcely visible gate at the corner of our road. At times, when we were still in bed, we could hear the sound of running footsteps and the loud sound of harsh, laboured breathing, which in time we learnt meant that a young girl, an asthmatic, was being brought to hospital for emergency treatment. And once we came out to the sound of loud shouts, of running feet, and saw a man being chased by a group of men, who finally overtook him. They surrounded him, concealing him from our view, and then ran back the way they had come, in silence this time, leaving the man lying prone on the ground, blood slowly spreading out from under him. Everyone on the road, including the watchman at the hospital gate, suddenly vanished, leaving behind a frightening silence. I guess someone must have rung up the police, because they came a little later.

Everything in Parel was tuned to the needs of the working class, people who flocked to Bombay to work in the cotton mills. Everything whispered of a Bombay that had grown out of the textile mills, of a time when there were rich industrialists, who believed that spending money for the good of others was part of the exercise of making money, or perhaps good for their souls! And therefore, they donated money for these hospitals which were over-crowded, even then, with sick people and their families. Would we ever have believed that in a decade or two after we left, all the cotton mills would be closed down, the workers dispersed, and the area undergo a sea change? When we lived in Parel, the mills, and the workers, seemed to be an intrinsic part of Bombay, something that was forever. But the mills disappeared at the end of a long strike, which was engineered, it was rumoured, by the mill owners themselves, who found that the mills were no longer profitable. And, of course, the land was prime land and as valuable as gold.

One of the leaders of the strike was my husband's classmate in medical college, Datta Samant. His was a very strange story. After passing out of college, he had started a clinic for workers.

He became, it was said, a genuine sympathiser of the workers and went on from there to become a powerful trade union leader. He was killed some time after the long strike (also called the Great Strike) of the Bombay mills ended. There were many rumours. One, that he had been killed by the workers who felt he had betrayed them, because the strike did nothing for them. The mills were closed down and all of them became jobless. It was a huge tragedy. There was also a theory that Datta Samant had been killed by the mill owners, with whom he had colluded to organise the strike. And the police believed he had been killed as part of trade union rivalry. The mill strike had been a bizarre story; rumours spoke of hit men of well-known dons like Dawood Ibrahim, being employed to get rid of people. Two mill owners had been killed. Whatever the truth, the strike, which achieved nothing for the workers, changed Bombay forever.

One thing was clear: with the disappearance of the mills, a way of life vanished. A life in which hardworking men and women sent money back home and brought family, neighbours and friends to work in Bombay. There was a kind of communal living that flourished in the chawls. I remember how often we saw groups of men, the bhaiyyas, as men from the North were called, cooking rotis and vegetables outside a tiny room in which a large number of them lived. The living space sufficed only because one lot was always out at work. There were also political repercussions of the strike. Even while we were living in Parel, a new political party, the Shiv Sena, had been coming up, and soon the clashes between them and the Communists, who had dominated the area until then, became common. The Kamgar Maidan, where most Communist meetings were held, was always a scene of agitation. We were used to crowds, to red flags waving all around and stolid policemen standing around the edges of the crowd. Actually, even before the strike, the Communist influence had begun waning. A Communist

M.P. was murdered, stabbed in a street close to our home, and a group from the party came home with his wife, who was the candidate for the seat which had fallen vacant on the man's death. I can still remember her blank face, her empty eyes. I think I voted for her, out of sympathy, perhaps. And possibly also because I felt a connection to the Communist ideology, to which I had, for many reasons, been sympathetic since I was a girl.

There was another very tenuous connection as well, for I got a few telephone calls, which turned out to be for a Rosa Deshpande, who was, I soon came to know, the daughter of the Communist leader, Comrade Dange. We had a common telephone for all the apartments in a cubby hole under the stairs. The watchman on duty would take the call and call out to whoever the phone was for. Hearing the name 'Deshpande', he called me. Much later, I read about Rosa Luxemburg, the revolutionary, and realised that Dange had, perhaps, named his daughter for her. From Rosa Luxemburg, to Rosa Deshpande neé Dange to me – connections, like coincidences, have always interested me.

Your address, which part of the city you live in, matters. There was a kind of pride in saying you lived in South Bombay. Parel was one of the worst addresses you could have. But I wouldn't trade it for any other place, it was so alive and the life which went on around the hospital so fascinating. There were all kinds of people who carried on various activities on the pavements, sitting under canvas or plastic shelters tied to the iron railings of the hospital. A man who told your fortune, via a parrot, which hopped out of its cage and picked up a card. I always wondered what was written on the cards and how the men, who crouched before the parrot and its owner, could believe that they could see their future in these randomly picked cards. Just outside the post office, next to Haffkine Institute, there were scribes, letter-writers, men who wrote letters for the unlettered. Bombay being a city of migrants, there were always people waiting to take their place before the letter-writer. I heard them slowly and solemnly speaking out their thoughts, which the writer rapidly took down. I sometimes wondered whether the 'writers' took down just what was told to them, or whether they embroidered the facts. This must have been the writer in me, still non-existent, peeping out.

I remember a woman selling herbs and roots, aphrodisiacs, I suppose, who had made a home on the pavement with her two infants. Evenings, when we came home from the market after our shopping, she would have begun cooking, making jowar rotis on a bright fire. Once, seeing me linger and look curiously at her arrangements, she gave me a big smile and asked, 'Want to eat with us?' I have never forgotten that woman. Never forgotten, either, Godaram, the man who was allotted the duty of cleaning the bathrooms and toilets in our building. Despite the work he did, and despite the clothes he had to wear (the official uniform did not give him even the dignity of long trousers, he and all the sweepers had to wear short pants), he was a man of great dignity. And with his willingness to help in any crisis, he became indispensable to all the women. Whenever he returned from a month's holiday to his *muluk* (native place), the cries of, '*Godaram, aap aa gaye?*', rang through the building. Not hard to know why. Your cleaning *bai* had not come? He would sweep and swab the house, leaving it spotless and shining. Your domestic help had left you? He would get someone for you. Honest and impeccably behaved, I remember his anguish when the nurse Aruna Shanbaug was raped by a sweeper. '*Ham sab ki naak uss* **** *ne kaat di,*' ('He has shamed all of us') he said, using a word of abuse I can't repeat here.

Now I think *I* am ashamed that a man like Godaram had to spend his life cleaning our toilets. With some education he could have gone far. I hope his children or grandchildren have broken out of that vicious circle of caste and poverty and have moved on.

As for me, I have never had anyone clean my toilets since I came to Bangalore. I have always done it myself. Become a comrade, perhaps, of Godaram. I like the thought. My best memory of Godaram is of him putting down his broom and bucket and bursting into a song for a birthday child, a film song that began, *Hum bhi agar bachche hote, naam hamara hota gabloo babloo* ... and ended with a triumphant, sonorous *Happy Birthday to you*. He never missed a child's birthday.

Parel was a place teeming with death as well as life. Funeral processions were a regular feature of our days, the noise and the songs changing according to which community the dead belonged. But they had this in common — the dead never went out quietly. There was music, singing, at times even a band. Local funerals were accompanied by a Marathi chant, *aamhi jaato aamcha gaavi* (we are going back home) — a poignant song for people who had left their homes to come to the city to earn a living. Those who were from the North, chanted *Ram naam satya hai*. I remember hearing this chant, solemn and monotonous, at night, while I was in bed. Once, I was horrified to hear our children playing a game with their friends, in which this dirge was chanted. Crackers were set off by some communities, coins scattered by another. A kind of morbid gaiety surrounded death; perhaps, a *carpe diem* philosophy was the only way to cope for people who lived in the slums.

I had read Thoreau's statement that most people live lives of quiet desperation. Here it was not a quiet, but a loud desperation. There was a very large slum just a short distance away from our home. All, or almost all, the people who lived in it had come from outside Bombay to earn a living in this city, whose streets, perhaps they had been told, were paved with gold. Instead of the El Dorado they had imagined, they lived this terrible life, in a place teeming with people. A place where there were only a few toilets for this huge mass, only a few water taps, and where water came only for limited times, so that there were always long queues at the tap, always a fear and suspicion of losing out, which erupted into loud fights. A place where, there were such few toilets, that the children used the pavements and anyone who went on those roads had to be careful where they put their feet. It was out of these slums that women, struggling to give their children a better life, came to work for people like us, it was out of here that girls and boys walked out confidently, as smartly dressed as if they had bathrooms with running taps at home. And the children were alive, eager and bright.

It was living in Parel that brought me out of the safe and cosy world of family and books that I had been living in until then, it was what I saw around me that woke me out of my somnolence. I saw and heard the workers marching with an almost military rhythm to work, even in the middle of the night. I saw the workers' meetings which often ended in chaos and riots, I saw alcoholics lying in the gutters, on pavements. I heard stories of women who were routinely beaten by their drunken, suspicious husbands, I saw women taking out their anger and frustrations on their children. I met women struggling to send their children to school, children I saw dressed in their Muncipal school uniforms. I was aroused to the knowledge of a world of injustice, inequalities, cruelties. Sometimes I think that I would not have become the kind of writer I am if not for my glimpse of the lives of these men and women, specially the women. Seeing the life around me, there was no way I could consider myself less fortunate because of the small salary my husband earned. I realised I was privileged. We had a comfortable house, our children went to good schools, we could afford occasional luxuries like going to a movie or a play. Hypocritical though it may sound, I was uncomfortable about being so privileged. Well, at least I never was able to take what we had for granted.

I also was deeply impacted by what I saw in my own home,

as well as in my own family, about the way women had to live their lives. For me, my mother-in-law was just a, well, mother-in-law, a woman whose way of life, riddled with ideas of purity and impurity, made my life hard when she came to stay with us. In time, I began to notice other things: that she had to cook her own food, whatever the circumstances. That she had no meal at night, and even if she wanted to drink water, she had to go through the tedious process of wearing her 'pure' sari, which she would have had to wash herself. I knew she had lost her husband before the age of forty, and was left with eight children, the youngest only a few days old. And, even though her husband had been a large landowner, she became a dependent after that, first on a male member of the family and then, when her eldest son became a major, on him. I saw that her sons, who were very protective of her, found nothing wrong in this, nothing wrong in her asking one of them for a few rupees so that she could gift it to a girl who was getting married, or was pregnant, or had just had a child. They thought this was how it had to be.

When I saw the way she had to live, I got a glimpse of why married women performed so many pujas and rituals, and observed fasts for their husbands' long lives. Because, when her husband died, everything changed for the woman. She had to follow some rules which dictated that she eschew all the pleasures in life. Whereas, nothing stopped a man from getting another wife. Not that no man mourned his wife; I am sure many did. But they did not have to enter into a life of deprivations, of hardships, like a widow had to. A widower's life continued to move on almost the same lines; only the woman in his life changed.

Going back to my mother-in-law: her tragedy was worse because she had lost three grown, married daughters, and for some reason, she had had to cremate one of her daughters herself. She told me that she had not shed tears since then. She showed me her calloused hands and said, 'I had to make sixty or seventy *bhakris* every morning (these were jowar rotis, patted out by hand and roasted on a constantly smoking wood fire). I think I was born for this.' A statement made by a woman who never complained about her life, in fact, never spoke of 'life'. A woman who was practical and pragmatic. Worst of all, I had to see her undergo the dreadful experience of having her head shaved by a barber. The thought of her sitting before him, offering her head to him, was like torture to me. I was filled with both shame and anger. But she never complained. This was to me even more unbearable.

All this was brewing inside me. And there was something else, a kind of strange inexplicable discontent. A discontent always accompanied by guilt. For, why was I discontented? I had it all, all the things I had been told as a child that women needed: a good marriage, two lovely children, parents, a sister and brother-in-law who supported me. So what was wrong? 'Women must prize this discontent as the first stirring of the demand for life': I was to read these words of Germaine Greer later. But at the time, I felt guilty, ungrateful. I had no idea that out of this seething, bubbling cauldron, my writing would emerge. All that I knew was that I had to do something.

I decided I would do my MA in English; the trauma of my poor performance in my BA still rankled. I completed the process of admission to the university, but at the last minute, before paying my fees, I faltered. Was I prepared to leave my two-year-old son at home all day? He looked so woebegone the one day I'd left him at home and gone out in connection with my admission. And could I spend so much of our scarce income on something which might never give us financial returns? I dropped the idea. I tried for a job, went to two or three places. Nothing worked out. Then our second son was born. It was a very difficult pregnancy and a difficult delivery. The state of my health after this made it impossible for me to think of doing anything more than looking after the children and home. Just at this time, my husband got the offer of a Commonwealth Fellowship, which would allow him to spend a year in England working at the National Hospital for Neurology and Neurosurgery, in London. The payment was not much, but it included an allowance for the family as well. This changed everything. It was the change we needed, a welcome change for both of us. Not only would it advance my husband's career, I would get out into the world from the cloistered space I had got myself into. Get away, perhaps, from the person I had turned into: Mrs Deshpande. Deshpande Kaku. Deshpande Vahini. Nandu's and Vikram's mother. More, I would see the places I had read about, I would enter the world I had glimpsed through books so many years back.

There are moments which you realise, only when you look back, were crossroad moments. You are faced with a choice; you have to take one road and reject another. You make your choice and sometimes, much later, you see that this choice changed your life. And you wonder: what if I had chosen something else? What if…? This is where fiction writers begin, this is the point at which they get into a story. And so, at times, I wonder: what if we had not gone to London when we did? What if we had made a different choice? Because we did have another choice.

Some time after the Commonwealth Fellowship was offered to my husband, he had another offer. An American pathologist had been invited to start a neuropathology department in K.E.M. Hospital because the neurologists and the neurosurgeons had felt the need of it. She established a neuropathology department and trained my husband in neuropathology. We became good friends with her and her painter husband. When she went back home at the end of a year, she initiated a move for my husband to get into a residency in neuropathology in a very good hospital in the USA. And so the quandary: which was better? The London fellowship or the American residency? I now know that if he had taken the American residency, we would never have come back, we would have stayed on in the USA. Shoals of Indian doctors went to the USA after their post-graduation at that time. The Vietnam war had created vacancies that were filled by foreign doctors. Each year, most of those who completed their MD in India left for America as soon as possible. Almost all of them stayed on and most of them did very well. Their children did even better, getting more and better opportunities than they would have got at home. It would have been the same with us. My husband would have made more money (which we badly needed), the children would have had better opportunities. But what about my writing? Would I have become the writer I did? At that time, there were some Indians in the USA who had made their names as writers. As *Indian* writers. I could have become one of these diasporic writers. Or would I?

'There are two ways of writing a novel. One is to ignore real life altogether … the other is going right deep down into life and not caring a damn.'

Words of that most underrated writer P.G. Wodehouse, who, in spite of saying things in a light, flippant way, said many wise things about writers and writing. My way of writing *was* to go deep down into real life. But that real life for me was the life I lived at home in India, the life I knew so well, the life I was an integral part of. Once distanced from that life, what could I have written about? Excellent though some of the Indian diasporic writers were, I often felt that, after the initial surge of writing, which came out of the nostalgia about their early years at home, there was a faltering. Many moved on to write about the lives of Indians as immigrants in another country, of the sense of alienation. But how long can a writer walk on that narrow path? Often, I sensed a kind of fatigue in the writing, a flagging. And for them to continue to write about India was to write from a distance, giving a sense of getting the material at second hand. But there is, it seems, no choice. It is rarely possible for an Indian writer, or any writer of foreign origin, to become part of the mainstream in another country. Almost no foreign writer can write about mainstream American life, no Indian writer can write a novel without having Indians as protagonists. Vikram Seth's *An Equal Music* is a rare novel, written by an Indian, but without Indians in it (I consider it even better than his *A Suitable Boy*). Such novels are rare. The problem starts with the publisher, who expects foreign writers to provide the exotic element, so that the books find a slot to fit into. Perhaps it is because of this that almost no foreign writer has made an impact on American literature. Perhaps it will, it might, become possible with the second or the third generation, the way it happened with Jewish writers, with writers who came from Europe and became part of American life. Maybe things are already changing, for, right now, there is the Vietnamese writer Viet Thanh Nguyen, a first generation immigrant living in the USA, who won the Pulitzer for his novel *The Sympathizer*.

I am selfishly glad we came back to India, that we did not make the choice of going to the USA, which would have surely ended in our staying on there. My novels have come out of our society, out of the world around me. And society is dynamic, it is constantly changing. It is impossible to feel this pulse of change unless you are inside it, unless you are a part of the change that happens from moment to moment. My novels, from *The Dark Holds No Terrors* to *Strangers to Ourselves*, have registered these changes. I do not think my novels would have had the impact on people, on the literary scene, in any other country, the way they have in India. And so, perhaps the decision to accept the Commonwealth Fellowship, which was only for a year (and which had a condition that the Fellow would return home at the end of the year) was the right one – for me, at least. Not that our decision was taken with this in mind. I was not even a writer when we went to London. But certainly it was good for both our families. My parents, my sister, my mother-in-law and my husband's siblings – I like to think that our being in India added to all their lives; though again I have to say the decision was not taken with this in mind either. At that age, when you are young and have young children, selfishness dominates. What is good for the children, what is good for us – these are the primary concerns. As they were for us. And so we went to England. The clinching reason that allowed the children and me to go was that one of my husband's very senior colleagues, a wealthy and philanthropic doctor, seeing him hesitant about accepting the offer, discovered that he was worried about the money for our fare, the children's and mine. He instantly wrote out a cheque on the condition that the money was not to be repaid and was never to be mentioned. *Those were the days* … Truly they were.

 The beginning of our visit was not very promising. It was March when the children and I joined my husband and the remnants of winter were still in the air. It was cold, too cold for us who did not have enough, and adequately warm, clothes. The home my husband was living in when we got there was lousy. Not only was it dingy and dark, we had to share the bathroom with the family living downstairs. It was an abomination to me, since I am overly fastidious – to the point of being OCD, as I am sometimes told ('Wash your hands, wash your feet, wash your face': these words were a constant accompaniment to my sons' days when they were children).

 In a month we moved into a better house in a better neighbourhood. The weather improved, it was spring, about which I had heard and read so much. I could see little flower heads coming out of the ground. We spent a lot of time outdoors. Our older son joined a pre-school very close by. We lived in the north of London, our tube station being Finsbury Park. In time our son got an accent which came close to the Cockney accent. He enjoyed his school, unlike St Mary's in Bombay, which, being a large school with a huge number of children, had intimidated him. My husband would drop him at school and I would pick him up, doing the shopping on my way back. Once home, I fed them lunch and parked the kids before the TV in the afternoons to watch the children's programmes, while I cleared up lunch and had a small break. Television was one of the novel pleasures of life here. We would not have a TV set for years at home in India, not until much after we moved to Bangalore. For us greenhorns, watching TV was a marvel – never mind if we had only a small black and white set. But it was a window to a wonderful new world. We watched *The Forsyte Saga*, we saw Cronin's stories dramatised, we saw some wonderful plays. We also watched the assassinations of Robert Kennedy and of Martin Luther King, the Soviet tanks rolling into Czechoslovakia, the French students' revolt in Paris, their battles with the police. Looking back, it seems as if that was an eventful year. And, thanks to TV, it felt like we were watching world events from a ringside seat.

Once, we splurged on a baby-sitter and went to see a play, Wilde's *The Importance of Being Ernest*. I knew the play almost by heart, I could speak the lines along with the actors. After the play, we went to a pub for a drink, and I felt incredibly sophisticated, miles distant from the shy girl in Dharwad and the staid housewife in Bombay. On our wedding anniversary, my husband bought a bottle of champagne, but a few sips left me so dizzy I had to 'retire hurt' from the celebrations. I have never taken to champagne since. We religiously watched 'Top of the Pops', even the children joined in – the Beatles were just coming into their own then – and I still remember a girl with an angelic face, a protégée of Paul McCartney. This girl, Mary Hopkin (thank you, Google, for the name, I'd forgotten it), was on the top of the charts for weeks. For years, the song, the music and the girl's face haunted me. And, above all, the words: 'Those were the days, my friend, we thought they'd never end …' Words that were magical and dripping with nostalgia. Words that, I think, speak to all humans. A lyric that came, strangely enough, I learned (thank you, Google, once again), from a Russian song. Finally, I used the song in *Moving On* and, as always, this act of writing about it exorcised the ghost and the haunting ended.

Life in London was, in a sense, even more confined than what my life in Bombay had been. No neighbours, no family, no friends, no maids and no Godaram. Just the children and I on our own all day, while my husband was at the hospital. What I sorely missed was the openness of homes in India. Here, doors and windows were tightly closed all day, not only because of the weather, but also because of an intense desire for privacy. It reminded me of Gandhi's surprise when he went to England and saw that a family lived behind closed doors in a home. To make up for this, however, there were open spaces everywhere, parks and commons in every locality.

Above all, I felt as if my mind had opened out after years of total domesticity. It was London that nudged me into the world outside, a world which I had known, but lost for a while. It was London that took me on to the path which would finally lead me to my destination. And yet, I did the same things here that I had done at home: I did the housework, I looked after the children, I cooked, I shopped, I cleaned. But during the weekends we went out – all-day visits to Hyde Park, or St James' Park, or Hampstead Heath, places where we could go with the children. We did some touristy sight-seeing as well, and at times, I had to pinch myself to make sure that I was not dreaming, that I was really looking at Buckingham Palace, or the Tower of London, or Windsor Castle. Even more exciting to me were Dickens' house or Keats' house.

Mine was an English literature lover's rapture, not a Colonial one, and the very names – Hyde Park, Trafalgar Square, with Nelson's statue and the pigeons, Piccadilly Circus with its statue of Eros, posh Bond Street, Oxford Street, Chelsea, Hampstead – came to me out of books I'd read, accompanied by the magic that was part of the books. Travelling from Paddington was like entering into a Wodehouse novel, in which the characters always travelled out of Paddington. This was the London I'd read so much about that everything seemed familiar to me. Yet strange, too, for many people spoke an English I could not understand. And at no time did we have an interaction with the natives. I thought the English were a strange people, combining in themselves an extreme politeness with total indifference. I don't think that, except in the shops, I ever spoke to a single native. But it didn't matter, for London was populated with so many old friends – Bertie Wooster and Jeeves, David Copperfield and Little Dorritt, Sherlock Holmes and Lord Peter Wimsey. And then, there was Bayswater Road – wasn't that where the Forsyte aunts had lived with their youngest brother Timothy? And surely that little shop in that small street was how the Old Curiosity Shop must have been? And wasn't that Lizzie Hexam rowing a boat on the Thames? Amazing the mark Dickens has left on London! He was always around, wherever we went.

The hospital where my husband was working had its associations, too, for it was situated in Queen's Square (familiarly called the Queen's Square Hospital), the square named after Queen Caroline, the unfortunate queen of the Prince Regent, later George IV, who was an admirer of Jane Austen. She, however, did not reciprocate his feelings because the Prince Regent behaved badly with Caroline, keeping her away from their only daughter and even closing the doors on her during his coronation. Abominable man. No wonder Jane Austen wrote, 'Poor woman, I shall support her (Queen Caroline, that is) as long as I can because she is a Woman and because I hate her Husband.' As far as I am concerned, the Prince Regent's only claim to fame is not Brighton, which was, in a sense, his creation, but the fact that his chaplain wrote a letter to Jane Austen, telling her about the Prince's admiration for her work and giving her suggestions about the kind of novel she should write next, and the kind of characters she should have in the novel. In her reply, Jane Austen gently disclaimed her ability to do what he wanted, because she was, she said (most famous words, these), 'the most unlearned and uninformed female who ever dared to be an authoress'. Modesty? That is what it is presumed to be. But I am not sure. I think it was the most diplomatic, tongue-in-cheek put-down made by an author to someone presumptuous enough to tell her what she should write about. The lady was truly amazing. The Regency era was also the time in which Georgette Heyer placed most of her novels. Even abominable men have their uses, it seems.

Looking back from this point of time, I realise that there was so much we did not do, could not do because of the children and lack of money. I never visited Jane Austen's Chawton or Bath, neither then, nor much later when I visited England once again, courtesy the British Council. Never visited the Lake District, either. Years later, we planned a trip specially to visit the Lake District and Scotland, but my husband fell ill shortly after we got to London and we had to come back home. No regrets, however. I have seen more than I ever imagined I would. And in any case, the things one has not done, not seen, are always a humongous heap compared to the things one has done and seen. That the large pile keeps getting even larger doesn't matter.

The one thing I did make up for during later visits was galleries and museums that I had wanted to see. When I went to England for the publication of *That Long Silence*, I kept popping between interviews into the National Gallery and National Portrait Gallery, both of which were very close to the Virago office. The highlight of our year in England, though, was a visit to Paris, where I remember visiting the Louvre. Here, too, we could not do much, but Paris was so beautiful, it was enough just to stroll along the Seine, to have a wonderful meal of fresh bread and salad, to watch the world go by while we sat in a café on the Champs-Elysées, sipping a cup of coffee. We made two visits within England as well, one to Oxford, of which I can only remember the river, and a trip to Wales, organised by the British Council, mainly for couples with very young children. They arranged some outings for us without the children; they had volunteers, who to us were angels, to look after the children. These angels made it possible for us to see a movie, the only one we were able to see in that year; I remember it was about the Crimean war and had Vanessa Redgrave in it. It brought back Tennyson and his dreadful, 'Half a league, half a league ...' Tennyson was never a favourite of mine, though his *Ulysses* startled me when I first read it. For me, that one poem redeemed him.

We had a bad scare once when my husband suddenly developed chest pains one night. His eldest brother had died of a sudden heart attack a little before we left India; he had been only in his forties at the time. That tragedy still hung over us. Terrified, I rushed to our downstairs neighbours, a family from Ghana. The gentleman drove us to the hospital and waited with me until the doctors said my husband was all right, but that they would keep him for observation until morning. I went back home where the children, unaware of everything, were sleeping peacefully. I couldn't sleep that whole night. It was one of the worst nights in my life. I think I saw for the first time how narrow, how thin was the line between us and disaster. I was far from India, with two children and no money. We had no home of our own and our tiny bank account had been depleted by the expenses of preparing ourselves for this trip abroad. What would I have done if the worst had happened? Thankfully, my husband was all right. But that experience left me with a great fear of possible disaster and a great desire to work, not just to fulfil myself, but to earn money, so that I would never become dependent.

At that time, I was yet to come across my father's words about his children 'standing on their own feet'. But this desire to earn enough to be independent remained an ache, an itch, an urge within me through the years, though never as strong as it was that night in London. In fact, all my life I have regretted the fact that I have not earned money, that I have not been financially independent, that I have not contributed my bit financially to the family. And yet, leaving two young children at home and going out to work never seemed the better alternative. I know many women did it, they continue to do it, my sister did it, many nights taking her little daughter with her when she had to go on night duty. But, for some reason, it never seemed the right thing for me to do, not even when we were very hard up.

I tell myself now that I am lucky I was at home; the children never had to come back from school and find no one at home, as I saw some children do. But I must admit that there were times when I also felt badly about being 'only a housewife', as the phrase went. Some more money would have come in very handy. Apart from the money, I felt I had lost myself, my identity. But the choice not to go out to work was mine; I learnt to live with it. So many women did not have a choice. And there were many others like me who made their choice. Somehow, all these choices went into creating the change that would soon come. I came across the words of Rosa Luxemburg much later: 'It is in the tiny struggles of individual peoples that the great movements of history are most truly revealed.'

To go back to that terrible night in London, thankfully, all was well. And equally thankfully, none of us had major health problems that year, except for this one episode. I did get headaches every morning though, and went to the doctor we were assigned to under the National Health Service. Waiting in the room outside, I felt even sicker. It was a malodorous place, closed in, made worse by people smoking and coughing. His room was no better; he had a cigar he kept puffing at, while he cursorily listened to me. 'Headaches, eh? All women have headaches,' he said. I'm sure he never imagined that behind the quiet brown face and innocuous look of the Indian woman sitting before him, there lurked a demon, who was imagining how wonderful it would be to trample on his cigar and perhaps even on his stupid mouth. The kind of medical care and attention we got at home because of being a doctor's family had spoilt us.

It was a year, not of physical inactivity, as when I first went to Bangalore, but a life in which, in some weird way, in spite of all the activity, I seemed to be in a state of suspended animation. It was as if life in London, and all that we did there, had little to do with our life in Bombay, with normal life. This sense of being distanced and the sense of isolation created the same feeling of living in a bubble that I had felt in Bangalore. I remember a woman I used to see every morning when I went to pick up our son from his play school, a woman in a window in one of the houses on our street. She was always there at the time I passed her house, doing something I could not see. To me, she seemed as distant as if she lived on another planet and much later I wrote a short story, which included this experience. That was the way life I saw around me seemed then – distant, impenetrable. When the year was over and we came back home, my mind was stimulated into sudden activity.

I knew it was not possible for me to be housebound again, I knew my life could no longer be contained within the four walls of my home. I knew that I wanted something more, that this life of wife, mother and home-maker, however satisfying it was, was not enough. I joined a journalism course.

Apprenticeship

The journey from the head to hand is perilous and lined with bodies. It is the road on which nearly everyone who wants to write – and many of the people who do write – get lost.

Ann Patchett, *This Is the Story of a Happy Marriage*

WHY JOURNALISM? PERHAPS BECAUSE of the three articles I wrote on our year's stay in London. For some reason, which I can't remember now, I sent these pieces to my father. He said nothing, but a little later I got cuttings of the three articles published in the *Deccan Herald*, the local Bangalore paper. My father had given the pieces for publication without telling me. I got the princely sum of twenty-five rupees per article, seventy-five altogether. I bought a 'scooter' for my boys (a contraption with two wheels, on which the kid stood, pushing it along with one foot and when enough speed had been gathered, 'scooting' along freely) and a shirt for my husband with the money. More importantly, it decided the future course of my life. I decided on journalism, not only because it had to do with writing, but also because the course timings suited me. Since it was meant for working people, classes were held in the evening. Which meant that I left the house after my husband came home and returned in time for dinner; by then the children would have had their dinner and be sleeping.

To go back to learning was like a rebirth, a resurgence. I must have been the oldest in the class, among the females certainly, for there were one or two men who seemed older than I was. I had been afraid that because of my age I would not be able to cope, I was afraid that I had lost all the intellectual capacity I had had as a girl before marriage. This came partly from Bernard Shaw's statement (I think it was his) which I had read at some time, in which he'd said that having children affects women's brains, their thinking power. I never forgot that statement. I was always fearful that it would happen to me, frightened after the children were born that it had happened. As a matter of fact, I had lost it all: my interest in films, in politics and, in fact, in the world outside. No time for newspapers or magazines, either. And for the first time in my life since I could remember, I went to bed without reading. There was nothing left in my life, it seemed, but the children. Certainly, I had changed immensely after the children were born. Perhaps Bernard Shaw (or whoever it was who had said that) was right.

I had to wait years to understand that nature makes this demand on women, and this, in the interests of nurturing the young of the species. The young have to be nurtured, given great care; human infants are far more helpless and vulnerable than the young of animals are. But once children no longer need constant care and attention, a woman's mind reverts to its early state of active interest in and curiosity about the world. Old hungers come back, old passions are reignited. Which is perhaps why I think that a mother who doesn't let go of her children, who continues to see her role as a mother as the main thing in her life, is an aberration, not those who put motherhood in its rightful place. All these ideas came to me much later. At the time I was only worried about how I would cope with studies and books again; I hoped I would not make a fool of myself. I need not have worried. In the classroom, contrary to my fears and Bernard Shaw's warning, everything fell away and I was only a mind, absorbing, responding, exulting in coming into its own. I understood then that the mind has no gender, no class, no age. The years I had done nothing but been a wife and mother had taken nothing away from me; in fact, these years had given me something I could not describe, but which I knew had enriched me. I had no idea where I was heading, but I soon made the discovery that I was on the right path, that this was where I belonged, that writing was what I could and would do. This time it was clear: *this* was my work. I had a skill for writing which I had not really known I possessed until my work was specially mentioned in the class.

One of the greatest gifts I got during this year was an introduction to Ernest Gowers' book on language, *The Complete Plain Words*. The teacher who taught us English (we had an English class, meant, I suppose, for students who were hoping to enter English journalism) was a great admirer of this book, he quoted from it extensively, he read out bits to us. Buy it, he told us, and I did. I still have it with me, the same copy, the pages yellowed with age, the hard cover softened by time, the corners pulpy. It has become my Bible in the matter of usage. Gowers is a man I not only trust implicitly, but with whom I completely agree. I later discovered from my husband that Gowers' father had been a neurologist and had worked at the same hospital my husband had worked in during his year in London. Gowers proudly tells us in his book that his father, who believed in simple language like he did (perhaps it should be put the other way round), invented the simple phrase for a knee tap; he called it – well, a knee tap. And so, a physician's tap on the knee became a 'knee tap'. Yes, that was Gowers: keep it simple, keep it straight. 'Writing,' he says, 'is an instrument for conveying ideas from one mind to another; the writer's job is to make the reader apprehend the meaning readily and precisely.'

Precisely. Nobody could have put it better. (Except for the pronoun. Why, oh why does English not have a pronoun to include both genders?) Gowers praises some sentences, because, he says, 'Every word is exactly right: no other word would do as well; each is exactly pulling its weight, none could be dispensed with.' Words of great wisdom. Very often, in the years to come, I would be condescendingly spoken of as a writer who wrote in very simple language, making it seem that I had a very small vocabulary, that I knew no words apart from basic four- or five-letter words. They little know, those who say this, the difficulty of writing simple language. Gowers knew. I have always had a leaning towards simplicity and austerity, always disliked flowery language, loaded with adjectives – and, yes, spiked with Capital Letters. I learnt, as I went on writing, that you use language to say clearly what you want to; you do not use language to dazzle or impress the reader. I still think that there is no better guide to writing than Gowers. Later, I bought the Oxford English Dictionary, Fowler, Webster, Roget's Thesaurus (another invaluable aid for a writer), Hobson Jobson. But nothing could take the place of Gowers' book, as far as I was concerned.

It was this same teacher, the man who admired Gowers (he was the only teacher who was not a journalist and he was the most interesting one), who lectured us on Current Affairs. There was much to talk about then, for those were tumultuous times. The Bangladesh (or rather East Pakistan, because there was no Bangladesh then) war was threatening to happen, because of the refugees flooding India from East Pakistan. Blackout soon became compulsory and we made makeshift screens with old newspapers. The siren of Haffkine Institute next door to us, which had gone off at nine in the morning and at five in the evening, signalling the beginning and the end of working hours, now became a siren warning us of air raids and of the 'all clear'. A large team of doctors went from K.E.M. Hospital to Bangladesh after the war was over. We heard later that most of their work consisted of performing abortions on raped girls and women. This was the second time that women in the Indian subcontinent had had to suffer the consequences of war – the first time was during and after the Partition. Later, I read in Susan Brownmiller's *Against Our Will*, how war is always accompanied by rape, which is another form of taking possession of the invaded territories. There was a strange chapter in the story of the Bangladesh war. A huge amount of money had been taken out of a bank, ostensibly in Mrs Gandhi's name. The man who drew this money later died and the rumour mills were busy connecting the money spent on training the Bangladesh army, the Mukti Bahini as it was called, with this money. There were also rumours that the man had been killed to hush this up. Nobody knows the truth; it is still a mystery. Rohinton Mistry wrote a novel about this episode, *Such a Long Journey*, a novel that gave a plausible explanation of this mystery. An example of a real-life story converted into a good novel. I can't say the same of his *A Fine Balance*, which brought in the Emergency. Too many details, many of which seem to have been culled from media reports.

Anyway, Mrs Gandhi had grown in stature with this adventure of hers, she had shown herself to be a bold and daring leader. She had brought about a split in the Congress party and had made herself the leader of the new party, skilfully ousting the heavyweights. Daring in her moves, as she would continue to be, she embarked on dramatic measures, one of which was nationalising the banks. Our teacher discussed this in our Current Affairs class the week after it happened. A banker himself, he told us, very clearly, what nationalisation of banks meant, what it would lead to. He spoke long after the hour when the class should have ended; he was brilliant. I walked to the bus stop, the things he had spoken of churning in my mind. A young woman, also a student of the same institute, but studying Advertising, travelled with me on the same bus every night. That night, I told her about all that I had heard in the class and she listened in fascination. I can still remember, as if it was yesterday, the two of us discussing the subject with animation, so lost in it that it was as if there were only the two of us in that bus, as if there was no one else. But of course the bus was crowded, as Bombay buses always are, even at that time, full of people going home after a day's work, men and women sunk in torpor, totally unaware of everything and everyone, miraculously waking up as soon as their bus stop approached.

It is only now, as I write this, that it occurs to me that we, in our entire discussion, never imagined that this was the first step taken by a woman who was in pursuit of total power. How could we, or anyone, have imagined that this woman would soon take us inexorably close to the end of the road of our hard-won democracy? I got home to find dinner on the table. My husband and I ate, I cleared up, set the curds, switched off the lights and, looking in on the sleeping children, went to bed myself. But I could not sleep. My mind was teeming with ideas, with words. The windows had been opened and my mind would never be cloistered again. And yet I knew that, even if I was finding a place in the world outside, this world of home and family was still mine, this too was where I belonged. I did not know then that I would live the rest of my life balancing these two, trying to acquire the skill of a rope-walker.

Some time that year (no dates!) the Congress session was held in Bombay. The father of a student in our journalism class was a prominent Congressman and she managed to get us press passes through him. I remember the pleasure of being in the press enclosure. (Though veteran journalists looked at us askance and one of them openly and loudly asked who the hell we were!) The sight of the party leaders sitting on the high dais, leaning against fat *takias*, was one I had often seen in pictures. To see it in person was to get a feeling of watching history being made. And in a sense, it was that. For this was the session in which Mrs Gandhi brought out her slogan of *Garibi Hatao*, a slogan that was to help her win the coming elections, which was the next step in her goal of absolute control of the party and absolute power over the country. A new era began with that session – of sycophancy, of dynastic politics, of ruthlessness and of corruption.

I had done no writing until then, except for the three pieces I had had published in the *Deccan Herald*. But as a part of my course, I had to do a good bit of writing and I plunged into it with confidence and ease. I wrote for the publication brought out by students – an article on bank nationalisation, another on the amendment of the right to property in the Constitution. This was one more of Mrs Gandhi's populist measures; she played the game of politics like a virtuoso. I wrote a review of the musical *Oliver* and, finally, before I got my diploma, I wrote a thesis on the two prominent women's magazines of the time. I had no idea, when I did this, that I would soon be contributing to these magazines myself. I ended the year with topping the class and getting three medals, including the Times of India Gold Medal. This did not mean what it would have meant to me once; but it assured me that I had come out of the walls that had enclosed me, that I had found the way to get back into the world. And that I could find a place in the world without endangering my place at home.

We had to do a month's internship with a newspaper or a magazine before we were given our diplomas. I have absolutely no idea why I chose the *Onlooker*, a glossy monthly, a society magazine. A magazine which was devoted to social celebrities, filled with pictures of them at parties with glasses in their hands. A society as strange to me as an African tribal's world. But I remember a piece I wrote for a State tourism department. The editor was delighted with it, because it was more literary than marketing, the commercial head was happy because her clients were happy with it. After my internship was over, they asked me whether I would like to continue working with the magazine – for a princely salary of 275 rupees. I agreed. I was working outside my home for the first time and I enjoyed it. The *Onlooker* office was a small one, with an all-women staff, except for one courtly old Parsi gentleman. It was a very friendly place, though there was a general hostility to the editor who, like me, had just joined; everything about her was as sharp as her stiletto heels and her tongue. I committed a solecism in the first week, coming late, unused as I was to rushing through my work in the morning. She made her displeasure clear and it was like being back in school again. I almost resigned on the spot! I can't stand anyone telling me what to do. Or what not to do.

There was a constant conflict between the advertising manager and the editor; each wanted more space. Of course, advertising won. I saw for the first time, from the inside, the power of money and advertising, and its control on publishing. But I did not have to worry about that. My job was to write what I was told to. And what I wrote was appreciated. I enjoyed the interviews and personality pieces I had to write. I wrote an interview with the CEO of a company. For some reason, he became nostalgic during the interview and I included that. He rang the editor and told her how much he liked the interview. I wrote a piece on Willy Brandt, then Chancellor of West Germany, which came out much better than I expected. I was slowly learning that for me the personal was important, that I enjoyed writing about people, enjoyed the peep into their selves, which they sometimes gave an interviewer. As I wrote for the magazine, I learnt many other things: about editing, about brevity, about counting words – skills that would help me greatly even as a creative writer. I also learnt to write captions and headlines, to make up pages – each of us had our own pages to do. We made up the pages manually in those days, a true job of cut-and-paste. I learnt to proofread, I went to the printers to go through the final proofs. One of the highpoints of the magazine was the nude they had every month in the centrefold. We women, happily unaware that we were taking part in something which was politically totally incorrect, enthusiastically searched for captions to go along with the nude. (Shakespeare invariably obliged.) Feminism had no presence in our lives then, political correctness even less.

And I wrote a short story, my very first short story, for the magazine's annual issue. The annual was being brought out by one of the staff and I don't know why, but she asked me to write a story for it. I as little remember why I agreed. But I did and over the weekend (yes, in two days!) I wrote a story, *The Legacy*, which was used in the annual. A story that was very Somerset Maugham-ish, with a punch line at the end, a story told in a male voice, a cynical male voice at that. It came partly out of a Kannada film based on a Kannada novel, Byrappa's *Vamsha Vriksha*, which centred round a man's great desire to continue his family line. The story feels so distant now, it scarcely seems mine.

After a few months, I decided to give up the job. They offered me a huge raise of twenty-five rupees but I rejected it. I had realised by then that I had been rash in accepting the job. I had not thought about how difficult it would be to be out all day, with one child at school, the younger one still at home, and my only help being a young boy, fresh from his village, willing and affectionate, but ignorant and incapable of responsibility. So, if all was well at work, at home I saw that my older son seemed suddenly more grown-up, aware of being responsible, and the younger looked like a neglected waif, which filled me with guilt. I gave up the job. I have always admired women who go out to work leaving young children at home; I can imagine the stress and guilt it brings on. Often there is no choice. For me, there was a choice. Not only was the salary I got from my job so pitifully small that we would scarcely feel the loss of it, I could also write from home. That was my choice: I would stay at home and write.

It was not easy. Working from home is never easy, as anyone who has done it will agree. You need to have a great deal of self-discipline; but that is not enough. Others have to learn to take your work seriously, *they* have to understand that even if you are at home, you are still working. This was going to be a long, never-ending and never-easy struggle. Perhaps it got a little easier as the children grew up, but vacations meant I had to put my writing aside, for it was no use feeling torn between their needs and my work. Besides, by this time we had a great deal of family in Bombay. My sister and her family, of course, had been there for years. Now there was my sister-in-law and her family in Vikhroli; a brother-in-law and his family were not too far away, either, just a few miles out of Bombay. They came to Bombay for the weekends, occasionally we visited them. And then there were my mother-in-law's visits, when everything was turned topsy-turvy for the sake of her Brahmin-widow regime for which my routine had to be put on hold.

Working at home also meant I had to equip myself with the basics. I got an old writing table from my brother-in-law (which mysteriously disintegrated when it was transported to Bangalore) and I had a good Parker pen we had bought in England. But I didn't have a typewriter, so I used the typewriter, a giant-size Remington, in my husband's office in the evenings after his secretary left. The office was just above the mortuary and the autopsy room, and the smell of death and formalin would waft up from the basement. I don't think I paid much attention to these morbid things, focussed as I was on typing out what I had written. I did this until I got a second hand portable Olivetti of my own (for three hundred rupees), which seemed a great luxury.

My writing began, not with fiction, but with non-fiction. I approached some of my teachers who were working journalists; they helped by suggesting topics I could write on. I wrote on domestic servants, I wrote about the prevalence of TB in Bombay and on many more subjects. But the one I remember the most is the article I wrote on the Suffragette movement. Again, memory fails me and I have no idea why I chose the subject, where I had the piece published, or whether it was published at all. I don't have the manuscript with me, either. Yet, I can remember it clearly. I had heard of the Suffragettes in England and of their struggle for the right to vote in a novel called *Fame is the Spur* by Howard Spring – one of those English novelists, whose books filled a shelf of the British Council library then, but whose name is totally forgotten now. I don't think he was a great writer, but he managed to bring the Victorian era to life. This novel was about a couple, the man a Welsh miner, I think, who joined the budding Labour Party, and his wife, who came from an aristocratic family, but joined the Suffragette movement.

For some reason, the book impressed me greatly and to read about the birth of the Labour Party, and of the Suffragette movement, was a kind of eye-opener for me. I knew nothing about the Suffragette movement; unlike the Labour movement, it died early. And was forgotten. So wholly forgotten that with all my reading, I had had no idea of its existence. All that I knew about the Suffragettes was from what I had read in Howard Spring's book. I read some more books before I wrote the piece and got most of the material from a book by Sylvia Pankhurst, daughter of Emmeline Pankhurst, the leader and pillar of the movement

(I had seen Emmeline's statue near Parliament when we went to London, but she had meant nothing to me then).

The Suffragette movement was the first and only organised battle in the history of the fight for women's rights. It was an ugly and violent fight. It was as if the code of behaviour, by which men and women had lived together, was abandoned once women asked for the vote, for equality, really; women no longer had the right to be treated like 'ladies'. It seemed incredible to me that women, fighting for nothing more than the right to vote, should have been opposed so fiercely, violently and cruelly. I read with horrified fascination of the women's hunger strike when in jail (which pre-dated Gandhi's fasts), of the forced feeding and other physical indignities they had to submit to. I read of Emily Davies, who threw herself in front of the King's horse at the Derby, a flag with the WSPU (the organisation which fought the battle for votes) colours in her hand. Emily Davies died. (Queen Mary, who was present at the Derby along with the King, called her a 'horrid woman'!) I read of women who chained themselves to the railings on the street. Of the passion with which women went on with the struggle. I was flabbergasted. How was it that we, no, I, had never heard of this? Why was it so totally forgotten? I wrote the article about the movement. What happened to it? Now I can only guess that possibly I had my article published somewhere, though I have absolutely no idea where. Or, maybe it was never published. But the article was not the end of it for me. My knowledge of this movement was the beginning of something that would shape both my life and my work, though I did not know it at the time.

I soon gave up writing non-fiction. Once again, I seemed to have discovered that something was not for me, though I did write quite a lot of non-fiction later. I wrote a story for a competition run by *Eve's Weekly*, a prominent women's magazine of the time, and got a prize for it. Which was morale-boosting. I must add that I knew it was a very ordinary story. I was embarrassed when I looked at it later. A writer friend, Anupama Niranjana, once told me that I was lucky I started writing late in life. It saved you from writing the usual juvenile stuff most writers produce at an early age, she said. Well, there was some comfort, it seemed, in having begun writing late! Today, they begin so early that I, thirty when I began writing, would be considered the Ancient Mariner, no less. But I don't agree with Anupama. I think writing juvenile stuff is part of the evolution of all writers. And I did write stuff in the early days which makes me squirm. I don't think I shed any tears over the loss of many of my early pieces. At this time, I also got an introduction to the editor of *Femina*, the other women's magazine of the time. I gave her three of my stories. 'Call me after a week,' she said. I called her exactly on the eighth day and asked about my stories. 'I'm publishing them,' she said. 'Which ones?' I asked. 'All three,' she said. Standing under the staircase, in the cubbyhole where the common telephone was situated, I took a deep breath and exulted. It was a kind of joy I had not known in my life until then. Indescribable.

That was the beginning. By now, people were thronging my mind, asking for their stories to be told and stories poured out of me as if they had been waiting inside me for years, stories that came out of the people I had seen, met, heard about. Nothing, it seemed, could stop me. I had to spend six months in bed with an undiagnosed pain, the beginning of a problem that was to trouble me all my life, a problem which is still with me. It was a very bad time, because at the same time, both our sons came down with chicken pox.

I remember, now a grief-bringing poignant memory, that our older son, Nandu, went to the back of the house to cry when he found the pain too much; he did not want to trouble me because I was sick myself. The woman who was working for me then told me that. The doctors who visited me (almost all the senior doctors in K.E.M., it seemed) had no idea of what was really wrong with me. Nevertheless, lying in bed, I wrote a short story which I knew was not a good short story and which, I knew later, had to be a novel. But this too won a prize in a short story competition and eventually it became *The Dark Holds No Terrors*. I was lucky that soon both the popular women's magazines were taking my stories most of the time without hesitation. I never knew then what a great boon this was: it meant I had found a readership. For years after, I had people coming to me, saying, I read your stories in *Femina*, in *Eve's Weekly*. Speaking at a seminar on short stories organised by the Sahitya Akademi a few years back, I lamented the fact that there are such few openings for short stories in English in India. Politics, sport and cinema have taken over all the pages. Whereas, in the *bhashas*, the short story flourishes because of the space given to it in magazines, in the magazine specials brought out during Dasara or Diwali. Even veteran writers make it a point to have new stories for these issues. But English stories have very little space for publication today.

At that time, though, there were many outlets for short stories. I had my stories published in magazines, in Sunday supplements of newspapers, in journals. My ambition, however, was to have one published in the *Illustrated Weekly of India*. This was the foremost magazine in India then. It also serialised novels of prominent writers – I remember reading Ruth Jhabvala's novel *Esmond in India* in the *Illustrated Weekly* and something by Kamala Markandaya. I went to meet Khushwant Singh, who was the editor of the *Illustrated Weekly* then. He was very courteous, he listened to me seriously, he took me seriously, unlike another editor, who made it clear he would have nothing to do with my story, a *woman's story*.

I had occasion to meet Khushwant Singh once again in Bangalore. Penguin was coming into India and Khushwant

Singh was the commissioning editor. So I think. Anyway, he was in Bangalore looking for manuscripts and also to meet writers. Somehow, along the way, this was translated into 'Kannada women writers' and a whole lot of them were there in the hotel waiting for him. I can still see his sense of bewilderment battling with his innate courtesy when he saw the women. When he had a moment with me, he confessed he was totally confused at what was happening, he didn't know what to do. I must say he said and did all the right things, he came out of the incident with flying colours. To go back to my story, I sent it to the fiction editor of the *Illustrated Weekly* as Khushwant Singh had asked me to. She sent back the story I mailed her, but with the reasons for rejection spelt out. Which was a rare and a kind thing to do. I rewrote it and sent it back and it was published.

But my main supporters were the two women's magazines. With Vimla Patil, the editor of *Femina*, I had a relationship that was ideal between a writer and editor. 'Why don't you write me a story for Independence Day?' she asked me. And to my surprise, I did, a story which, in spite of being written to order, so to say, felt good. Write me a love story, she requested me, and I wrote one which I knew was like just any other love story. Ordinary. I had to wait for over thirty years before I could write about love without the clichés, without being mushy.

There has always been, and still is, some kind of a prejudice against fiction that appears in women's magazines. Of course, like the stories I'd read as a girl in *Woman & Home*, most were romances, targeted at young girls and lonely women. Young women and girls wanted to read such stories and dream of romance in their lives. It is as natural for women to read, write and dream about romance, as it is for men to read or write about sex. But for some reason, a man writing about the male libido is taken seriously, whereas, women writing about romance, or women reading romances, are looked down upon. Just a step away from this, is the idea that fiction is 'soft' as opposed to 'hard' non-fiction, and that fiction is meant for women. I don't know how often I have heard a man say, 'I don't read fiction.' I think everyone should read Jane Austen's brilliant defence of the novel in *Northanger Abbey*, where she speaks sarcastically of novels as 'performances which have *only* genius, wit and taste to recommend them'. Only!

Actually, at the time when I wrote for women's magazines, things were changing. Women were becoming increasingly aware of a growing desire to articulate, to express their thoughts, to speak of their condition, they were slowly questioning the tacit acceptance of the limitations of their lives. Some of the stories I wrote, like *Why a Robin?*, or *The Intrusion*, came out of the questions teeming in my mind. I had never been comfortable with the place allotted to women in the world, with the easy authority that men wielded over women, with the general assumption that men know more, they know better, except in domestic matters. I had always hated stupid jokes about women, which were so easily and casually passed around; I never failed to express my dislike of such jokes. And I was uncomfortable with stereotypes and generalisations, dissatisfied with the way men portrayed women in books. I once heard a West Indian writer say that she wrote because she could not find herself in the books she read. I cannot make such a strong and easy connection. But certainly, the fact that I (which included everyone like me) was not in any of the books I read, felt like a gap, an absence, a dotted line on which I had to write.

At this time, when stories flowed out of me, I began to understand that the involvement, the total absorption in writing, is the same as it is with babies and toddlers: the world is blanked out. For long, I was not very satisfied with my stories. I felt there was something wrong, something lacking. And then, I wrote *The Intrusion*, after which I knew what it was I had lacked: it was my own voice. In this story I found my voice. This was the story of a girl who finds the first night of her marriage a painful experience, feels that her husband, by having sex with her when she is not ready for it, is violating her right to her own body. Of course, she is not able to articulate her thoughts so clearly. (This, a woman's right to her body, is an issue which is being talked about now. But when I wrote this story – I think in 1971, for once I have the date because I have a cutting of the story with me – the idea was not even in women's minds. Perhaps, women felt that marriage meant their husbands had a right to have sex with them.) In this story, the theme, the language, the emotions and the craft came together in a harmony that does not often happen. I wrote it in one stretch, almost furtively, as if someone was looking over my shoulder as I wrote, because I was writing for the first time about sex, about a young woman's response to sex. After this I had no inhibitions, I never held back from writing about sex, except for aesthetic reasons. To write of two bodies and bodily parts is not something that interests me. While the body is the active participant in the act of sex, while it is the body which enjoys all the sensations, the major part of the urge and of enjoyment lie in the mind.

When I asked the editor of *Femina* whether she would be using my story, *The Intrusion*, she asked, 'Which one? The one about rape?' I had not thought about it in that way. The concept of marital rape did not exist then. Even now, it is a thorny issue, one that can divide men and women; which divides even women among themselves. One of the arguments against making rape in marriage a crime is its impact on the institution of marriage and the family. It reminds me of the long-back debated question of votes for women, when the right to vote, it was feared, would destroy the sanctity of family life. So, what is good for women is always bad for the family! So, it is always women who have to make a sacrifice for the good of the family! If we want women without any opinions of their own, women who think that their bodies and minds belong to their husbands, not to themselves, if we want, in other words, peaceful angels in the house so that family life is one of peace and tranquillity, why don't we lobotomize all women then?

Recently, while reading some divorce cases when I was writing *Strangers to Ourselves*, I came across a statement made by a judge in a divorce case that happened many years back: 'The categories of cruelty can never be closed.' It chilled me, it hit me hard, that remark, reminding me afresh that so much of cruelty takes place in a home, among the most intimate relationships. I used the words as an epigraph, but they were something more than merely the right words to be used in the right place: they expressed a thought that informs my attempts to understand the relationship between two humans. A relationship which can be full of great love and tenderness, as well as of great cruelty.

My own belief that women – and men as well (though this question rarely arises) – have a right to their own bodies, their own minds, came into another story I wrote at this time, *The Death of a Child*, which was about a woman who decides to abort a child, accidentally conceived, a baby she finds herself unable to accept. This story came out of my own experience when I conceived for a third time. Our younger son was less than a year old then, I was in pretty poor health and the thought of going through the process of pregnancy and delivery all over again filled me with panic. I just could not do it. Abortion was illegal as yet, but a doctor friend of my husband's we went to for help, seeing my state of near-panic, immediately agreed to help us, though it was he who was more at risk. He did it on ethical grounds (anti-abortionists, take note!), which for him meant putting the woman's emotional and physical health first. He was one of the finest humans I have met, and his face, concerned and serious, was the first one I saw when

I came out of anaesthesia. My immediate thought was, 'I've had a baby, why is he so serious?' A moment later the truth of what had happened came to me. A vague sense of loss, of an absence, haunted me for some time.

Not too long ago, I read a review of two books on the issue of abortion and on the history of anti-abortion in the USA. It seems amazing that there should be such an opposition to abortion, that there was a time when abortion clinics were bombed in the USA, when doctors who performed abortions were murdered. (We may yet see such a hard stance emerge in the Trump years.) These pro-lifers, as they call themselves, consider abortion to be murder, they look at it as the killing of an infant. This is something which can be endlessly discussed, and the ethics of it may weigh on the side of the pro-lifers. Nevertheless, I think the woman's needs are paramount. She is the one who is going to bear the child for nine months, to give birth through pain and blood; it is her body that pays the price.

The laws in India are finally changing, the judges waking up to certain social and health realities of women's lives. Just the other day, the Supreme Court came out with a judgement which stated that a woman did not need her husband's consent for an abortion. I think this is how it should be. We saw a play on BBC the year we were in England about an Irish Catholic woman who gets pregnant yet again after many children. She does not want the baby, but knows there is no way the Church or the law will support her. One day she just disappears from home. I could so well understand her tormented thoughts, her desperation. She didn't want the child and yet to think of putting an end to its life was unbearable. A reviewer commented on my story *Death of a Child*, saying that the ending was not feminist enough. If a woman had the courage to take such a decision, why anguish over it? It seemed strange to me that the reviewer did not realise that we do not live our life according to an ideology. This is what fiction is able to do: to give a more true picture, because it brings in the grey areas, the nuances, the contradictions, the complications which are part of any human's life or thinking.

I had begun to understand, as I wrote my stories, that one learns the craft of writing only through the process of writing. I discarded many stories, I wrote many drafts of each story, I wrote *A Liberated Woman* (which became a novel, *The Dark Holds No Terrors*, finally) more than a dozen times, each failure teaching me something about the 'how' of writing.

'Art stands on the shoulders of craft.' Ann Patchett.

'The art must be respected ... for if you let the mind run loose, it becomes egotistic; personal, which I detest. At the same time the irregular fire must be there.' Virginia Woolf.

Control, yet passion. Control in the crafting, passion in the emotions. Irregular fire. Easy to say, but hard to practise. And it takes ages to learn. For me, the intensity was very important. I could never glide on the surface, I had to drown myself, lose myself in the character's feelings, emotions. A novel demands even greater intensity and it demands that the intensity be sustained over a longer period of time.

By this time I was aching to write a novel, I was eager to get out of women's magazines, for I found I did not like being typecast as 'the woman who writes for *Femina* and *Eve's Weekly*'. It was not ingratitude; I was feeling stifled, claustrophobic. There was a restlessness which drove me into writing two books for children. But it was not what I really wanted to do. A novel was waiting patiently inside me. And I know now, that, while I was writing short stories, I was preparing myself for writing a novel. Short stories, much more than novels, provide an opportunity for breaking the mould, for trying out something new. My father used one-act plays as laboratories in which he worked out new techniques for his full-length plays; short stories can be used in the same way. I wrote over fifty short stories, then tried out longer stories which were serialised in magazines, before I embarked on a novel. I had a rough idea of the novel I wanted to write, but it was still difficult to get hold of. And then, two things happened: my husband accepted a job in Bangalore, which meant a major move. And a little before we left Bombay, Indira Gandhi declared a state of Emergency in the country.

'D'Ocracy, D.E.M., son of L.I.Bertie and T.Ruth, brother of Faith, Hope and Justice, expired on 26th June.'

We read this notice among the death announcements in *The Times of India* the morning after the declaration of an Emergency. This, together with a blank editorial page, or a blank first page in newspapers, told us that overnight we had ceased to be a democracy. It was the death of D'Ocracy indeed.

A Balancing Act

I will write my books and raise the children. Anything else just fritters me away.
Anne Tyler, *The Writer on Her Work*

I CAN STILL DISTINCTLY remember the day we decided to move out of Bombay. We were in a grocer's shop in Dadar, giving our orders to a young shop assistant, who repeated the orders in a dull monotone and packed the stuff with the efficiency of a robot. The shop was crowded, the pavement outside teeming with jostling, shoving pedestrians, the road choked with loudly honking traffic. We must get out of here, my husband decided that day. Even as he was looking for a suitable job outside Bombay, he was fortunate to get the offer of a job in Bangalore as Professor of Neuropathology in NIMHANS – formally, the National Institute of Mental Health and Neurosciences. It seemed ideal. It was a job which would give him independent charge of a department and a chance to build it up. Besides, we would be in Karnataka, and he would be much nearer his ancestral village home where his mother lived. As for me, I knew the city well; I had lived in it and my parents lived there still. Nevertheless, I had misgivings. I was by now completely at home in Bombay, I had become a real 'Mumbaikar' – except for the fact that I could never travel by a local train, or a 'local' as a real Mumbaikar would call it. (We had once got into a local after a late night movie, which soon got so crowded that when it was time for us to get out, I found I was stalled by my sari pallu being trapped between two bodies. Such was the density of the crowd!) There were also valid reasons for my reluctance to leave Bombay. Bombay was a much better place for the children's education. Bangalore was (then) a smaller place, with fewer educational opportunities. And it was caste-ridden. Were we doing the right thing? But the opportunity could not be missed, and so we moved to Bangalore to make a home in the NIMHANS campus.

The Bangalore we came to in the seventies was very different from the Bangalore I had come to in the fifties with my parents. It was a changed city, though not as changed as it would be in the next two decades. Little independent homes still outnumbered large residential apartment blocks, stately old bungalows were still standing, and it was as yet very much a city of flowers and gardens. The change in the city lay elsewhere. When we came to Bangalore for the first time, Bangalore had only just become the capital of the newly formed Karnataka State. It was not used to the role, Mysore having been the capital of what had earlier been the princely Mysore State. Geographically too, Bangalore was perched at the southern tip of the State of Karnataka, and closer to Madras State (as Tamil Nadu was known then), spatially, as well as in many other ways, than to the rest of Karnataka. Now, the city looked as if it had got used to its role as the capital of the State. The Vidhana Soudha, which housed both the legislative houses as well as government offices, had just been built when I came here the first time and it had had the look of an upstart, both in its shining newness and its pretentious architecture. More, it had contrasted unfavourably with the gracious old red High Court building which stood just opposite. Now, the Vidhana Soudha seemed to face the High Court with greater composure, as if it, too, had found its place.

My father had been in the forefront of the movement to unite all the Kannada-speaking areas into one state. In Dharwad, most functions used to begin with a song that sang of the 'Kannada flag'. I am sure my sister and I also sang as part of the chorus once or twice, because of being our father's children. But as I grew up and began to think for myself, I was never in favour of linguistic states. I thought that this would be one more dividing factor in our country, that it would encourage linguistic chauvinism. This did happen, not only in Karnataka, but everywhere, the border areas bearing the brunt of the agitations. There were language riots in Karnataka, too, though much later. And after the State of Karnataka was formed, there was an uneasy relationship between the various Kannada people who had earlier belonged to different regions.

This time, when we came, things had changed. Not that there was much more of an amalgamation of people from different areas; in fact, there was a new enclave in the city where all those who came from North Karnataka (they had been part of Bombay State) lived. This became one more enclave added to the Muslim, the Tamil, the Christian and the Anglo-Indian enclaves. But in spite of this divide, there was a kind of cultural renaissance, a flowering in different cultural fields, due perhaps to a flowing in of different people, different ways of life. The renewal was most obvious in films. In the fifties, the theatres on K.G. Road, a road lined with theatres, had mostly had Tamil films running, and posters of a moustached, swashbuckling MGR, or of Sivaji Ganesan dominated the area. Now there were an equal number of Kannada movies being shown. Kannada heroes, like Rajkumar or Vishnuvardhan, had their fan clubs just like the Tamil stars. The films of Puttanna Kanagal, a director, were both critically acclaimed, as well as box office hits. I saw one of his films on TV, saw it twice, actually, a film about a woman who had grown up and lived in the professional theatre world, and who, at the height of her fame, married a wealthy man and tried to live the respectable, domestic life of a rich man's wife. But her passion for the theatre conquered her and she went back to acting. It was one of the usual over-the-top, hand-wringing, chest-beating, tear-jerker melodramas. But the woman's passion for the theatre and her inability to fit into any other role caught me.

This apart, new directors were making different kinds of films. Even while in Bombay, we had heard of *Samskara*, based on the writer U.R. Ananthamurthy's novel. Much acclaimed, it became a brilliant movie. Later, there was *Vamsha Vriksha* which was based on Byrappa's novel. The mingling of cinema and literature seemed to yield wonderful results. We saw a new young director Girish Kasaravalli's debut film *Ghatashraddha*, a powerful film, once again based on a story by Ananthamurthy. There was Girish Karnad's *Ondanandu Kaladalli* (Once Upon a Time), in which a young and talented Shankar Nag made a great debut as an actor. Kannada writers had begun claiming the national Jnanpith award, then (and still) the biggest award for literary works in Indian languages. Masti, Bendre, Kuvempu, Shivaram Karanth were all Jnanpith winners.

In the world of theatre too, there was a resurgence. My father was in the midst of a lively theatre scene, there were many new amateur groups. My father's dream of more professionalism among amateur groups, of small theatres scattered all over the city, of repeated performances of any production, was still distant. But certainly the theatre scene was different from what it had been earlier. I remember one of the first plays we had seen after we came to Bangalore the first time. Actors happily forgot their lines and looked for help to the wings from where the prompter's voice came loud and clear and the audience was full of squalling children. Now the theatre seemed lively and growing. Perhaps I may be wrong in attributing these changes to a unified state. Or exaggerating. For certainly I have neither the knowledge, nor the kind of understanding needed to come to such a conclusion. Yet, what was undeniably clear, was that a composite Kannada identity was slowly evolving. People who had been unseen, almost lost in the 'Madrasi' or 'Southerners' mass, were finding a new confidence in themselves, making their presence felt on the cultural map of India. Was this the result of a unified Karnataka State? Was I wrong then in thinking that the idea of linguistic states was wrong? The answer is no, I was right if one looked at the linguistic fanaticism which soon made its presence felt in Karnataka, at the linguistic chauvinism that followed and was used by politicians, through mobs, for their own purposes. The anti-Tamil riots in Bangalore, the anti-Marathi riots in North Karnataka and the persistent anti-Hindi, anti-Northerners campaigns, the blacking of all boards in English, Hindi or any other language which periodically erupt, are examples of this. (The Metro is the latest enemy, Kannada fanatics vehemently protesting against name boards of stations in Hindi.) It seems that it is only by hating the other that you can proclaim your love for what is your own. And yet, as against this, there was the emergence of an identity, a confidence that had not been there earlier. I suppose this can be endlessly debated.

On a personal level, our life in the staff quarters in the NIMHANS campus was very different from our life in Parel, perhaps much better in many ways, though it was a long time before I could think so. It was a huge area, there was certainly no shortage of land, and the old mental hospital dominated the campus. That it was on the edge of the city was made clear by the fact that there were cemeteries and crematoriums on both the approach roads to NIMHANS. One Christian cemetery was a very old one, the size of the trees planted among the graves giving an indication of its age. The trees were lush and green, as if – I had a macabre thought – there was a symbiotic relationship between the trees and the dead: the dead helped the trees to grow, and therefore the trees hung protectively over the graves. I always wanted to go into that cemetery and find out about the kind of people who were buried there and the time they had lived in. It never happened.

Like in Parel, we lived in the midst of doctors. The campus was a close and friendly community, the greatest asset being that our children were roughly about the same age. Which meant that the children had friends and, just as important, a lot of space to play in. The house itself was a large four-bedroom house, but like all buildings built by the Government Public Works Department, fault-ridden. Lights fused all the time, the bathroom floors sloped the wrong way, so that water never ran in the direction it was supposed to, doors and windows could never be properly closed. Nevertheless, it was a great place to live in, even though we were very isolated, a long distance from any place. There were no shops, no houses, nothing like a neighbourhood close to us. Nights were silent. In fact, I who was used to buses screeching all the way from round the corner of our home in Parel, before stopping outside, under our window with an over-sized screech, found the silence unnerving. It was long before I could get used to it. There was no fencing around the campus, nor around our houses. Anyone could just walk in. Our neighbour had a strange experience one morning, when, trying to get out, he realised the door had been bolted from the outside. He banged on the door, he called out. A sleepy voice replied, '*So jao.*' Our neighbour, a psychiatrist who delighted in the unusual and the quirky, did just that – he went back to sleep. When he woke up a little later, the door was unbolted. A family of nomads had camped on their porch for the night.

Our isolation was made worse because of the lack of transport; Bangalore has always had an abysmally poor public transport system, which is why almost everyone had/has a two-wheeler. Buses were infrequent and few, rickshaws whimsical and reluctant to come all the way to this area. My husband was lucky, he had just a five-minute walk to get to the hospital. The children were not so lucky. Initially, they went in a cycle rickshaw along with our neighbour's two children. But they soon rebelled against this form of travel and we bought cycles for both of them. Looking at the road now, with the traffic thundering all day and night, I can't even imagine that there was a time when children could safely cycle on this road. We still had our car, but Madam Temperament stayed snugly in her home (for the first time we had a garage) most of the time. There were a few occasions, state occasions, when we took the car out, like for a visit to my parents.

If we were physically isolated, I was even more isolated as a writer. In Bombay, there had been the two women's magazines; I had regularly visited their offices, met the editors, talked to some of the staff. Here, there was no one. In Bombay, there had been a kind of English literary world, though I had never been a part of it. But in Bangalore, there were almost no English writers, none that I knew, or had heard of, anyway. A small group of Kannada women writers, who met regularly, invited me once or twice. But I had no desire to be part of any group (I have always been solitary), and I did not believe in dividing literature by gender. These women believed that by uniting they could fight the subtle discrimination they met as women writers. I thought that such segregation only made it worse; that what was needed, was to just go on writing. But the women had a right to their beliefs and they later grew to a surprising strength.

I did make two good friends, though, who contributed greatly, not only to my literary life, but also my personal life. My father knew the leftist writer Niranjan and his doctor-wife Anupama very well. They became good friends of ours as well. Anupama was a writer and a feminist – there were not many feminists then, or perhaps not many declared themselves to be feminists – and in her, I found a friend and a good intellectual companion. I also met Laeeq Futehally, sometime editor of *Quest*, and our chance meeting at a seminar was the beginning of many years of friendship. (I distinctly remember that both of us were struck at that seminar by the resemblance of a young man to Hugh Grant. We confessed that we both admired him, no, his looks, perhaps the beginning of shared views!) Laeeq had a great talent for friendship. Witty (her letters were gems of wit and brevity), warm and wise, she readily gave me her shoulder to sob on when I was troubled about anything. And, a rare and wonderful trait, she never offered any advice. Truly a wise woman. Anupama, on the other hand, was a loudly enthusiastic supporter. When my husband gave up his job and decided to open his own diagnostic laboratory, she offered him some money to start off with. Dr Shivaram, a senior doctor, had helped her when she had started, she said, and when she tried to return the money, he told her to help someone in her turn instead. It was that kind of a world.

The fact of my parents being in town added another dimension to our lives, certainly to mine. It had been difficult for us to go to see plays or movies in Bombay, because of the children. The only movies we went to were those that were meant for children. However, once the children were old enough to be left by themselves, we did go (though very rarely) for movies, music performances and plays. Marathi plays, specially. I remember *Swami*, about Madhavrao Peshwa, whose personality impressed me deeply and who came back to me when I was writing *A Matter of Time*. We saw Tendulkar's *Gidhade* and *Kanyadaan*, both deeply disturbing plays, *Ti Phularani*, a Marathi adaptation of Shaw's *Pygmalion* by the famous P.L. Deshpande, Girish Karnad's *Tughlak* in English (with Kabir Bedi showing off his muscles in the opening scene), and Alyque Padamsee's *Evita*. We saw some experimental plays too, including my father's play in Marathi, with Amol Palekar in it, in a small theatre in Dadar.

In Bangalore, we could enter that world more easily, because I was connected to it through my father. I felt less of an outsider, a little more than a mere spectator. My father had found his place in the literary and cultural life of the city and I could feel the pulse of this world myself. I accompanied my father to a panel discussion organised by Ananthamurthy, when the British novelist Angus Wilson was visiting town. My father and the poet Gopalkrishna Adiga were on the panel with Angus Wilson, Ananthamurthy moderating. We went to Mysore with my father when he was awarded an honorary doctorate and, later that day, my father took me with him to visit R.K. Narayan, who had also been given a doctorate at the same time.

Sadly, I have no memory at all of the conversation between the two writers. I am, as I said, neither a notebook-carrying person, nor do I rush home and record memorable moments in a diary. Which is why a conversation between two great writers has been lost to posterity. I remember, though, that I was tongue-tied, and said almost nothing, except to speak of Dev Anand's film, *Guide*, based on Narayan's novel. Narayan dryly commented that he was not paid for the story by Dev Anand. I don't know if this is true, but I can believe it. We Indians like our writers to be noble and perhaps wise, but they shouldn't talk about money, let alone ask for it. (This was how it was then. The time would come when an advance amount, provided it was large enough, would be written about in the papers.)

On my father's suggestion, I gave some of my stories to R.K. Narayan, hoping to get his opinion. After a very long time, he sent back the stories, with a letter saying he had not been able to find the time to read them. I was a little annoyed then (though, at least he had been honest), but now I understand him better. I am asked at times by young writers to give my opinion on their work. It is true; there is simply no time. Nor do I think I am qualified to judge anyone's writing. I'd be terrified to take on the responsibility.

Once we settled into our new home and the children were admitted into their new school, I went back to writing. With the children at school all day, and with better and live-in help, I had more time. It was then that I organised my day to get the maximum time for writing, something that set the pattern for my daily living since then. I wrote in the early hours of the morning, before the children had to be woken up, and I wrote after I finished my cooking and household chores, until it was time for the children to come home. It was also a kind of peripatetic writing. I wrote at my table in the bedroom in the mornings, later in the spare bedroom and then at the dining table, because I had to prepare something substantial for the children, who would come home ravenously hungry from school.

I am amazed when I think of how much I wrote in those years. Amazed, because I was also a full-time hands-on housewife, who cooked three meals a day for two grown-ups and two growing children. And, I now recollect, that with my mother's help and because of her enthusiasm, I made pickles and papads, sandiges and dried chillies. Our first Diwali in the NIMHANS house, I prepared all the things that were conventionally prepared for Diwali – laddus, chaklis, chivda, anarasas, kodboles. In fact, the lot. Looking back now, I see that I was playing my role of 'the woman of the family' to the hilt. Whom was I trying to impress? Myself, perhaps. But after that burst of enthusiasm (I had even baked a cake for one of my son's birthdays. I remember it now with disbelief!), I lost interest in these things. And after the children left home, I was so disinterested in cooking that my cooking deteriorated and, later, when they were home, my boys would look at what was on the table and say, 'I'm not hungry.'

Soon after we came to Bangalore, I began keeping a diary for the first time, a kind of self-communing, a place where I wrote about and tested my ideas, searched for names, got clues to characters' lives. I found some of these recently when I was going through my books before moving out of the house we had lived in for thirty years. I was surprised to find a refrain of entries saying, *I can't write. I can't write. Words, phrases, sentences have deserted me. I am finished. I am a big ZERO.* I am surprised when I read this, remembering the amount of work I did in those years. There is written evidence of the work. A great many stories. Two novels. Two, no, three children's books. A number of articles. Correspondence with editors. Which version do I believe? Both, I think. For soon after we came to Bangalore, I got into a state of depression. This is something I often suffer from, specially after changes in my life, changes which are not of my choice.

After seeing my brother's illness, and my parents' struggle to keep it a secret, I learnt to be open about my problem. I remember visiting a psychiatrist friend in his consulting rooms once, and, since my name was not on his appointment list, the receptionist asked me whether mine was a personal visit. No, I said, it was a professional visit. When I went in, the doctor asked me, 'Must you be so honest?' I saw no reason not to tell the truth about my need for professional help. I think facing the problem squarely helped. Above all, work helped; writing was both catharsis and therapy.

At this time, I wrote confessional stories for a magazine. True stories, ostensibly, written in the first person, on a variety of themes. My name did not appear as the author of these stories and I felt uneasy; it seemed dishonest. But the writing helped me get out of my 'writer's block'. What was more important was that I was also able to earn a regular sum for a few months, though I am afraid I had to pay a price for it. I found it hard to get out of the confessional tone afterwards, I found it difficult to go back to my own writing, to my own style. I decided then, I would never do such a thing again. I think writers should be responsible for every word they write, their name should be attached to all that they write.

This was the time when I did a great amount of reading, as well. I read Irawati Karve's *Yuganta* which was to have a great impact on my thinking and writing. Even before reading *Yuganta*, I had written a story about Sita – *The Golden Deer*. In it, I had probed Sita's thoughts about her husband, Shri Ram's, image as the perfect man, and of the price others had to pay for this image. It was the beginning, for me, of going back to mythological women. I wrote a story about Amba, about Draupadi, Kunti, and surprisingly about Duryodhana, the villain of the Mahabharata. I realised that as a writer you do not judge a character and so it was in *The Last Enemy*, the story about Duryodhana. This story surprised even me, for he was certainly not a character I was sympathetic to. But there it was, a story that came to me when I was waiting in the car, swatting at mosquitoes, while my husband went into the bank. A story I wrote out, unusually, in one sitting, as soon as I went home and finished with my chores. Surprisingly, Duryodhana was not a villain in this story. I moved into a different phase of short stories at this time – *My Beloved Charioteer* came to me after seeing a movie. Not an inspirational one, just an ordinary movie about a woman struggling to cope with the death of a loved one. *A Wall is Safer*, which I wrote after we finally had a fence for our house in NIMHANS, is one of the stories I am fond of, because I think I was able to work out an idea through the very mundane. This story appeared in one of the Writers Workshop collections, and when a reviewer commented on the triviality of the story, P. Lal sent me the review with his words written on it. 'Forgive him, he does not understand.'

My first collection of short stories had come out at this time, brought out by P. Lal. My father had been suggesting I have a collection of my stories published and someone had recommended Prof. Lal and the Writers Workshop to me. I wrote to him, not expecting much. He wrote back saying that he would publish my stories, but I would have to buy a hundred copies. Hundred copies! I had seen how my father's venture into publication – of an English translation of his novel – had ended in disaster, with unsold books lying all over the house. No, I wrote back to Prof. Lal, while I was prepared to earn no money from my writing, I would not spend any money on it, either, except for paper, ink and postage. After a while, he wrote back that he would publish the book, even if I didn't buy the hundred copies, and he would also do something he rarely did: he would write a small blurb for it. It was the beginning of a long association, which gave me what I badly needed at the time – someone who believed in my writing. Prof. Lal was the first literary person to think my writing mattered. Through all the years I knew him, he continued to be supportive of my writing. I still have many of his letters, treasures, because of his beautiful language, the pithy manner in which he said so much, his beautiful hand, and his strong belief in my writing. I remain eternally grateful to him; I badly needed the kind of affirmation he gave me. My first collection, *The Legacy*, surprisingly got some reviews. I still remember one that said, though not in these words, it was not great stuff, but promising. I thought these words were honest and true. I had a very long way to go.

Mainly, I was waiting to start on my novel. I knew that the short story *A Liberated Woman* had to be a novel. But it was hard to get hold of it, it kept sliding away from me. In addition, I was unable to move out of the short story form, I kept coming to a kind of pause after three thousand words. I was glad when another novel offered itself to me, a novel that was simpler to write. This was *Roots and Shadows*. It was initially going to be a mystery novel. I have always been a great reader of crime novels. My father must have been, at some time, an enthusiast, because there were a number of crime books at home on which I cut my teeth – a few Peter Cheyney's (I remember one, *Your Deal, My Lovely*) and some of the green-cover cheap Penguin paperbacks that were brought out during the war. There was *A Bullet in the Ballet, Death and Mary Dazill, The Postman Always Rings Twice, Trial and Error, The Black Gloves* and some others. All extremely good books. My novel, I thought, would have a nasty rich old woman as the victim, with a large number of suspects – Agatha Christie style. Somehow, this never took off. Instead, it morphed into a study of power in a family, and what it does to everyone, including the person with power. In fact, *Roots and Shadows*, which I now look at with some embarrassment, took off with my mother's Pune home.

Houses have always mattered a great deal to me, and the Pune *wada* was so much a part of my childhood that when I heard that it had been demolished – too old, too many owners, nobody to live in it – I was very disturbed. Night after night I dreamt of it. In my dreams, it was always thronging with people, as it had been when I was a child, there were many known and some unknown faces and a jangle of voices. And then, it came to me that this was the location of the novel I was trying to write. A cousin, who is thinking of writing a family history, recently lamented that there are no photographs of the Pune *wada*. 'I can sketch it out for you in detail, the entire plan of the house,' I told her. A house built around three courtyards, with over a dozen staircases, two beautiful long halls with arched windows from which light streamed in, the large front door which was kept open all day and closed with loud creaks only at night – even today I can see the house vividly. In *Roots and Shadows*, it was transformed, as it had to be, but it came entirely out of the Pune *wada*. In this house, and in the family which lived in it (not my mother's family, but my own creation), I wrote a story of power, an idea which came from Mrs Gandhi and the Emergency, and what happened, not only to the country, but to her as well, as a result of her craving for absolute power.

Recently, I resigned from the Sahitya Akademi because of it's failure to comment or take any action on the killing of a writer – Prof. M.M. Kalburgi. My action was part of a protest by many writers and artists after the killing of three rationalists, a protest against the government's failure to protect people from those who tried to curb intellectual freedom and the right to freedom of speech. Curbs which came from mobs and fringe groups, rather than the government, which cannily allowed them a very long rope. I was asked, then, by a number of journalists, whether I thought this situation was similar to what had happened during the time of the Emergency. No, I said, it was not. The Constitution itself had been suspended during Mrs Gandhi's Emergency; suddenly we had no constitutional rights at all. There were arrests all over the country, people were jailed without trial. Jayaprakash Narayan, leader of the opposition to Mrs Gandhi, who was very ill at the time, became a symbol of the resistance. George Fernandes, another of her opponents, was hunted with the same zeal with which the Americans searched the world over for Osama bin Laden. A pall of fear lay over the country. Mrs Gandhi's younger son, Sanjay Gandhi, was the man behind some of the worst excesses of that time.

My father was a very active and vocal opponent of the Congress, Mrs Gandhi and the Emergency, and he wrote a play, which was used in the election campaign when Mrs Gandhi inexplicably announced elections. My husband and I played a small role, too, in the resistance. His nephew belonged to the RSS, an organisation that rested on the foundation of patriarchy, religious intolerance, and a kind of quasi-Fascism, with children – no, boys – being trained from very young to become good and militant Hindus. The organisation was against Mrs Gandhi and the Congress party, which from Nehru's times, had been sympathetic to the Muslims. Our nephew – like many others opposed to Mrs Gandhi and the Emergency – went underground as soon as the Emergency was announced. He somehow got a message through to us, asking whether they could use our house for their meetings. It was risky. We were living in government quarters and to give any help to those who were opposing the government, especially at such a time, could have had disastrous results. Now, when I think of it, it seems to me surprising that we never thought of the risk, our feelings against what was happening were so strong. We agreed. And so, a group came at night to our house to hold a meeting in the dark. We never saw anyone. They came silently – just leave a carpet for us, we were told – and the next morning everything was as it had been, the carpet neatly rolled up.

My husband's nephew was soon arrested and, once again, a secret message came from someone in the organisation, asking whether I would meet him in the prison; they would arrange the meeting. Which they did. I did go to the Central Jail, where a number of leaders, including L.K. Advani, were held, and passed on a little note to our nephew during the meeting. I had been asked to do this. I guess I was chosen because I looked eminently respectable, a sedate family woman. Too tame to be dangerous! I had no sympathy at all with the RSS. I thought, and still think, it is a very chauvinistic organisation and one which, by refusing to accept the idea and the fact that we are a multi-religious, multi-lingual, multi-cultural country, has built up an idea of a very narrow, intolerant India.

They have some queer and not very intelligent ideas about India's past, as well, which no thinking person can accept. Now, with the BJP in power, they have suddenly emerged as a strong and sinister force. I am strongly opposed to the ideology they so fiercely believe in, one they hope all of India (Hindu India, that is) will embrace. But at that time, I put my own feelings aside; for that little while, we were on the same side.

Despite these 'political experiences', my novel refused to become a political novel. It became, instead, a story of power within a family. I do believe a family is a microcosm of society. Put it under a microscope and you will see the same things – greed, ambition, envy, dishonesty – that you see in the politics of a nation. And so, this novel, which came out of Mrs Gandhi's ruthlessness and desire for absolute power, was transformed into the ruthlessness and desire for power of a woman who had suffered all her life under her husband's power. I had already become aware of the powerlessness of women, which begins in families and goes on to women in society and in the nation.

Like most first novels, *Roots and Shadows* was flawed; I knew it was flawed. It embarrasses me now. But it convinced me that the novel was the form which not only best suited me, it gave me immense satisfaction. For one thing, it gave me more space to explore people's lives, their minds and emotions. It allowed me to explore ideas. *Roots and Shadows* taught me that writing a novel could be full of surprises; you never know which way it will go. I'd drawn up a sketch of the characters and of the plot before I began. I had to abandon it. This plan had absolutely no connection to the novel I finally wrote. I have never planned a novel ever again. I also learnt that, if with short stories the problem was how to begin and how to end, with a novel the problem was how to sustain the story at length, how to hold on to it through the months and years it takes to write it.

Now I was ready to write my second novel. But for a long time, the structure evaded me. Until I read *Kinflicks* (by Lisa Alther, an American author), a novel that was part of the growing feminism of those times. This novel veered between the first person and the third person. And I immediately thought that this was how my novel had to be. Mine was a novel about marital rape, sibling envy, about guilt and parental neglect. Obviously, it was hard to write. (A reviewer called it a simple novel. Perhaps even *Oedipus* would be simple to her/him!) However, I could not get the beginning of the novel even when I came to the end. Then one night, or rather one early morning, I had a vision – like Leigh Hunt's Abou Ben Adhem. I could almost see the words before my eyes. I got out of bed and wrote it out; this became the beginning of the novel. The passage stayed that way, it needed no editing, no revision. Such a thing has very rarely happened to me.

I sent the novel to Vikas, a publisher whose name I had begun noticing as fiction publishers. I got a letter saying that since they had a great number of manuscripts to read, it would be at least six months before they could get back to me. And then, within a fortnight, I got a letter from the same gentleman (Samuel Israel, his name is engraved on my mind in letters of gold), saying that he had picked up my novel during his lunch hour, that he could not put it down and yes, they would publish it. It was an unforgettable moment. Getting the published novel in my hands was another. It came in hardback. I had seen a copy of Anita Desai's *In Custody* some time earlier and had envied her. I had dreamt of seeing my novel in such a form. And here it was, my own novel, in hard cover.

Surprisingly, the book received a large number of reviews. I say surprisingly because today, even after forty years of writing, my novels don't get as many reviews. (I guess the reason is that fiction has been superseded in importance by non-fiction. And also perhaps because there are too many books and too many writers today.) When I completed *The Dark Holds No Terrors*, I knew that there was no novel like it in English; at least I hadn't read any. I was not being boastful; I just knew this for a fact. This novel was not a victim's story, or Everywoman's story; it was the story of a woman trying to understand her condition. The quest ends for her when she hears what her mother had discovered just before she died: that we are alone, that we have to be alone. That there's nobody but us. The words of the Dhammapada, which I used as an epigraph, 'You are your own refuge; there is no other refuge,' fitted perfectly. This is the philosophy that has connected all my novels: the essential loneliness of the human being. Yet we keep forging connections throughout our lives, hoping they will give us what we need, hoping they will last. The ultimate human paradox.

It was with *The Dark Holds No Terrors* that I learnt to separate the person from the writer. Some things in *The Dark Holds No Terrors* came out of my life – inevitable that it should be so – and I know that the novel made my parents uncomfortable. 'We never made any difference between you and your brother,' my mother said to me ingenuously once, apropos of nothing, and I knew she was referring to my novel. But I had to write what I had to write. If something is relevant to the novel, there is no way you can keep it out.

Although I had two novels and a number of short stories by now, I was completely isolated from English writing. I didn't know a soul who wrote in English. In Bombay there had been some English writers, and Kamala Das, the poet, I was told, had a kind of salon, where everyone was welcome. 'Why don't you go?' a friend had asked. I couldn't. I was too shy, too wary of eminent people and reluctant to call myself a writer with only a few stories to my credit. In Bangalore, it suited me that, except for my parents and the Niranjan family, nobody knew I was a writer. It was better than being asked inane questions like, 'What do you write?' or 'What are the titles of your novels?'. Or being told, 'It's a good hobby.' All my work was done through the post – sending my stories, corresponding with editors, publishers, etc. For years, I must have been one of the greatest patrons of the Indian Post. (Much later, to my great pleasure, I was invited by them for an event and given a first day of issue stamp. It gave me equal pleasure to talk at the event about Jane Austen and how she, and everyone else who could write, were inveterate letter-writers.) I continued to write short stories for some more time, though only when commissioned. The novel was now my choice. I had no idea, when I began writing novels, of the kind of involvement novels demanded. How it would take over my life for three, four, five years. How desperate it made me to grab all the time possible for my writing. How it would haunt me even when I was not writing. My life narrowed down after this to just two things: my family and my writing.

While my writing seemed to have found its way, our life was once again on the brink of change. Even while we seemed to have let down roots, it looked like it was time for us to leave NIMHANS. Mainly, it was again lack of money which made this necessary. Our older son would be going to Bombay for his undergraduate studies, the younger would leave soon as well, most probably for a professional course. We had to support them in whatever they wanted to do; they were very intelligent boys and deserved all the support we could give them. At this point, suddenly there seemed to be a possibility of going back to Bombay; a well-known hospital offered my husband a job, with a house thrown in as part of the deal. This apart, he got the offer of a WHO Fellowship, which would take him to the USA. But he decided to take a third path instead, of starting his own laboratory in Bangalore. I was very unhappy. I thought Bombay would be ideal for the children. His friends and colleagues came to convince me that a job was a job and no salary would give us what we wanted – enough money for the children's education and a house of our own. My parents, who dreaded the thought of our leaving Bangalore, had been anxiously waiting for our decision. When we finally decided to stay in Bangalore, I rang up my father to tell him about it. Later, he told me that the moment he put down the phone and conveyed the news to my mother, she burst into tears (my mother rarely shed tears). I was very glad, at least for their sake, that we decided not to leave Bangalore. But we would leave NIMHANS.

Our older son left Bangalore to join college in Bombay that same year. I remember how I sobbed when he left home (I used to shed copious tears very easily, until I got dry eyes, part of an autoimmune problem). In two years the younger one would leave as well to join a medical college. Family life would never be the same again. We had had a wonderful time in NIMHANS. Of course we had had problems – problems of my health, problems of money. Above all, the shadow of my brother's illness lay over us, especially over my parents. He had been brought to NIMHANS for treatment and he had improved to some extent. He went back with instructions to come back in a month. He did. We, my husband and I, visited him once in Dharwad, after this. He seemed all right, if a little subdued. He took us around his department in the university, introduced us to his departmental head, a very sympathetic man. When we were leaving, I made him promise to take his medicines, to come to Bangalore for his check-up. He never did. That was the last time I saw him. Any attempt to get close to him made him slip away a little more. And so we lost him.

Except for this dark cloud, we had been happy. Halcyon days they now seem when I look back at the time we spent in NIMHANS, when we were all together. Even the snake in the backyard, which no snake catcher had been able to trap, which no one was willing to kill (it was a cobra), remains part of the enchantment. I can still remember the day we spotted it, sunning itself in our backyard, unopened hood held high, sunshine gleaming on its shining skin, wholly unaware of all of us, adults and children, who were watching it in fascination.

We had made a home for ourselves, the children had done well in school, they had made good friends, they had spent time with their grandparents. We had planted trees – shade-giving trees, flowering trees and fruit-yielding ones. We had greened what had been a barren area, we had got rid of the Congress grass – a weed that grew wildly all over the place; it had given us much trouble initially. My husband's farming instincts had come back and he had planted vegetables, optimistically hoping for a bumper crop. Kilos of chillies, kilos of beans, he promised us. We had hooted in laughter at his optimism. For water was scarce and the soil rocky and hard, reluctant to allow anything to grow.

But like gardeners learn and know, there is always something in a garden which gives you pleasure. In our garden, there were bunches of bananas, sweet papayas, a creeper of beans which grew over the garage roof and yielded enough beans to supply four families. Best of all, a sampige tree in the front yard took root and showed signs of healthy growth. And the so-wonderfully-named creeper, the Scarlett O' Hara, provided a blaze of colour on the fence. We learnt from the garden we planted, about the miracle, the unpredictability of life. Expensive seeds, planted and carefully nurtured, refused to open up, while on the manure heap, tomatoes grew in healthy abundance. We had to leave all this and go. But we had left our footprints on the land: that was the comfort I took away with me.

Making Sense of Life

Writing is making sense of life. You work your whole life and perhaps you've made sense of one small area.
Nadine Gordimer, *Women Writers at Work: The Paris Review Interviews*

Too many choices can be confusing, almost paralysing, as we found out when we visited the USA for the first time and were confronted by an array of choices, whether it was in beers, ice cream flavours, just plain drinking water (gas? no gas?) or hotel rooms (King size bed? Queen size? Smoking? Non-smoking?). If making a choice was hard, the regret that invariably followed was worse. Why did I choose this and not the other? Or another? When we left NIMHANS, we had opted for the choice of staying back in Bangalore. I can't remember now whether I regretted the choice – it has been overlaid by so much that has happened since then. Perhaps I was pragmatic: we're here, so let's make the best of it. Or perhaps I was taking it one day at a time. Or possibly, the real truth is that I did not think of it at all; if I had, I would have howled like a banshee. For, we had left a large and comfortable home with live-in help for something which was almost the stuff of nightmares.

Homes are very important to me, as anyone who reads my novels will know. For a person who gets attached to her home and hates change, I must say I have moved house a great many times. Nine times in Bangalore alone, until we built our own home. I had thought that would be the last, my final home. But we had to move out yet again, a year back – it was too large for just the two of us, it made me feel too insecure. Of all these homes, the house we lived in after we left NIMHANS must be one of the worst we had to live in. I can remember only one place worse, the little room we lived in, in Bombay, our first home, where we had to share the toilet and bathroom with our landlords. The women in the family, I am sorry to say yet again, were slobs and to enter the bathroom required great courage.

The house we moved into, after we left NIMHANS, was in a fast-growing suburb called Banashankari. It was infested with more cockroaches than I ever thought could live in one house. It also smelt of drains, a stink that pervaded the whole house. I remember I used to go out into the tiny, partially open entrance hall, where the smell was not too bad, to eat my meals. My husband was just setting up his diagnostic laboratory and we were not sure what his earnings would be; this house, whatever its faults, fit our budget. It was one of two rows of identical houses facing one another. I didn't meet a single neighbour in the four months we lived on that street. But when I walked on the road, I could see curtains twitching and knew that curious eyes were having a good look at me. After the liveliness of Parel and the friendliness of the NIMHANS campus, it was dull and boring, a killing deadliness. There were two centres of excitement on that street, two houses opposite us, which relieved the boring nothingness. A group of Iranian students inhabited one house; they were a large and noisy crowd. Why were they here in this Bangalore suburb? Anne Tyler, in one of her novels, speaks of how one could guess where a war was going on in the world from the restaurants that sprang up in the American cities. But I am sure these Iranian students were not in Bangalore for any political reason – the revolution had been long over, the Shah deposed, the Islamic Republic established. I don't think they were against the Islamic Republic, either. No, I am almost sure that these students came only because Karnataka had begun the 'education for sale' policy. Students could buy seats in engineering and medical colleges by paying a large sum of money, called a capitation fee. Karnataka was a pioneer in this dubious enterprise and, later, there would be many complaints about the quality of doctors and engineers turned out. But students came from all over India, some from outside India, as well. The Iranians kept to themselves, they did not talk or even look at a single soul apart from their own group. And they were noisy. Music blared out of their home all day, their motorbikes zoomed loudly and noisily each time they came in or went out. One day there was total silence in the house; we heard that one of the students had died in a road accident. The silence was eerie. I was filled with sadness to think of the young man dying so far away from home.

    The other house that was active and almost equally noisy belonged to an astrologer. She was so loud-voiced that everyone on the street could hear all that she said to her clients. If they wanted privacy, they certainly didn't get it. She had an old father over whom she tyrannised mercilessly. He had his revenge on her by sneaking out and pissing against the wall of the house, perhaps the one just outside her bedroom window. Invariably she would catch him and her loud and angry tirade, peppered with a rich repertoire of abuses, would provide entertainment for the entire street. I guess.

We were only three of us living at home by this time, our older son, Nandu, having gone to Bombay. The three of us had to struggle in our own ways. My husband, who had all these years headed a large department and had had a staff, with a secretary, now had to do everything himself. There was no bus in the area which would take Vikram, our younger son, to school. He, therefore, had to leave early every morning with his father to the lab, take a bus from there, and return the same way in the evening. Which meant he had a twelve-hour day, with scarcely any time to study after he came home. And I was alone all day, except for an hour when my husband came home for lunch. While he ate, I typed out his reports; he didn't have a typist as yet. My '*asdfg*' exercise was proving useful in yet another way. I did this for a year, during which time I learnt to spell many obscure medical words, I learnt how many diseases and how many investigations there are, I came to know how vulnerable the human body is and what a miracle it is that so many of us are fit and well and walking about on the streets. At the end of the year my husband could afford to pay a typist. And so I was supplanted by a very young girl from Kerala, who looked as if she had just come out of school, a girl who could speak no English, but who proved herself such a competent typist that, nearly forty years later, she is still working in the laboratory.

Our car was slowly giving up the struggle, though she was kept on a life-support system all night, the dynamo connected to an electric point inside the house. Nevertheless, I began to learn driving, more because it was a relief to get out of the house for a while. The only person I knew on the street, the sister-in-law of our landlord, was my co-trainee. She was everything that 'lady drivers' are supposed to be, and when she got her license, the inspector told her not to drive. Which she did the very next day and drove straight into a gutter! As for me, I didn't dare go on the roads. I tried short distances and had a mortifying experience once. I drove past a policeman's stop signal and I managed to stop only after driving some distance. He frantically waved me to go on, because I was now holding up the traffic. But I couldn't start the car. By this time Vikram, who was with me, was hunched in his seat, his face covered in his hands, ashamed of the spectacle his mother was making of herself! Well, I did learn to drive later when my husband had his surgery and was told not to drive. I was pleased that I could drive him to the park nearby for a walk, and even more pleased that in time I could drive myself to my mother's house (a long distance, that), and that I didn't have to depend on anyone to drive me.

The worst thing in our new house was that we had no telephone. Those days you had to wait a long, long time to get a telephone connection. Only the government could give you one and, as always with government monopolies, there were long queues. With the world teeming with mobile phones now, anyone under twenty-five will find this incredible, they will wonder how people could live without phones. But so it was. There were many things you had to apply and wait patiently for: a gas connection, a phone, a car, a two-wheeler. In fact, there was a shortage of everything, except of human beings. We had to wait for nearly a year-and-a-half for a phone – and ours was a priority case, my husband being a doctor. I remember how we rejoiced when the phone arrived. One of those terribly ugly black rotary telephones, which went a harsh *krrrk krrrk* as you dialled. Without a phone, I was cut off from the world all day. I remember an evening when I was waiting for the boys, who had gone to Jayanagar. They didn't come home even after dark, nor did my husband. I was frantic, but there was nothing I could do. When they came home, I learnt that the boys had taken the moped and didn't have a license or something, and they had been taken to the police station. They rang up their father who paid the necessary fine, only after which all of them came back.

One of my occupations was walking every evening around the area we lived in. This was a spanking new suburb and houses were coming up everywhere. I looked at them with longing. I have never so wanted anything as I wanted a home of our own at that time. I went on the terrace sometimes, and looked at the city beyond us – vast open spaces dotted with very few houses. I stood there watching the sun set behind the hills in the distance, almost nothing between me and the hills. A few years back, I drove past this area and saw that not an inch of space was vacant. Every bit of land had been built on. It was almost terrifying to drive through this urban nightmare. And there were still lorries full of sand, of long steel rods, driving in for the houses coming up. At times, I have a frightening sense of the earth caving in under the weight of all this steel, sand and cement. It might just happen, but I won't be here, thankfully, to be a part of it. After me, the deluge.

Writing had obviously come to a standstill. A magazine asked me for a short story for a special issue and I somehow managed to write one. For the first time, they returned the story, the editor, who had always been very appreciative of my work, called it 'clichéd'. I was shocked. But the high standard I had set for myself forced me to admit that she was right. It was a bad story. I would have to wait to get out of there before I could even think of writing. Only four months in the place, four months which seemed like a lifetime, we moved to Jayanagar, one of the best suburbs in the city at the time, into a house just a stone's throw from Lal Bagh – a wonderful location. It was a brief stay, but we returned to Jayanagar some years later when we built our own home. It has been home since then; it still is. The house we moved into after our terrible time in Banashankari was quite large. We lived upstairs, the owners downstairs, and there were two families in two little 'outhouses' at the back of the building. It was a friendly place and, after our last home, almost a paradise. Our landlord was a sophisticated man who had worked for, I think, one of the UN organisations. I could hear him coaching his niece in her English text, during which he was constantly correcting her almost pure Kannada-accented English. Ours was an eccentric house. Literally so, because it had two wings: a large living room and an even larger bedroom on one side, and a tiny room on the other where the floor crackled as you walked, as if you were causing a minor earthquake. These two wings were connected by a long, narrow corridor, divided by a partition, which became the dining room and the kitchen. My husband's lab was just a ten-minute walk and I would go there in the afternoons to type the reports. Writing was still not possible. I tried to get back to the novel I had been thinking of when we moved out of NIMHANS. I remember sitting at my table, watching a bumble-bee banging against the window, making an angry buzzing sound as it tried to get in. I felt I was doing exactly the same thing, trying to get the novel out of my head and, instead, banging my head against the glass. It was frustrating. To add to this, our neighbour had a dog that went crazy any time it saw a human being. We had to keep away from the windows, because the moment it saw us, it would begin barking and never stop.

Writing had to wait until we moved again. This time to a place my father built for us above their home. A tiny apartment. It was on my suggestion that he did this. I was tired of landlords and rented houses and he liked the thought of having us nearby. It could have been a double blessing; instead it became a double-edged sword. It didn't work. My mother, unable to cope with the loss of her son, had become more difficult. Her grief was transformed into an anger against the world, and hostility towards me. I deeply regretted my decision. I knew my mother, I had been warned by my sister; but I had no idea it would be as difficult as it turned out to be. My father's health was deteriorating. Instead of finding comfort in our presence, my mother resented my attempts to help, she resented me doing anything for my father. But my father, knowing his end was near, was comforted by the thought that we would be there, that my mother would not be alone.

In the meantime, I had stupidly registered for an MA as an external student in Mysore University. I hoped I would do a more disciplined reading because of this, that I would read the kind of things I hadn't read before. It was a huge strain. I told my family then that if ever I spoke of doing my PhD, they should hit me on the head with a blunt instrument (the Agatha Christie influence again)! With my husband out all day and returning only very late in the evening, exhausted after the long day and difficult drive home, and Vikram in the crucial year of preparing for admission to a professional college, I had to do everything in the house. I had to also cope with my mother's hostility and my own anxiety about my father's health. And, of course, my MA studies. Huge parcels of notes came from the university with work which I had to complete within a certain date.

The only good thing about this whole exercise was that I read much that I enjoyed. I had never appreciated Henry James, but now read *The Portrait of a Lady* with pleasure. I never changed my opinion about D.H. Lawrence, though; I continued to have problems with the way he looked at women. However, the poetry of Donne, Marvell, Emily Dickinson and T.S. Eliot was a revelation and a delight. Long back I'd read John Gunther's *Death Be Not Proud*, a heart-breaking account of his teenaged son's death by cancer; it had affected me deeply. Now I read Donne's poem where the title came from. I had read a great deal of contemporary drama, and some of the Restoration plays, but Christopher Marlowe's *Doctor Faustus* and John Webster's *The Duchess of Malfi* were new to me and fascinated me. Both seem to me equally relevant to our times; Faust selling his soul to the Devil makes me think of the craving for success in the world today. And the hint of incest in *The Duchess of Malfi* tells me that there is nothing new under the sun, neither evil, nor good; it has all happened at some time. The line in this play, 'Cover her face. Mine eyes dazzle, she died young,' haunted me. In fact, it was this line which led me to P.D. James, to her book, *Cover Her Face,* which was her first book I read. Reading Shakespeare at a mature age was also startlingly different. I remember tears running down my face at the end of *King Lear*, at Lear's grief at Cordelia's death. How that man – Shakespeare, I mean – could write!

Anyway, my results didn't reflect any of this interest and enthusiasm. I wasn't surprised, because I had lost out on the chunk of marks given for attending a fortnight of classes in Mysore. I could not possibly have left home and stayed in Mysore for fifteen days. How could I go, with my father sick, my husband over-worked, and my son working like a maniac, not only for his college exams, but for various competitive examinations? In any case, my motivation for studying for my Master's had been different. And I had done it. My father, in a final accolade, said, with reference to my poor marks (well, not poor, but certainly not marks to be proud of), 'Perhaps they could not understand your answers.' I was glad I had not disappointed him. By then, he had read both my early novels. Though he said nothing to me, he spoke to a friend praising my writing; so I was told after his death. He also paid me the great compliment of asking me to check the first few chapters of his English translation of the Natya Shastra on which he was working at the time. He never completed it.

Whatever my problems with my mother were, my relationship with my father was very good in these last days of his life. He had always been closer to my sister; she had been, since she became an adult, his greatest support. After we went to live in his house, he saw more of us as a family. I like to think that he was pleased with what I was making of my life. When he gave me his English translation of the Natya Shastra for my opinion and comments, I was embarrassed and pleased as well. And when I got an award for my first novel, *Roots and Shadows*, he was very pleased.

But his health was failing. I remember a night when he was almost delirious. He kept getting out of bed, saying his long-dead uncle was calling him. It was frightening. My mother and I spent the entire night trying to get him back into bed. He improved after that, but two months later he was bad again. This time I had a kind of premonition. I rang up my sister in Bombay, and asked her to come. Right away, I said. Don't wait. By evening, he was in such distress he had to be taken to the hospital. He died in the early morning of the next day, without meeting my sister, who could not get a ticket until the first flight the next morning. That was my main regret, that he was unable to meet her.

The death of a parent is always traumatic. There is a sense of loss, not only of a parent, but a loss of a part of your own life, a part of your past. And suddenly there is no shield between you and that Great Enemy, that Great Leveller – Human Mortality. I had not been as good a daughter as my sister. I had questioned, disobeyed, argued, doubted … He was troubled by my relationship with my mother. 'You understand people so well, can't you put up with her?' he asked me once. Nevertheless, his attitude towards me remained unchanged, perhaps because having already lost his son, he did not want to distance his daughter. Though the tragedy of his son had hit him hard, he was stoical and never showed his feelings. He had become philosophical even about his work, which had been the biggest and most important part of his life. 'I will soon be forgotten,' he said to me in those last few days. He had not given up working. He had corrected the proofs of his last book the evening before he was taken to hospital. He rarely spoke of his illness, except to say once, 'Time is running out for me.' And there was his regret that he had to give up smoking after his cardiac problem had been diagnosed. He had bought two packs of cigarettes just before this happened and, patting the box one day, he told me, 'I am waiting to smoke these soon.'

His death shook me up tremendously. It was hard to come to terms with his absence. Indira Gandhi died just two weeks after his death. I heard the news on the BBC and immediately went rushing downstairs to tell my father about it. The moment I entered the house, I remembered he was not there. Now I had to deal with my mother. She had been composed and dignified after his death. Very soon, she decided that we must complete the translation of the Natya Shastra. Five chapters had been left undone – these were the chapters on music. She asked me to do them. I could not say no. I put aside my own work, even my own family, as my sons complained, and sitting in her home, completed the translation. It was one of the hardest things I have done in my life. This was not my work, I had no knowledge of Sanskrit. But I had my father's Kannada translation, a copy of an old English translation, as well as Kannada-English and Sanskrit-Kannada-English dictionaries, and I completed the job. My mother left for Bombay after that and I had the respite I needed.

I went back to my novel. For a long time, even before my father's death, I had been struggling to write it. My writing table was in a corner of our tiny bedroom, so tiny that it was easier to climb over the bed to get to it, than to squeeze through the narrow space between the bed and the wall. I remember sitting at my table, trying to work, listening to the cries of schoolchildren who came out during the break to play on the street. Opposite our house, just across the road, was a small old-style house with a tiled roof and verandas all around, set in the midst of a large tree-filled compound. The owner had deliberately kept the house small; he wanted more open space around the house, more trees. He was an environmentalist before the word became trendy. One day, I idly watched two young women come out of the house and sit on a bench under a tree, both of them totally absorbed in their talk. For some reason, the scene, the image of the two young women sitting under the trees, deep in their conversation, stayed on my mind and, later, one of the young women morphed into Sumi, a character in *A Matter of Time*.

In the meanwhile, I had got stuck at a particular point in the novel I was writing. But just the day before my father's death, I had been able to get over the obstacle. This was the part about Jaya's father's death. I wrote it out in the few hours I got that afternoon. The next day my father was worse and then he was gone. Life imitating art? For a long time I was terrified of writing something dire, afraid that it would happen because I wrote about it. But I have since understood that you can no more stop yourself from writing something that you have to write, than you can avoid experiences you don't want to go through in life.

I completed my novel, but I was not happy with it. I knew there was a problem, but was unable to see it. I decided to give the manuscript to Shama Futehally, the writer, my friend Laeeq's daughter, and by then also my friend. For some reason I trusted her to give me reliable feedback. I had never done this before, nor since. I can never share my unpublished work with anyone. My husband is always the first to see it after it is complete and he never says anything, no, not a word. (Which is why we have lived together for so many years, I guess!) Then it goes to the editor. But now I looked to Shama for help. Shama, sincere and honest as always, read the entire novel and sent me her comments. Through her comments, I got an idea of where I had gone wrong and how to reshape the novel. Finally it was done. This is my only novel, apart from *The Dark Holds No Terrors,* for which I found a title fairly easily. I came across the words of a suffragette, Elizabeth Robins, about the long silence of women which seemed ideal: 'If I were a man and cared to know the world I lived in, I almost think it would make me a shade uneasy – the weight of that long silence of one-half the world.'

Indeed, absolutely ideal, specially the words, 'cared to know the world I lived in …' I think this has been the main problem with the way men have looked at women and their lives. They did not, they do not care to know about them, they were/are happy with their own ideas of them, with generalisations and stereotypes.

Where to send the novel was the next question. I was not entirely happy with the publishers who had published my novels so far. Apart from this, I was doubtful about any publisher taking this book. This was so much a woman's novel, a woman's ideas about her life, about her relationships. A novel confined within the four walls of a home, located mostly in the spaces of a woman's mind. Who would take this novel? But I had to try. I thought I would try a foreign publisher this time. Prof. Amur, my father's student, a professor of English and an eminent critic, had told me it was time for me to take this step. I got a book from the British Library, which listed the names and addresses of agents and publishers. I zeroed in on Virago, a women's publishing group. I thought I would have some chance with them. And so I wrote to them.

I still have a carbon copy of the letter I wrote to Carmen Callil of Virago. A short, factual letter giving a brief summary of the novel, along with the first three chapters (I think). I wrote, 'I'm afraid this sounds like a hundred other novels. I hope, however, when you read it, you will see what it is really trying to say.' They asked me to send them the novel. I did and I got a reply saying they would get back to me. So far so good. And I waited, not patiently, but with an author-impatience, which is like a child's impatience. 'When, oh when?' was the constant question on my mind. The reply came after eighteen months. The letter was under-stamped and I had to pay the postman eighteen rupees before he gave it to me. Never have eighteen rupees given me such a wonderful return. It was an acceptance letter, the kind of letter any author would dream of getting. The joy of that moment is still with me. No awards, no cheques, no reviews, can equal that moment.

Later, they wrote that they wanted me to go to London at the time of its publication. Would I be able to go? *Would I?* Of course, I would. Fortunately, we could now afford it – if only just. Otherwise, I don't know what I would have done. And if I hadn't, I know that not only would I have regretted it all my life, my writer's journey would have been a very different one.

I was fifty when I left for London, the age at which, in some professions, people are nearing retirement and, in some others, they are at their peak. And here I was, after three novels, a great many short stories and some children's books, thinking this was a kind of beginning for me. And, for a reason which I would fully understand only later, this *was* actually a beginning. I had started writing quite late, but I felt like a young woman when I set off on my journey. I was a little apprehensive, though, because this was the first time I was doing things on my own; yet there was a sense of excitement and anticipation as well. The last time I had travelled abroad, the children had been with me (and having small children who depend on you doesn't allow for anything but courage) and my husband was waiting for us at the end of the journey. Now, I was alone. No, actually, I was not entirely alone; my old friend guilt came along with me. I had left my family to look after themselves, something I had never done until then. Then, there was also my mother, who would never admit, even under torture, that she felt insecure when I was not in town; but I knew she would feel lost, nevertheless.

In spite of all these things, there was enormous pleasure in knowing that this was *my* trip, that it had come out of *my* work, out of something I had achieved myself. Once, during my father's faith-in-astrologers days, the astrologer had told our futures, as well as our parents'. Three futures thrown in free for two paid ones, perhaps. He had said I would never earn any money, I would just have a great many children. Any achievement since then has been for me a thumbing of my nose at that man. This trip to launch my book abroad was the biggest thumbing of my nose I ever did, I guess.

Like my last London trip, it was not a very happy start. It was January and London was very cold. And rainy. It was worse for me as I didn't have the right kind of clothes. I didn't have enough warm clothes and I wore saris, I remember, which squished wetly around my ankles. I also wore open-toed sandals (shoes make me claustrophobic, if that makes any sense). An Indian woman who saw me on the road exclaimed in horror and told me to get some shoes right away. But somehow, these things didn't matter. I was to stay with my editor, Ruth Petrie, who gave me the little apartment on the top floor of her house, consisting of a bedroom, sitting room and a tiny kitchen. Her friend, who normally stayed there, moved downstairs into Ruth's home. Strangely, I still have the schedule given to me when I got to London, yellowed with age and with the round mark of a tea mug on it; it has somehow survived all the years since then.

One of the staffers at Virago – the newest, I think, and a novice in publishing – was my escort throughout the trip. We became good friends by the end of my stay, but she could be quite maddening at times. She had absolutely no sense of time management and somehow managed to be *almost* late for all appointments. I remember one trip to the BBC studio for an interview when we got caught in a traffic jam on the way. She kept wringing her hands all the way (the first time I'd seen someone do it, it was quite impressive), crying out, 'I'll lose my job, I'll lose my job.' She was lucky. We reached only just in time and a staffer, who was waiting for us outside, whisked me to the studio where I reached barely a minute before I had to begin. Nevertheless, I couldn't help liking my escort; there was something very honest about her. And she threw herself fully into my programme. She was thrilled at the BBC interview (the interviewer was a very eminent journalist, she told me) and when we went to the writer Aamer Hussein's beautiful flat for me to be interviewed by him, she was more excited than I was. Of course, I didn't know who Aamer Hussein was then. Lois and some of the younger women in Virago took me to a pub one day. The atmosphere was not for me, yet I envied these young women their freedom to enjoy life, as well as work. Soon they left me alone and went off with their young men. I watched them and wished this kind of easy friendship between the sexes had been possible when I was young. So many taboos, so many fears. I am glad things have changed now.

I had a packed programme, yet not so hectic as to tire me out. I was lucky in my publishers. They were efficient, friendly and warm. They had a tiny office space, littered with books, and buzzing with activity. Everybody believed in what they were doing, they were committed to it; there was a spirit in the place which made them different from the usual commercial publishers. Lennie Goodings, when she was heading the publishing house, spoke of Virago as 'a brand with a genuine philosophy'. It is this philosophy, which has made it possible for them to survive for so many years. They had told me the very first day that I arrived, that a friend of mine had been ringing up and asking when I would be there. Her name, they said, was Maria Couto. Maria Couto? I was puzzled until she stepped into the office, and I knew this was Aurora Figuerado, who had been in school and college with me in Dharwad. She had been a tall, attractive, serious-looking girl then, and she was a tall, elegant, beautiful woman now. She hugged me with such warmth that I almost forgot I was in London in January. All the women in the office smiled and rejoiced, I could see, in this meeting of old friends – a moment I still vividly remember. My schedule was packed with interviews with radio and print journalists, with book-signings, a large public meeting and party on the last day. There were also trips to Birmingham and Leeds. Publication day was lunch in a restaurant, along with some of the Virago staff and a journalist or two. Everyone drank a toast to *That Long Silence* and they gave me a cover of the book with the signatures of everyone working in Virago then. That was that. This was my first launch and, for nearly a decade, my only launch.

For me, the most wonderful moments were when I realised how books can reach across space. I had read books by English authors and responded to the writing. Now, for the first time, I saw that my books could reach readers here as well. The BBC interviewer, a woman at the top of her field, told me that she had seen herself in the book. In Jaya. I was astonished. A successful professional woman to see herself in my poor Jaya? It was hard to believe, but she said it. And she said this, not during the interview, but after the interview was over, once we got off the air. Another woman, a journalist, told me during a private moment at a public meeting that my book had made her look at her own marriage with a clarity she had lacked before.

But the best response to my book came from Lakshmi Holmström who lived in Norwich. She was not as known then as she was to be later; to me, she was only my friend, the translator Gita Krishnankutty's friend. Gita had introduced us to each other through letters before I left for London. Lakshmi rang me up late at night, when I was in bed, snuggling into its warmth. She told me she had just finished the book and she thought it was 'bloody good'. There was a note of surprise in this statement, which delighted me. (As a reader, I had enjoyed being surprised by a writer. Now, as a writer, I was delighted to surprise a reader.) Only then, she apologised to me for disturbing me at such a late hour. 'You're welcome to disturb me at any time,' I assured her, 'if you call to say such wonderful things.' Later, Lakshmi would ring up Virago about an interview with me in *The Guardian*, which she thought was condescending. This eventually led to Virago's asking Lakshmi to compile and edit an anthology of short stories by Indian women writers in all the languages, not just English. The result was *The Inner Courtyard*, which remains, in my opinion, one of the best of its kind. Lakshmi would go on to do many translations and become one of the best, and best-known, translators from Tamil into English, the same way her friend Gita Krishnankutty was in Malayalam. I consider it my good fortune that through my writing I got to know such remarkable women, who then became good friends.

While in India, I had received a letter from a small German publisher, Wolf Mersch. Earlier, he had told me that he had published a German translation of *The Dark Holds No Terrors*, one of a series of German translations of Indian books he was publishing. He had not been able to contact me because the publisher disclaimed knowledge of my address! He had got my address finally from P. Lal. When he learnt that I was being published by Virago, he had wanted to come to London and meet me, but he was not well and sent two people, a journalist and photographer, instead. He bought the German rights to *That Long Silence* and brought it out soon after. He was a great admirer of Indian writing and his list of translated works was quite impressive: Tagore, Kolatkar, Madgulkar, Vatsyayan (Ajneya), Bhisham Sahni, Mannu Bhandari and some others. Wolf Mersch had also invited me to Germany for a conference. I couldn't go that year, so he had me invited the next year to Mannheim. Since Wolf Mersch could not come to Mannheim, he invited my husband and me to Freiburg, one of the prettiest towns I have seen. I remember the roses and strawberries and the little stream running in the middle of the street. And the magnificent castle on top of a hill where we had lunch with Wolf Mersch and the translator of *That Long Silence*. He died soon after. His wife wrote to tell me of his death. She also told me that he had come out of hospital for just a day, only to meet us, but he never mentioned it to us. He is one more of the wonderful people I have met through my writing. After his death, a larger publishing firm bought his list and *The Dark Holds No Terrors* and *That Long Silence* came out once again in German, in rather jazzier outfits. I did not know it then, but I would soon learn that translations open the door to the world. Without translations, you are voiceless, you are invisible abroad.

It was a good time to be published abroad, I think now, in hindsight. Some years ago, I came across a little note I had scribbled in an old notebook about a review by Anita Desai, in an American newspaper (*The New York Times?*), of a novel written by an Indian, Salman Rushdie. This was long before I wrote *That Long Silence*, when I was only just beginning to think of it. The review gave the book fulsome praise and when it got the Booker, it was a sensation in the international literary world. Suddenly Indian writing, which had quietly been occupying a place in a corner of the room, came centre stage. In Anita Desai's review, I had read that the novel was about India after Independence. I had been a little anxious. Was my novel going to be like his? (This was before *Midnight's Children* became the success it did.) I need not have worried, oh, I so much need not have worried. *That Long Silence* was a quiet, introspective book on a very small canvas. A novel about a woman's ideas of herself, of her roles in life. Virago had done a great job of publicising my novel, but it was clearly not an epic novel, not a novel about national issues. My novel belonged to a different category, it was a 'woman's novel', a label I soon realised would never come off.

My visit to England had done me good. It had made me realise that I was a writer who was taken seriously. Always unsure of myself, diffident, socially awkward, hating to be in public and among crowds, I discovered that when it came to professional activities I was confident and sure of myself. I knew what to say, and said it without hesitation. In a public meeting I was asked why, if I was a feminist (of course I was, why else would Virago publish me?), had I acknowledged my father, but not my mother, in my bio. I think I said that my father was connected to the thinker, to the writer, in me, not my mother.

This question came back to me later, and I had to think whether feminism meant a rejection of your father, or of any male, and his role in your life. I wrote a small piece on feminism later, which was published as a middle in a national newspaper where I pursued this thought. I think it was here that I was able to articulate my thoughts on feminism most clearly. But I have realised since that feminism is the most misunderstood ideology, it is like the elephant which many blind men try to describe; each sees it as something different.

It was this experience of going to London which gave me, more than anything else, a sense of having made my name – not in the sense of becoming famous, but more in terms of having forged an identity of my own. This mattered to me, not only as a writer, but also as a woman. Of all my novels, *That Long Silence* took the longest time to write. It had been a struggle all the way – a struggle to find time, a struggle to keep going in the midst of all that was happening in our lives, including my father's death, a struggle to pick up after long breaks, a struggle with health problems, and a struggle to continue to believe in my novel. I rewrote the first fifty pages at least a dozen times. I changed my mind about the narrative style (after having agonised about it for long) until I stumbled upon the fact that this was Jaya's story and that she had to tell it herself. I find it hard to read the novel now. I don't like to read my own words, I'm not one of those writers who enjoy the sound of their own voice. But to read this novel is particularly painful. The raw emotions, the suppressed anger, the humiliating feeling of a loss of self-worth, the claustrophobia that envelops the novel – they came out of the life I was living then. To revisit that time is painful. In a small way, this was my story, but mostly it was not. Many first novels are autobiographical. *That Long Silence* was not autobiographical in the personal details, but it was so mainly in the ideas, in the thinking. I said things here I had been struggling to get out of me for years. In this novel, I asked questions I had never articulated even to myself. Above all, it was an attempt to penetrate the dense forest of lies and half-truths in which we live our lives, the lies and half-truths which make life possible.

This is the novel that made me known. It has become a kind of classic and is now being taught and read in many colleges and universities in India. Even today I have readers who come to me and say, 'I read your *That Long Silence.*' Not only is the book still in print, it has just come out in a new cover, along with *The Dark Holds No Terrors,* both the novels now nearly forty years old! One of the greatest compliments I have received was from a reader who is now a writer and a friend, K.R. Usha. She told me that it was *That Long Silence* which made her feel she could bring together her material and the language in a happy harmony. She realised she could write the novel she wanted to in English and she did. I launched her first novel; it was one of the most satisfying moments of my life. One thing that continues to surprise me is that, since *The Long Silence* ends with Jaya going back to her husband, people, specially academics, think that the book advocates a return to tradition. How could an intelligent woman's agonised thinking about her life end in her going back to the same point she had started from? She would have to be an idiot to do that. The way I see it is, Jaya rediscovers herself, and the woman who goes back to her husband is not the same Jaya who has lived with him for so many years. Whether they will continue to live together depends on if her husband can live with this different woman. The revolution that takes place in this novel happens in Jaya's mind. Most, no, all revolutions begin in the human mind. I have said this many times, but soon, yet another student working on the novel will come to me, with a paper or a thesis, which sees Jaya as veering between tradition and modernity and ultimately returning to her traditional role. Phew! What do I say?

Though on the whole critics were appreciative, one critic was very angry that I wrote about Jaya, not about the women who worked for her – that I ignored the working class woman! I thought, and still think, that it is the writer's prerogative to choose what she is going to write about, who her characters are and so on. The critic's job is to see whether she has done this well enough, not to ask her to write an entirely different novel. (Jane Austen should have written about the fear of Napoleon invading England, about the war with France, not about courtships, balls and marriages!) And whatever the critics may say, it has been my most successful novel. It has been translated into many languages, both Indian and European, and has made me more money than all my other books.

Thankfully, it was not such a great success that I could not move past it; I was able to build on it. (I think of *The God of Small Things* and wonder whether, if it had been less of a success, Arundhati Roy would have been able to move on more easily to her second novel.) I know that I had to write it so that I could move on. In writing about Jaya's silence, I broke my own, in writing about Jaya's claustrophobic world, I liberated myself from my own constricted life. In writing this novel, I got rid of many of the fears and doubts that had always dogged me and I emerged lighter. At the core of a story of a 'middle-class housewife' (as Jaya is always described), I found a woman with a beating heart, a human being with talent, desires and aspirations. A woman who came to know that she was much more than the roles she played as wife, mother and daughter. A woman who realised that her life mattered, that it was important to her, if not to anyone else, because she is a human being. And that she, only she, was responsible for it. My father was a great lover of the poems of the saint-poet Purandaradasa, as is my husband. (Both of them got their knowledge, as well as their love of Purandaradasa, from their boyhood in their villages, where community singing by children was part of the fabric of their lives. Such an easy and wonderful way of imbibing one's culture.) I had therefore become familiar, especially after we came to Bangalore, with some of Purandaradasa's poetry.

One of the songs, '*Manava januma doddadu*', affirms the greatness of human life and that to be born human is a wonderful thing. To me it means that there is a seed of greatness in every human life, however seemingly unremarkable. To know this, to look at your own existence through this prism, is what transforms any human life. To try to find, *and* to understand this not-common quality of a seemingly common human being – this is what inspires a writer.

These thoughts were not consciously, or even unconsciously, part of my life then. At the time, it was primarily a matter of learning to cope with both living and writing, because the choice was clear to me: I would look after my family and I would write. I would do both. A balancing act, in fact. And, therefore, it was a matter of practically making time for writing. It helped that writing crept slowly and gently into my life, millimetre by millimetre, making space for itself in my day, space which it never gave up, space it would not share with anyone or anything. Deviously, insidiously, it inserted itself into whatever gaps it could find in my day, stretching its allotted hours, whenever possible.

It helped, too, that when my writing was taking up more and

more of my time the children were growing up and moving away from home. Now I needed only self-discipline, all the self-discipline I was capable of. Strictly dividing time between writing and household chores, giving up all else, writing at regular times, for regular hours, sitting at my table even if I could not write a word – this was a battle I won. It became clear that writing was now my life, and as the novels came to me, it was this discipline which would stand me in good stead.

Where Do We Belong?

English has proved its ability, as a language, to play a creative role in Indian literature through original writing and transcreation.

Credo of the Writers Workshop

Iᴛ ᴍᴀʏ ʙᴇ ʜᴀʀᴅ to believe, but when I began writing it did not occur to me that I was writing in English. And, with the way things are now, it is harder to believe that writing in English was considered to be odd, even wrong, in India at the time. There was a strange hostility towards Indians who wrote in English; to the very idea of writing in English. S.H. Vatsyayan, a Hindi writer, during a conference of Indian writers, proclaimed with great finality that, 'India cannot have a literature except in an Indian language.' It was not a case of 'let a thousand flowers bloom', but that this particular flower should not bloom.

I may be wrong, but it seems to me that I was asked the question, 'Why do you write in English?' more often than other writers. Was it because I did not have the usual profile of an English writer in India — fairly upper class, studied abroad, living, or having lived abroad, etc.? Or was it because my father was a Kannada writer?

Or because I did not 'look' sophisticated enough to be an English writer? I remember an old Parsi lady who, hearing that I was a writer, said, 'You write in Marathi.' It was more a statement than a question. No, I said, I write in English. I can still remember her puzzled look, as she took in my crumpled cotton sari, my hair knotted into a bun, my un-lipsticked lips. 'When you came to meet the editor, we thought you were just any middle-class housewife,' a journalist who had worked in one of the women's magazines told me later. And when I cut my hair much later for various reasons, a friend, as soon as she saw me, exclaimed, '*Now* you look like an English writer!' I do? I thought.

At that time, writing in English was made to seem like treachery. I once heard a language writer call English writers traitors during a large public meeting. I also heard a Kannada writer being praised on a public platform for writing in Kannada, though, it was said, he *could have* written English. (At the time there were many Kannada writers and critics who were English teachers.) But does one have a choice? I think not. I believe there is one language, which is the language of a person's creativity.

I know that for me it was a matter of having something to say, and I had to say it in the only language I knew well enough to articulate my thoughts in. English was the language that came to me naturally and easily when I was writing. In fact, it was the only language I could write in. This apart, I never even thought I was part of the Literary World, with a capital L. I scarcely had the courage to call myself a writer; how could I think that I was part of any literary world? Literature then meant to me Austen, the Brontës, George Eliot, Dickens and all the rest. Closer home, writers meant my father and others like him, mostly men, who wrote in their own languages. I had seen how completely my father was part of the Kannada literary world. There were always visitors at home – no one rang up for an appointment then (there was no phone at home, anyway; he got a phone only for, maybe, the last twenty years of his life); people just dropped in. There was a constant interaction with other writers, with people from the theatre world. I heard them discussing issues that mattered to writers – issues about the theatre, about literature, I heard the spirited debates and arguments that went on between them. I, on the other hand, knew no other writer who wrote in English. And there was my writing itself which seemed to fall into a deep dark hole. I had no readers, at least no feedback from readers. So where did I belong?

When I went to London for the launch of *That Long Silence*, I was considered an *Indian* writer, as if going abroad had brought out my passport and underlined my identity as an Indian. Being published by Virago made me a 'woman writer'. In London, I was also an 'Asian writer'. Asian writer? This was truly puzzling, for it was a category that embraced all the writers who were not of the Western world. In truth, writers hate being slotted, they dislike labels being hung round their necks. So do I. Writers think of themselves only as writers. So did I, so do I. I discovered that all writers feel the same way, Indian or otherwise. Not only have I always rejected labels, I have identified myself as *not this, not this, not this*. A *neti neti neti* kind of classification.

I said this aloud at the first seminar I ever attended in my life. At the time I had written two novels, a large number of short stories and, I think, three children's books. Or was it four? But I was certainly not known in any writers' circle. Which is why I was surprised to get a letter from a Professor C.D. Narasimhaiah (popularly knows as CDN), inviting me to a seminar he was holding in Mysore in the institution he had founded – Dhvanyaloka. This was my first recognition from academia. And, though pleased, I was nervous. I accepted the invitation, nevertheless. Unfortunately, my father died just about a fortnight before the seminar. Prof. CDN wrote me a brief condolence letter and in my response, I said that I would not be able to attend the seminar. He wrote back, gently persuading me to go, 'at least for a day', he said. This might help, he said.

And so I went. Reluctantly, because my mother had gone to pieces after my father's death; it was hard to leave her. When I got to Dhvanyaloka, I wished I had stayed at home. Always a coward at meeting new people, I had more than enough reason here to be terrified. I soon realised it was a very eclectic and distinguished group of writers, academics and scholars from all over the country. Worse, while I knew no one, they all knew one another. I felt completely out of place. This was my first time at such a meeting. I knew nothing about writing papers, I didn't know what a keynote address was, what a plenary session meant. (Phew! What a relief to get this ignorance off my chest!)

Thankfully, Prof. CDN had let me off from writing a paper. Instead, I wrote a small presentation which I had titled *The Dilemma of a Woman Writer*. It was the first time I was speaking to a literary or a scholarly audience, and my paper, when I now look at it, seems so unscholarly, so amateurish, I wonder how I dared to present it to such an audience at all. (Though I have learnt since then that creative writers are, on the whole, kindly looked upon by academics. Their ignorance, their unscholarly ways, are treated as minor peccadilloes.)

Despite its simplicity, it was an important statement I was making, because this was the first time I was articulating my thoughts about writing, about being a writer and about being a woman and a writer. It was the first time I was understanding some of these things, as well, for understanding came, as it always, or very often does, in the course of the writing. I spoke of the isolation in which I worked, the personal isolation of sitting at home and writing without any connection to readers, or other writers, without any link to any literary world. Besides, there was a kind of self-imposed isolation which came from my lack of any feeling of kinship with the few Indian English writers I had read. If I thought of them at all, it was to tell myself: I will not write like this, or like this, or like this … Yes, I said this to the distinguished gathering before me.

Afterwards, when I thought of this statement, I was not only embarrassed, I was aghast. How could I have been so abominably rude? What I said was the truth, but surely I could have phrased it more diplomatically? Specially when I was speaking to people far more learned and knowing than I was. I am glad that I had the grace and sense to try and atone, even if it was more than two decades later. Speaking at a celebration of R.K. Narayan's centenary organised by the Sahitya Akademi, again in Mysore, I confessed my rudeness on the earlier occasion and tried to make amends.

I looked at R.K. Narayan in a new light, not because it was his centenary and I had to pay a formal tribute, but because by then I had learnt that the early writers – R.K. Narayan, Raja Rao, Mulk Raj Anand, Bhabani Bhattacharya, Manohar Malgonkar, etc. – were pioneers. They had had to tread uncharted paths, and find some kind of a way for themselves in this field of writing in English in India. They had to write the way they did, and, by this, they made it possible for the writers who came after them to move on and to walk, perhaps, with a greater sureness of step. It was like the many drafts I have to write before I get close to getting it the way I want it to be. So too with each generation of writers. I now know this, too, that rejection of an earlier generation is a necessary step to enable the next generation to move on. Jane Austen turned her back on the then much-loved and much-read Gothic novel, with its combination of romance, horror and melodrama and created a new kind of novel. It was fascinating to know that when Jane's father sent *Pride and Prejudice* to a publisher, he rejected it, 'thus calling down upon himself hoots of derision from an unfeeling future,' as Fay Weldon puts it.

'Without those forerunners, Jane Austen and the Brontës and George Eliot could no more have written than Shakespeare could have written without Marlowe or Marlowe without Chaucer or Chaucer without those forgotten poets who paved the way and tamed the natural savagery of the tongue.'

Virginia Woolf's words opened my eyes to a new understanding of the existence of a long chain of writers, of connections between writers of different generations. But when I spoke in Mysore, the first time, I had spoken more as a reader than as a writer. It was as a reader that I had first found Indian books in English wanting in some, or in many respects. There were some exceptions: Attia Hosain's *Sunlight on a Broken Column*, later, Anita Desai's *Clear Light of Day* and, even later, Amitav Ghosh's *The Shadow Lines*. Narayan's *The English Teacher* had moved me; but the book's extreme simplicity, both in language and style, had dulled my enthusiasm. The other two of the Big Three of the time, Mulk Raj Anand and Raja Rao, left me cold (though Raja Rao's *Kanthapura* gave me a kind of puzzled satisfaction), as did Manohar Malgonkar and Bhabhani Bhattacharya. I had enjoyed Bhattacharya's *Music for Mohini*, but that was when I was a girl; later, I could not look at it in the same way. Ruth Jhabvala's books scarcely concealed her contempt for India, which made me angry, and Kamala Markandaya wrote about a land and a country which I could not recognise.

Strangely, I could respond with greater enthusiasm to stories and novels translated from Indian languages. There was Shivaram Karanth's Kannada novel, *Marali Mannige,* translated into English as *Back to the Soil*, which I enjoyed so much that I read it over and over again, though I was told it was a bad translation. The epic story of a Brahmin priestly family eking out a living by the sea, and the rejection of this life by the next generation, was an eye-opener for me. I enjoyed a Marathi novel (I can't remember the author, but I think the title of the novel was *Manini*) which was about a woman's struggle to assert her dignity in a broken marriage. There were also some wonderful translated stories; I can remember Ismat Chughtai's Urdu story of cruelty towards a little girl (*Tiny's Granny*), a cruelty done so casually, it was terrifying; N.S. Phadke's Marathi story about a little boy selling boiled eggs to Indian soldiers during the conflict in Kashmir, soon after Independence; Ashokamitran's Tamil story about a young girl entering the film world. And many, many more. Later, I read some excellent translated stories in the anthologies brought out by the Sahitya Akademi, by Katha and other publishers. Like Vaidehi's *Gulabi Talkies*, or Bolwar Mahammad Kunhi's *A Piece of the Wall* (both Kannada stories), Asha Bage's *Wings* and Gauri Deshpande's *Maps* (both Marathi), C.S. Lakshmi's *A Kitchen in the Corner of the House* (Tamil), Maitreyi Pushpa's *Basumati ki Chitthi* (Hindi).

I not only appreciated these stories as a reader, but as a writer I felt that my writing was much closer to them than to the works of known writers in English; it seemed that this, perhaps, was where I belonged. But there were some English stories also which belonged to this body of writing, like K.R. Usha's English story *Sepia Tones*, which delighted me. I remember Meenakshi Mukherjee, the critic (a very gentle one), and I sharing our pleasure in this story, in the discovery of a new writer who both of us thought would go far. But as far as English writing was concerned, when I started writing, there were no writers I admired, no writers in whose footsteps I wanted to walk. Part of it was because I was speaking in a woman's voice, and, except for Anita Desai, no writer had brought this voice into her/his writing.

On the other hand, I found the Indian English poets far more readable. They were able to wed the language to the Indian context with much greater felicity than the novelists. Of course, it helps that poetry does not have to go into minutia, like the novel. Yet it was more than this; some of the poets, some of the poems, got the tone right, which the novelists, at least in my opinion, were not able to do. An offshoot of being published by Writers Workshop was that Prof. Lal regularly and generously sent me some of the books he published. One of these, an anthology of women's poetry (*Hers*, edited by Mary Ann Dasgupta), gave me immense pleasure, for here they were, the writers in whose company I seemed to belong. Writing the kind of writing I was doing, though mine was prose, not poetry. Kamala Das was here and Gauri Deshpande, a splendid poem by Shama Futehally, and many others. There was a poem called *Barnstorming* by a poet, Lalita Venkateswaran Massy, which I loved, but sadly I never saw any poem of hers after that, never heard her name again. Even earlier, when I read Indian English poetry in my sons' school texts (by then schools and colleges were giving students a taste of Indian Writing in English, I had found the poetry far superior to the fiction written by Indian writers. Reading Nissim Ezekiel, A.K. Ramanujan, Arun Kolatkar, Gieve Patel, Kamala Das, Gauri Deshpande and some more poets for the first time, I thought that the poets had found their voice and language, which the fiction writers were still struggling for. These poets knitted me into the literature in English in India. They gave me what I had been looking for – a sense of kinship. Kolatkar's *Jejuri*, when I read it, did more: it excited me. Like Keats, when he first read Chapman's Homer, I too felt I had suddenly discovered a new world, a new planet.

'What is god/And what is stone/The dividing line/If it exists is very thin/At Jejuri'

There was a time, I remember with some embarrassment now, when I had said that my influences were the British writers, specially Jane Austen, the Brontës, George Eliot, Mrs Gaskell, Dickens and so on. Yes, it was from these writers (and others as well), that I had learnt about the amazing grace, beauty and strength of the novel, just as I had learnt from the Russian writers about passion and intensity. It was as a reader that I had imbibed from these writers an understanding of the use of language, of narrative structure, which were to stand me in good stead as a writer. Nevertheless, I would soon understand that this was not where I came from. I read F.R. Leavis' *The Great Tradition* when I was doing my MA, and found this statement right at the beginning: 'The great English novelists are Jane Austen, George Eliot, Henry James and Joseph Conrad.' Leavis also says, 'Jane Austen is the inaugurator of the great tradition of the English novel.' While I marvelled at the certainty with which he said these things, his statements made it clear that Indian English writing had no place in the literary world he was speaking of. A common language was just not enough. My visit to London, where I was classified as an Indian writer, as an Asian writer, and later, my visit to Cambridge, made me understand how far removed I was from the British tradition.

However, in time I began to understand that I did not come out of emptiness, but from a far more complicated place. I had three languages – my father's language, Kannada; my mother's, Marathi; and the one that became my own, English. I read some more languages, including Sanskrit, in translation. As children, our father made us learn the *Amarkosa*, a kind of Sanskrit Thesaurus, by heart (I can still quote some lines). I absorbed, like all Indians do, the myths and legends, stories from the epics and the Puranas, along with fairy tales and English children's books – from *Little Women*, *What Katy Did* and *Heidi* to *Treasure Island* and *Alice in Wonderland*. In later years I read, again in English translation, the Ramayana and the Mahabharata and, much later, the Gita and the Upanishads. As a girl, I read stories in Marathi women's magazines along with stories in *Woman & Home*.

I was exposed at an early age to the devotional poems of Purandaradasa and Basaveshwara, through my father's love for and knowledge of these poems. I listened to Marathi natya sangeet in my mother's Pune home and to *abhangs* and *bhavgeets* in Marathi. I saw and thrilled to the spectacle of the Yakshagana, I loved the beat of the staccato music and loud singing that accompanied the dancing and the dainty mincing steps and gestures of the dancers, which were at such variance with their large grand costumes and garish make-up. I responded with fervour to Mirabai's poems, especially when sung by M.S. Subbulakshmi, I enjoyed Hindi film music, adored Geeta Dutt (oh, her *Mera sundara svapana beet gaya*!), and found Hollywood movies satisfyingly exotic. I enjoyed the romance in Bhasa's *Svapnavasavadatta* as much as I enjoyed Daphne du Maurier's *Frenchman's Creek*. In personal life, I knew I was a Hindu (though, as our father's children, we were never overly conscious of it), but studying in a Roman Catholic school had made me familiar with the church. We entered the church, dipped our fingers in the holy water, genuflected, knelt, knew how to recite *Our Father who art in Heaven* and *Hail Mary full of grace*. As a grown woman, I visited the Ajmer Dargah, as well as the Church of Infant Jesus. There was never any sense of conflicting contrary selves; everything was harmonised and melded into one. Like Walt Whitman, I could have said: 'Do I contradict myself? Very well then, I contradict myself. I am large, I contain multitudes.'

And yet, when I was writing my second novel, *The Dark Holds No Terrors*, I knew what not belonging meant. It meant I was entirely on my own, it meant I had no predecessors in whose footsteps I could follow, it meant I had to write solely out of myself, creating and shaping a language to meet my needs. Peter Ackroyd, in his biography of T.S. Eliot, speaks of Eliot complaining to Virginia Woolf that, 'in the absence of illustrious models, the contemporary writer was compelled to work on his own.' The illustrious models were even fewer for women. And for an Indian woman writing in English, for the kind of writing I was doing, the lack of any kind of model, illustrious or otherwise, was even more evident, the lack of a safety net of other writers' work, which Ackroyd says Eliot needed, even more glaring. In fact, I wrote out of a blankness which had only my self in it, out of a large silence which I had to fill with my words. Words, which I had to discover, to conjure out of thin air, for there were no models for me to follow. Indian writing was in the Indian languages and English writing was done by writers whose language it was the way it could never be mine.

Nevertheless, it was a good time to be a part of Indian writing in English. Indian writing in English was on the brink of a great change; very soon this writing would become known and read through the world. But this change would be closely linked to being published in the West. I soon realised the advantages that being published in the West could give an Indian writer. A happy result of being published by Virago was that, very soon after my novel came out, I was invited by the British Council to the annual Cambridge seminar, which brought together writers and academics from English-teaching and English-writing countries from all over the world.

The invitation was a total surprise to me. It put me in the dilemma that invitations always did, always do. I would have to be away from home for nearly a fortnight, something very hard for me. But it was a prestigious seminar and would be fully paid for, including a visit to any place of my choice within England (I chose Haworth, the Brontë home. I now wonder why I didn't choose Jane Austen's Chawton instead). I had also accepted an invitation to Sweden just a short time before the Cambridge visit. Two trips out of home in quick succession! I dithered, agonised, but finally went.

It is now more than twenty-five years since my Cambridge visit. Much is forgotten, yet some things remain: stray wisps of memory, of images, faces, words. I can distinctly remember the beautiful Master's garden where we were officially welcomed, the various colours of the participants' faces, which gave one a glimpse of the vast spread, the sprawl of the English language and literature. I remember the beautiful green of the lawn on which, we were told, no one was allowed to walk. Impossible not to think of Virginia Woolf and *A Room of One's Own* then, of Virginia Woolf's anger when she was chastised for walking on the sacred grass, symbolic to her of women being kept out of university education. 'This was the turf; there was the path. The gravel was the place for me.' The beautiful buildings of the colleges and churches, the towers and spires, on the other hand, brought back Dorothy Sayers' *Gaudy Night*, one of my favourites, a novel set in a women's college in Oxford. Progress, perhaps, yet the mystery in Sayers' novel centred around the fact that women academics were hated for trespassing on male territory; women were not meant for scholarship and academics. And yet, Christ's College, where the seminar was being held, was established by a woman, Lady Margaret Beaufort, the scholarly and pious mother of Henry VII.

Not that these thoughts came to me at the time. I make the connections now as I write about that evening when I was jet-lagged and tired, and also perhaps a little woozy with the glass of wine with which we had been welcomed. I listened to the well bred voices welcoming us, making little jokes, apologising for the building in which we females had been housed. It was an ugly modern building and like in all hostels, the bathrooms were a disaster. There was a large frightening notice in the dreadful bathroom saying, 'CLEAN UP YOUR OWN MESS.' Thankfully, somebody had cleaned up before we came, there was no mess! But the water was never more than a trickle, and the shower sent sprays of water all around, except on the person standing under it. The food, however, was satisfactory. I was the only vegetarian among more than sixty participants and each day I had something new, something special to eat (I remember the day I had samosas! Almost everyone was drooling over them). The lectures were interesting, exciting or dull, depending on who the writer speaking to us was. I saw for the first time the importance of the writer being a performer; not all writers are good performers. But at that time, I had no thoughts, except to wonder at my being in Cambridge – never mind in what guise I was there.

Memories are much clearer after the first evening. The beautiful dining room with its panelled walls, satisfyingly ancient looking benches and long tables, old portraits on the wall looking down on us. The seminar room, beautifully panelled as well, but a little crowded with many participants. Once again I had to pinch myself to make sure I was really here, listening to authors I had read and admired. Margaret Drabble was at the time a favourite of mine, her *The Middle Ground* seeming to speak directly to me, reflecting my life, my thoughts. Antonia Byatt (Drabble's sister, though we were told not to speak of one to the other) who had just got the Booker for *Possession*, was intellectual, but friendly and unassuming. Doris Lessing was the most awkward and least eager to make a good impression, but to me it didn't matter. Her *The Golden Notebook* had spoken to me far more clearly than she did. Which is how it should be, though in today's world the good performer starts off with an advantage. David Lodge was such a humorous writer, but why did he look so morose? All of us who had read him had this thought. Penelope Lively, whom I had read and whose books have continued to give me great pleasure, was very matter-of-fact and approachable.

When I now think of the writers there (I wrote a piece for the British Council journal and so have all the names), I realise how English the writers who spoke to us were. Caryl Phillips was the only 'outsider' – he was from the Carribean. The British, clearly, were showcasing *their* literature, English literature, for us. With the Empire, their colonies and all their territories gone, they still had this, their language and literature. I have no problems with any country offering its literature to the world to be admired. And most of us were willing accomplices, for hadn't we learnt this language, beginning with nursery rhymes, and hadn't we later devoured their writers, looking at them as our own? Nevertheless there was sense of disquiet, a feeling of something wrong.

But during a visit to Stratford-on-Avon over a weekend, all was forgotten. We became like the many pilgrims who had flocked there to get a glimpse of the great writer's home. Here, the Englishness of Shakespeare was announced in the cottages, the gardens. But I thought Stratford too pretty-pretty to contain the vast genius of Shakespeare. Not surprising that he went away very early to London. I am sure he felt more at home among London's crowds, its vitality and sturdy independence more to his taste. The play we saw in Stratford, *Henry IV*, like all Shakespeare's plays about English kings, is steeped in the English spirit. And yet, looking at the crowds, many of whom had come from all over the world, I thought that Shakespeare was one of the writers who, though quintessentially English, had leaped over the boundaries of the little island he was born in, and belonged everywhere. A combination, which is the true mark of a great writer.

On then to our last lecture in the Cambridge seminar, which was by George Steiner, obviously, from the excitement of the academics, a much-admired scholar. Within minutes of beginning his lecture, he showed us why he was so admired. He spoke without notes, without a pause. Taking a line from Dante's *Inferno*, he gave a brilliant speech, weaving in innumerable ideas and quotations. But question time proved a little difficult with many awkward questions. How could he say Africa had no unifying text? Did he discount oral texts completely? And how could he dismiss feminist criticism so cursorily? And what did he mean by ignoring all civilisations except the Western Christian and Greek civilisations? What about Indian and Chinese civilisations? I could have asked this last question, but didn't, uncomfortable about making myself conspicuous. I could have asked about Indian writing, as well, which was one of the oldest in the world: the Vedas, the Upanishads, the epics, the dramatists who wrote long, long before Shakespeare. But I didn't; again my reluctance to draw attention to myself drew me back.

Even if I did not ask these questions, it was becoming clear that Indian writing had no place in the literature of this country. In fact, it was foolish of us to imagine otherwise. The only Indian writer who had been mentioned during the seminar, and only once, was Rushdie. And he was spoken of in connection with the fatwa against him. Margaret Drabble, in the course of her talk, said that his editor had suggested some cuts which Rushdie had refused. 'And look what happened,' Margaret Drabble said. We looked and there was a respectful two minutes' silence after that.

After Cambridge I was eager to go home, but there was still Haworth, the Brontës' home, to visit. *Wuthering Heights* had made a great impact on me when I had read it as a girl. And unusually, I never changed my opinion of it, even later. Even today, I think it is one of the greatest novels in English. Besides, there was the story of the Brontës, the story of their secret writing and of their brief and tragic lives. I have seen a number of authors' homes, preserved over the years, but none affected me as much as the Brontës' home in Haworth. I was amazed at the thought that the four of them and their father lived in such a small house! All of them loved their privacy (and privacy they must have had to write), so, how did they manage? Something of them still remains there, in spite of the fact that it has become a tourist place, full of souvenir shops and restaurants. However, the old cemetery just outside the house reminds visitors that these women had lived very close to death.

Walking up the cobbled street, which was almost unmanageably steep, I remembered reading about Charlotte's anxiety about their faithful help Martha's problem of walking up every day when her knees were giving way. There was something melancholy about the place. Did I see the church? I don't remember. But I have the information, from Mrs Gaskell's biography of Charlotte, that there are tablets for all the Brontë dead in the church, beginning with the mother, then the two older sisters, then Patrick, Emily and Anne. There was, Mrs Gaskell writes, ample space between the lines of the inscriptions of the first memorials. Then, the letters became more cramped, the lines closer together, as the dead followed one another in quick succession. Finally, sadly, there was no space for the last of the siblings to be buried. And so there was another tablet for Charlotte. Yet *Jane Eyre* and *Wuthering Heights* came to the world out of this place. Melancholy vanishes when I think of it. And I have a special fondness for the place because it was here that I had a glass of wine with my lunch, *all by myself*. I felt that I had crossed an invisible Lakshman Rekha!

I returned from my trip, convinced that it was foolish to imagine that Indians writing in English could have any connection to English literature. Of course, for me it didn't matter, because I just had to write what I wanted to write. Where my writing belonged was not my problem. But change was coming to Indian writing in English, it was just round the corner. Soon, Indian writing in English would be known and read the world over. A number of Indian writers would emerge who would win the appreciation of the West, soon IWE would be one of the major literatures of the world. Not Indian writing, but *Indian writing in English*. An article by Rushdie in *The New York Times*, with a picture of a galaxy of celebrated Indian writers, all of them writing in English, all of them published in the West, most of them living abroad, at least for much, or some of the time, nailed this fact. An article in which Rushdie bravely and rashly stated that English writing was the best of the literatures in India. (What a furore he created in India with this statement!) The subsequent Bookers for Arundhati Roy, Kiran Desai and Aravind Adiga, and the Pulitzer for Jhumpa Lahiri seemed to prove Rushdie's words. In these years, I found fresh questions gathering in me: why had I thought of my being published in England as a new beginning? I had by then got a reasonably good readership in India, a great deal of it because of my stories. Nevertheless, I had put all that aside and regarded the publication of *That Long Silence* by Virago as a fresh start. And why had it given me so much pleasure to be accepted by a British publisher? Of course, the professionalism of the publishers, and the money, were part of it, but it was also because it gave me, strangely, greater recognition at home. And yet, equally strangely, as Indian writing in English took its place in the world, I found that I could not be part of the success story. I discovered that to be published abroad, very often you had to pay a price. Which I was not willing to do.

The Private and the Public

How else but by invoking the Muse, to understand the writing of a novel?

Fay Weldon, *Letters to Alice: On First Reading Jane Austen*

I DON'T KNOW WHETHER it was a good time for women's writing, or whether it was due to *That Long Silence*, but I got more invitations after the book came out than I could ever imagine. Had I ever imagined that I would travel to so many countries when I wrote *That Long Silence*? Travelling abroad with all my expenses paid, being treated like an honoured guest, meeting some very interesting people – all these things should have been enough to give me a heady excitement. But my nervousness about travelling, my reluctance to leave my home, and the anxiety of leaving my mother and my husband, whose health had suddenly become suspect, didn't allow for any excitement.

Mannheim in Germany, where I was invited, thanks to my German publisher Wolf Mersch, was the first international conference I ever participated in. What did I do there? Except for our visit to Freiberg to meet Wolf Mersch, I remember nothing. Oh yes, I remember a lecture I gave in Frankfurt in the university, again a first for me, and I also remember that when we got to Frankfurt station from Mannheim, I was aghast and totally bewildered to find people lying about on the ground all over the place. It was like a scene from Dante's *Inferno*. Drugs, Prof. Dieter Riemenschneider, who was with us, tersely said. And how can I forget our nightmarish experience in Mannheim when we got into a bus without tickets? We knew there was a ticket-machine at the stop, but since we did not know where to get off and could not read German, we thought we would buy the tickets on the bus. But the young conductor did not agree; we should not have boarded the bus without tickets, she said. She ticked us off for 'ticketless travelling', asked for our passports and said we'd have to go to the police station. To the police station for not buying a bus ticket? When we had had no intention of cheating? The police! German police! In my mind I saw them like the Nazis in Hollywood war movies. I panicked, I tried to explain, I pleaded our ignorance. But it was only when I told her that I had been invited by the university, and told her the name of the professor who had invited me, that she changed. She told us she was a university student herself. She let us get off, told us which bus to take, bought us our tickets and then left us. But those few moments, when I thought of us in the police station, our passports confiscated, were hellish. Perhaps it was then that my fear of losing my passport began. Since then I have the habit of checking for my passport all the time – the surest way of losing it, my husband says.

Gothenburg, Sweden, was an all-women's conference. And it was low-budget as all women's events tend to be. Virginia Woolf speaks of how women are traditionally poor and refers to the differences between men's and women's colleges in *A Room of One's Own*. In her inimitable style she speaks of a splendid lunch she had in the men's college, where the 'wine glasses flushed yellow, flushed crimson; had been emptied, had been filled'. And the dinner in a women's college, where a plain meal was followed by biscuits and cheese, 'and the water jug liberally passed around'. She asks, 'Why did men drink wine and women water? Why was one sex so prosperous and the other so poor?' I have no idea if things have changed. I can only hope they have, though women's comparative poverty is still a hard fact. But the conference in Gothenburg was, if small and intimate, very rewarding in many ways. Unusually, I find a note on this conference in an old notebook, which says, 'All of us spoke of integrity and commitment to the truth as we saw it.' We did? That sounds wonderful. I don't think any other conference spoke of these things. For me, once I began writing, the idea of integrity, integrity to myself and to what I wanted to say, was always most important; I'm glad it was echoed by others.

The conference was remarkable for the women I met there, as well. Amazing women, some of them. I can never forget Anna Rutherford, and our host, Prof. Britta Olinder, who worked like a Trojan and managed things as thriftily as a wise housewife. She not only made possible a great forum for discussions, but also induced a spirit of camaraderie I never saw afterwards in any conference. Amsterdam was cold and we spent much time searching for a coat for me. (Always hard to get my size. I just read Isabel Allende's memoirs and noticed how obsessed she is by her small stature. I want to say to her, 'Me too!')

I had been invited to Amsterdam to lecture on a subject given to me and I realised only when I went there that it was a very prestigious lecture organised by the publishers, Novib, who, each year, invited one of their authors to give the lecture. (Novib had published the Dutch translation of *That Long Silence*.) There was a large audience and this was where I first learnt to lecture and realised that as long as I had a written text with me, I was all right. Learnt, as well, that when one went out of the country, one represented one's country in a way, and therefore had to grapple with all kinds of questions. As I had to cope with the Kashmir question, the Sikh agitation, human rights, dowry deaths and many other problems India was facing then.

But I could not live off one novel for long; no writer can do that. A writer, a film maker, or any artist for that matter, is as good as her/his next work. For a novelist, the second novel is crucial. It is often said that all of us have one novel inside us. I have so often heard someone say, 'I want to write a novel, I will when I get the time.' The time never comes for most; and even the few who write the novel lurking inside them rarely go on to the second novel, because the first novel was purely personal. And there is only so much anyone can do with her/his life. Most such first novels are nondescript, they are a kind of catharsis for the writer; but beyond that, as literary works, they don't count. Of course, there have been geniuses whose first novels were remarkable: Dickens' *Pickwick Papers*, Jane Austen's first published work *Sense and Sensibility*, the Brontë sisters' *Jane Eyre* and that masterpiece *Wuthering Heights*. But these authors had written a great deal earlier. The Brontë sisters had their Gondal and Angria chronicles, Jane Austen her delightful spoofs, including a novel, *Lesley Castle*, Dickens was a journalist and so on. (All these authors were also great readers when young.) In our own times, we have had first novels like *To Kill a Mockingbird*, or *Gone With the Wind*, and even though it is in a slightly different class, *The God of Small Things* – all of which are truly inexplicable.

After the success of Indian writing in English, I remember a large number of novels came out, written by writers who were never heard of again. It is with the second novel that a writer finds out whether she/he is a real writer, it is with the inability to write a second novel that a writer begins to understand that she/he is, perhaps, not a real writer ('she/he' again! This is terrible. High time someone invented a usable pronoun to include both the genders).

For me, it was not the second novel, but the fourth that was a significant step. It was this novel that took me out of the intensely private into the public space. Not that *Roots and Shadows*, *The Dark Holds No Terrors*, or *That Long Silence* had come out of my life. No, they came out of thoughts that had been simmering within me for long. But with *The Binding Vine*, I not only crossed the line and became a writer who knew she would go on, I moved out of myself – a very necessary and important thing for a writer. Self-absorption and self-indulgence can go only so far. As a matter of fact, when *That Long Silence* was done, I had two novels jostling in my mind; I was not sure which one I would write first. And then suddenly, one day, out of nowhere it seemed, a third novel came to me.

Martin Amis speaks of the 'mysterious business' of a novel arriving. It is truly mysterious, the way it comes. One moment, there is nothing. And then suddenly, there is a kind of nudging, something pushing itself into your mind, asking, no, clamouring, to be let in. This, my fourth novel, came out of the rape of the nurse Aruna Shanbaug, in K.E.M. Hospital. It had been a terrible incident, how terrible it was becoming clearer as the days passed, and Aruna remained imprisoned in her dark world. We were living next door to the Nurses' Quarters when it happened. The editor of *Femina* had asked me to write a report about the incident for the magazine. I had interviewed the Matron and filed my story. Later, a journalist wrote a book on Aruna's rape and each year, on the anniversary of her assault, a few newspapers revisited the story. The young woman continued to live, a vegetable existence, her cognitive faculties all gone. And yet some fear was still lodged within her; she would scream, a doctor told me, if a man entered her room. Shortly after the rape, when it was clear she would not improve, the authorities tried to move her out of K.E.M. into a suburban hospital. The nurses went on strike; they wanted her in their midst, they would look after her. Which they did so well that, forty years later, though she had become a wasted body, she was still living.

When she came to me as the centre of a novel, she had been living this way for nearly twenty years.

However, my novel was not about the young and beautiful Aruna Shanbaug. Fiction requires recreation, at least to me it does. The character has to be mine, wholly mine; a real life character remains a puppet. To take anything *in toto* from real life stifles the imagination. And so, the girl in my novel was Kalpana, smart and ambitious, who lived in a slum and craved for a better life. As fiction demands, everything was transformed. And it was not just the story of Kalpana and her rape, but of Urmi, the narrator, as well, and of Urmi's long-dead mother-in-law, Mira, who had been a poet. Mira had not been part of the novel at first; she came to me out of a book, Holbrook Jackon's *Bookman's Holiday*, a book I'd found at home as a girl, not knowing where it had come from. A book I so enjoyed and loved that I treasured it for decades, holding on to the tattered state it was in finally. I have only recently found a replacement. In my first copy, someone had scribbled a note on the flyleaf at the back of the book, a note about a scene of three little girls playing, with a description of each one of the little girls. It was the language of a writer (I still don't know who wrote this) and, reading it, I saw Mira, quietly watching the scene and writing about it. And so Mira was born.

By this time, we had built a home for ourselves in Jayanagar and this was the first novel I was writing in our own home. Now, I had a room of my own to work in. Well, almost; it was an adjunct of the bedroom. But I had a large table now (I need large tables to spread my papers); a comfortable chair; a huge, almost wall-to-wall bookcase, filled with all the books I'd collected so far; a smaller one with the books I needed when I was writing: the Oxford Dictionary, Roget's Thesaurus, a large book of quotations given to me by my brother, Gowers, Fowler, Shakespeare, as well as Sanskrit, Marathi, Hindi and Kannada dictionaries. My table faced a blank wall. The idea that a wonderful view, or that beauty inspires you, is so wrong. A blank wall is good; it provides no distraction. In any case, inspiration comes from within. You are looking only at the paper on the table; nothing else exists. That part of the room, which was my study, had a sloping roof, so there was no ceiling fan. Summers were terrible; Bangalore had already lost its temperate weather. I worked with a pedestal fan and a tiny fan closer to me, and, at times, with a basin of cold water for my burning-with-the-heat feet. Much later, when summers became truly unbearable, we had an AC installed in the bedroom. But I thought it wasteful to switch on the AC during the day. My middle-class upbringing always rejected any idea of comfort if it smacked of luxury! 'Think of it as necessary for your work,' my husband said. 'You can work more if you have the AC on,' a writer friend said. But would I earn enough to justify this expense? It was doubtful. And so, I worked with fans around me. I had exulted when I got this room, I thought I could close the door on the world and write. It never happened. There were constant interruptions about household matters. But I clung to my timings; discipline was how I managed to work. Which is perhaps how, in this room, I wrote seven novels, besides a great deal of other writing.

It was with *The Binding Vine* that I learnt to use the computer. My husband persuaded me to get one, since my arthritic pains made banging on the manual typewriter difficult. The computer I got was, looking at what we have today, an antediluvian machine. It was also both whimsical and hostile to me. It would suddenly behave badly and do something called 'hanging', which meant it just refused to go on. It also gave me weird messages, one of which was, 'You have committed an offence.' I think it said 'Federal offence'. I, who am terrified when I see a policeman approaching me, convinced I must have done something wrong, perhaps unknowingly, was at first almost paralysed by this message. I thought the machine was smarter than me; surely it knew what it was saying? In time, I decided to brazen it out. 'Bring on the handcuffs,' I would mutter, a little fearfully, I have to admit. As for getting a connection to the internet, it was one of the most time-consuming and futile exercises. It emitted a number of queer squeaky sounds and letters which looked like the Russian alphabet – this went on and on. You got a connection only by fluke. My friend Githa Hariharan, who is fiendishly smart with gadgets, finally convinced me that the way to deal with computers was never to be afraid of them; there was little that could go wrong. Eventually, I became smarter and the computers improved, though even today I do not have a laptop. I don't want one. I am happy with a desktop. I don't write anywhere except at my table, so why do I need a laptop? I often think that if all humans were like me, we would be still moving on all fours, we would never have learnt to be erect, to stand, to walk, to run.

I had given the manuscript of my new novel to Ruth Petrie of Virago when I met her after my Cambridge visit. Once again, the waiting period began. This time I knew it would not be such a long wait; Ruth had promised she would get back soon. Another novel was knocking on the door, but I could not admit it until this one was off my mind and out of my hands. In the meantime, Penguin had come to India – great news and very significant for writers and, indeed, for Indian writing in English. Virginia Woolf, that wise woman, speaks of how material circumstances influence writing. 'Dogs will bark; people will interrupt; money must be made; health will break down.'

I consider, that having a publisher in India – who would look at Indian writing through a different lens from the one foreign publishers would use – changed the whole course of Indian writing in English. It made all the difference to me. Penguin had bought the rights for *That Long Silence* from Virago, they would be redoing *The Dark Holds No Terrors* as well. All good news. But the news about the new novel was not so good. It received a mixed response. Ruth and the other editor, Melanie, who had both read the novel, thought that it did not work without Mira's poetry. It was not enough for me to 'talk' about the poetry; it had to be actually there in the novel. I had feared this, but I was not, and never had been, a poet, not even as an adolescent. I could not write poetry to save my life. I realised I needed someone to write the poetry for me.

It was fortuitous that I had only recently met a poet who came to interview me after I got the Sahitya Akademi award. (Have I mentioned that I got this fairly prestigious award for *That Long Silence*? If I haven't, how could I have forgotten to write of it?) She was a Kannada poet, and I wanted a Kannada poet because Mira had written her poetry in Kannada. Hesitantly I approached her. I need not have worried. She agreed to write the poetry for me. She even agreed to my condition that I would not give her the manuscript to read (I am superstitious about showing my unpublished work to anyone except to my husband, and even that, only when I complete the final draft). I would tell her, instead, about Mira, about the time she lived in, the kind of person she was, a little about her background and her short life and the kind of subjects she wrote poetry about.

Pratibha Nandakumar, the poet, was an enthusiastic partner. Poems poured out of her, she read them out to me on the phone from her working place, she came home with pages full of scribbled lines, and read the poems aloud to me. We discussed them, she let me choose the most suitable poems and then we translated them together. In fact, I was so enthused, so inspired by working with a poet, that I wrote a few, maybe three or four poems, myself. Snatches of what could be Mira's poetry. I remember I quite liked the one I titled *The Day of the Astrologer*, and I must confess I was tempted to include the poem here – where else could I place my poetry? – but I could not find it. I am glad about that, for it is certainly not fair to push bad, no, terrible poetry on an unsuspecting, innocent reader. Good sense told me I was no poet, I am a story-teller. I thought the poems I finally chose were most appropriate for Mira, for the times she lived in, for her particular situation. Later, an Australian poet who read the novel, called the poetry 'iffy'. I had to go to the dictionary to find out the meaning of the word. I suspected it was a negative word, and so it was. I don't agree with her. I think the Australian writer did not see the poetry in its context – a very young girl who was trying to capture her world, her fears, her doubts, and above all, her ideas, in poetry. A girl living in a place, and at a time when there were not many women poets, and almost no role models for a young girl beginning to write poetry.

I was later witness to a very strange incident during a seminar in a local women's college in Bangalore. The chief guest was a much known and admired poet in Kannada. In the course of the seminar, a young woman, obviously an aspiring poet, and an admirer of this poet, asked him for some words of advice. His advice was: why do you want to write poetry? Leave it to us men. Children are your poetry. I can swear he said this, though I find it hard to believe it myself today. My friend Anupama Niranjana and I looked at each other open-mouthed. We spoke of it later, but at that moment we said nothing at all. I am pretty sure if it had happened today, someone would have got up and challenged him, and would not have let it pass like we had done.

To go back to my novel, Virago accepted it with the poetry. Once again the title gave me trouble, I agonised over it; Githa Hariharan finally gave me the title *The Binding Vine*. The novel was later published in India by Penguin. For some reason, after the initial sales (which were very good in England, Ruth wrote and told me so), the novel did not do too well in India. I don't mean only the sales figures; I rarely go into them. Too morale-sinking.

What I mean is that it was not as talked about as *That Long Silence*. I have realised through the years that books, like humans, come into the world with their fates written on their foreheads. Or is that escapism, is it fatalistic? But there is no doubt that while one book takes off, another, just as good, perhaps, doesn't. The quality of a novel is not always proportionate to how well it does. Though I believe that *Small Remedies, A Matter of Time, Shadow Play* and *Moving On* are better novels, readers, when they talk to me, still speak of *That Long Silence* and *The Dark Holds no Terrors*. However, as far as *The Binding Vine* is concerned, my suspicion is, the feminist ideology is too visible in it.

'I always try to write on the principle of the iceberg. There should be seven-eighths of it underwater for every part that shows,' Hemingway said in an interview. In the case of ideology, I would think that the right proportion is all of it under water. Ideology should come through people and their stories. 'The work needs to escape from the message and transcend it' – the words of a critic, Ferdinand Mount. I think that didn't happen in this novel. I have to admit that in the years before I wrote this novel, and even as I was writing it, I steeped myself in feminist books – Simone de Beauvoir's *The Second Sex*, Virginia Woolf's *A Room of One's Own* (both these books have been the greatest influences on my life), Margaret Mead, Elaine Showalter, Ellen Moers, Susan Brownmiller, as well as Irawati Karve and many, many others. I also read the novels of Margaret Drabble, Erica Jong, Doris Lessing, Anita Brookner, Margaret Atwood and so many more. Virago, when I had gone for the launch of *That Long Silence*, had generously allowed me to take away as many of their books as I wanted to. I had brought back novels from their classic series by Antonia White, Rosamond Lehmann, Winifred Holtby, Margaret Kennedy, Molly Keane, Kate O'Brien, Rebecca West, Charlotte Yonge… I had also got to know a women's activist group in Bangalore. Though never an activist myself, except through my writing, I admired the work these women were doing and I marvelled at their selflessness. Brave and compassionate women, they sat by women dying of burns, surely the worst death, the worst suffering, any human has to endure. They held the suffering, the dying women's hands, supported their families, helped them to liaison with the police, and made sure the dying declarations were recorded. Harrowing work.

A volunteer told me once how long it took her to get used to watching the suffering of these dying women and what it did to her. I myself saw one of their founder members, who had been doing this work for decades, break down during a meeting and burst into uncontrollable sobs. It was at a meeting of this organisation, Vimochana, that I heard about the dilemma they often faced, torn between the need to make the cruelties and wrongs public and yielding to the desire of the families to keep it private. This became part of *The Binding Vine*. It became a source of conflict between Urmi, who wanted to make Kalpana's plight public, and Kalpana's mother who cried out, 'We will be shamed. Who will marry my younger daughter?' It was a source of conflict between Urmi, who wanted to publish Mira's poetry (about her great aversion to her husband's constant demands for sex), and Urmi's friend and sister-in-law, Vanaa, who thought it wrong to make family matters public.

The Binding Vine came out at a time when the first wave of feminism was over and there was a kind of backlash against it. The women's movement was derided, it was ridiculed, feminists were treated as men-haters and family-haters. Many women turned their backs on feminism as well. There was a kind of disdain for it among the privileged few, and a huge misunderstanding about it among others. Am I trying to find excuses for this novel? No, I am not. I am trying to say that it was with this novel that I learned that overt ideology has no place in fiction. The first time I said this aloud was in the course of my visit to a university. I have visited a great many universities in the country in the course of my writing life and it is impossible to remember all of them. But this is a visit I do remember, because the teacher who had invited me and organised the visit was unusual. I found him committed to his work, to his students and to the ideology he believed in – a rare combination in teachers. He asked me a question: did I believe in Art for Art's sake? He had read somewhere that I had said that ideology has no place in a novel. (I often wish people wouldn't quote things I said long ago in a different context, back to me. Surely we are entitled to change our view! Surely a thinking person must change her/his views?) I don't remember what my reply was, but I think I said what I believe: in a country like ours, rife with injustice and inequalities, nobody, least of all a writer, who is constantly responding to society, can ignore these things. But the writer's ideas or ideology cannot be pushed through in a novel. To do so would be to produce a bad novel. And a bad novel sinks to the depths, without leaving a trace. So what use is it to the ideology then?

There was a time when women's novels were loudly angry. Marilyn French's *The Women's Room*, for example; I thought it was just a bad novel. On the other hand, there were writers like Margaret Atwood or Margaret Drabble, who were splendid novelists as well as feminists, their feminism scarcely visible, and yet the foundation of their writing. Jane Austen has often been criticised for not bringing contemporary events into her novels and for not speaking up for women, like Charlotte Brontë or George Eliot did. But Jane Austen was a novelist first and last. And a perfect novelist. She wrote about women's lives in such a nuanced, subtle way that it did not mar the novel with a message.

Mrs Bennet's matchmaking, for example, her desperation for Elizabeth to marry Mr Collins – these come out of the situation of the Bennet family: the family estate entailed to the closest male relative and the widow and daughters left with nothing. Charlotte

Lucas' acceptance of Mr Collins comes out of her fear of remaining a spinster, dependent on her father and then on her brothers – a fate which Jane Austen and her sister Cassandra knew very well. Oh yes, Jane Austen knew all about the injustices in a woman's life and she knew how to knit them into a novel so that they never obtruded. Look at Miss Bates and her mother in *Emma*. Amazing creations. And Fanny, the poor dependent in *Mansfield Park*. Yes, Jane Austen was the perfect novelist. A novel is not the vehicle through which a writer can clamour for social or political changes. The wrongs can be hinted at, the solutions are never part of a novel. It is for the readers to see these things in the novel, to think them over, to find some answers within herself. Non-fiction is the vehicle for propaganda, for polemics. So I have always believed. In any case, the nation had other things to think of at the time; feminism was not a priority. Many things happened that shook the nation.

The nineties began with violence; Rajiv Gandhi was killed. It was the first time suicide bombing had been used to assassinate a political leader in India. I remember one of our sons was at home at the time, and we were having our early morning cup of tea when the phone rang. It was my mother. Like my father, she had the habit of listening to the first radio news at six in the morning, which was how she had heard of Rajiv Gandhi's death. There was a sense of déjà vu. Inevitably we remembered his mother's death, which had been equally horrifying – she had been riddled with bullets by her own guards. I had never admired her; I thought then, and still do, that she was responsible for many of the ills that India is still struggling with: corruption, political sycophancy, dividing people for the sake of votes and creating vote banks. She had been ruthless and, in a way, her violent death seemed inevitable, though no one should have to die the way she did. Rajiv had been, or had seemed to be, a gentler person; yet, after his mother's death, he had allowed the killing of Sikhs to go on, though he could have stopped it. Sometimes I wonder whether Nemesis, the gentleman the Greeks believed in, is still among us, still at work. Recently, when some veteran BJP leaders were asked by the Supreme Court to stand trial for their role in the demolition of the Babri Masjid, I thought I could see the old gentleman putting on his black cap, ready to pronounce the sentence. Nobody gets away, you have to pay at some time.

When I had heard of the BJP leader, L.K. Advani's plan of a rath yatra, from Somnath in Gujarat to Ayodhya in Uttar Pradesh, in support of the building of a Shri Ram temple at what was considered the birthplace of Ram, I had been overcome by a sense of unease. When I saw Advani, a senior political leader, standing in his 'chariot', hands folded in a perpetual namaste, a sanctimonious smile on his face, I was horrified. I wondered: does he know what he is doing? Yes, he did; he was putting in his claim for becoming a leader to be reckoned with. But more, he was dividing the country into Hindus and Muslims. His entire exercise of a yatra was not just in favour of building a temple; it was also *against* the masjid that had been built on the spot where the temple had been. I thought of Hampi, the seat of the Vijaynagar kingdom, India's richest kingdom at the time, which had been destroyed by the four Muslim kingdoms of the Deccan. There was large-scale looting and senseless destruction, and the idol of the God Vithala had been carried away to safety just in time. But even that war had not really been about religion.

Wars are/were fought for acquiring territories and riches, for getting political power. Moreover, history does not coerce us to correct past wrongs, as is believed by so many now; instead, it is for us to see that what happened once does not happen again. But it is easier to inflame people, rather than tell them to think for themselves. And so it happened. It was the rath yatra that led to the Babri Masjid being stormed and razed to the ground by a mob which had come from all over India to offer this 'seva'. The 'sevaks' as they were called, or rather as they called themselves, destroyed an old mosque which they were told was built on the place where Shri Ram was born. Once again, we were witness to an event happening far away. We saw a lone man on top of the dome of the masjid signalling victory and then watched people swarming all over it, until nothing was left of the building but a heap of rubble. What amazes me, when I think of it, is that the so-called 'leaders' watched it all as if it was a drama being staged for their benefit. Did they not foresee what would be the result? Or did they not care? As long as they got their votes, and stayed in power for the next five years, it obviously did not matter to them that the country was divided by religion. This was a watershed moment in India's history. It shattered the hard-earned harmony between different communities, it destroyed the complex, intricately woven fabric of Indian society. What happened after the demolition of the Babri Masjid was worse than what anyone could have imagined.

I had lived in Bombay for more than fifteen years. A crowded, dirty city, it had entered into me, I was linked to it in so many ways I could not understand myself. Besides, we had family living in the city, both my family and my husband's family, as also many friends. When the Bombay riots began, it was a personal shock. My brother-in-law, a doctor, practised in a predominantly Muslim area; he had a great many Muslim patients and often spoke of their generosity, their warmth and courteous behaviour. Suddenly they were enemies, suddenly the Hindus were their enemies. At first it was Muslims who ravaged the city, then it was the turn of the Hindus. Finally came what is now known as Black Friday, a day on which bombs went off across the city, spreading death and destruction indiscriminately through it. I remember talking to my writer friend, Saniya, at a time just after President Bush (the senior Bush) had taken the USA into a war, supposedly to help Kuwait! Both of us confessed that we were finding it hard to write at a time when the world seemed to be exploding. TV had brought war into people's homes and we saw the angry red skies, we heard the gunfire, the bombs going off, the jets screaming across the sky, the oil wells burning – it was like a picture of the Inferno. How could we write of human relationships and frailties when this terrible dance of destruction was going on around us?

Ultimately, of course, we went back to writing; writing was what we wanted to do, writing the way we always did. I think of Theodor Adorno's words: 'To write poetry after Auschwitz is barbaric.' Profound though it sounds, there is an element of non-understanding of what writing is, in this statement. It is important for the writer to write, to keep writing, to write what she/he wants to. But to consciously respond to events never works. I have the examples of McEwan's *Saturday* and John Updike's *Terrorist*, both of which were written under the shadow of 9/11. They don't work because the writers are consciously writing about a significant event, doing their writerly duty, so to say. That, I must add in all fairness, is how the novels struck me. Two other writers, John le Carré and Harold Pinter, on the other hand, wrote a letter to President Bush about the futility of going to war. That didn't do any good, either. Nevertheless, it was a better way of doing one's 'writerly duty'. And so I went on to my next novel, leaving *The Binding Vine* and its reviews, both good and bad, behind me.

Learning to Be 'An Author'

A novel worth reading is an education of the heart.
Susan Sontag, *Women Writers at Work, Paris Review Interviews*

By the time I had completed *The Binding Vine* and moved on to my next novel, things were slightly easier at home and I was hopeful that I would now get more time to write, that I would be able to write this novel without interruptions. Or at least, without too many interruptions. Our sons had got married a little earlier, both of them in the same year, a few months apart. They had not been living with us for some years; they had both left home before graduation. Of course, they had always come home during holidays and spent their free time with us. But now that they had their own homes (both outside Bangalore) and companions of their choice, we knew the visits would be much less frequent. We were very pleased, though, that they had chosen their own partners; we were reluctant to go through the rigmarole of an arranged marriage. Nevertheless, I must admit the weddings were a strain for me. I know many women enjoy their children's weddings; at least, they find them exciting events. I don't find weddings exciting; I hadn't enjoyed even my own. (Of course, at the time I had been in a state of combined confusion and blankness.) I hate crowds, I dislike dressing up, I am uncomfortable with religious rituals, and I loathe shopping. So what's left? There was the pleasure of the young people, of course. And I have to admit I enjoyed buying the bridal saris. I am a great lover of saris. My aesthetic sense delights in their beauty, in the craftsmanship, in their beautiful weaves and colours. And I love the grace, elegance and dignity it confers on a woman. I have also occasionally experienced the joyous camaraderie of sari-shopping. I remember how, when I was shopping for saris in Calcutta, some women in the shop put aside their own shopping and enthusiastically helped me to choose, telling me about the saris and where they were from. And once, when I was buying a sari for my new daughter-in-law, everyone, customers and shop assistants, got into the act. Is she fair, or dark, they asked, and then started looking for colours which would suit her complexion. I look at the high-end sari shops today, air-conditioned, with security at the door and CCTV spying on you, and I wonder whether women are able to find the same joy in shopping in such places. I don't know, because I have given up shopping, except for necessities.

Our family (not the brides, of course), would have loved very simple weddings. I believe in simple and austere weddings; in fact, Aru's wedding in *Shadow Play* was a kind of wish fulfilment of mine. But the brides had their own ideas and dreams and we couldn't deny them those. Therefore, they had their full-fledged weddings. We tried to keep it simple on our part, though. Just fifteen of us went for our older son's wedding, and, perhaps, ten for the younger son's. When it was all done, there was relief that it was over, that we didn't need to worry about our sons any longer. So I thought, or rather hoped; a vain hope as most parents find out. But certainly there was no empty nest syndrome for me. I moved swiftly into my new novel which had been gathering force inside me. I already had two old diaries full of notes. It was time to begin.

This novel, the second of the three which had entered into my mind, came out of many streams. There was the old house opposite my parents' home, a house set in a large compound with many trees and the stone compound walls of an earlier period. It came out of a mother and her three daughters I had met once when I'd gone with my aunt to visit her ex-husband's family. The mother and her three daughters lived on their own in a large old house; there was no man around, and the girls' father was never mentioned. The novel came out of a story I'd heard, about a woman thrown out of her home after three decades of marriage and her daughter's battle to get her mother justice.

It came out of the predicament of a researcher/academic, who had got into trouble with a fundamentalist group. They had questioned some of his findings about a thirteenth-century poet, who had fought against the caste system, fought against the great inequality in the name of caste in Indian society. This group had forced the academic to retract his findings. My novel also came out of Maratha history, out of the disastrous defeat of the Marathas in the Third Battle of Panipat. For most Indian students of my time, Indian history meant the history of the North, of the Slave Kings and the Moghuls. Shivaji was part of it only because he stood up against the might of the Moghul Empire, because he defied Aurangzeb. Now I read about the vast sweep of the Maratha kingdom after Moghul power had weakened. I still have a quote from a book by Richard Temple, which had given me a flutter of discovery:

> 'In the days of Balaji Bajirao, full one hundred thousand Maratha horses were slaking their thirst in every stream that flowed between the Cape Comorin and the Himalayas.'

The defeat of the Marathas in the Third Battle of Panipat by the Afghan, Ahmed Shah Abdali, was a watershed moment in Indian history, for it checked the power of the Marathas, who had been the greatest power in India at the time, and opened a window through which the British entered. Nanasaheb Peshwa died soon after Panipat, heart-broken, it is said; the Peshwa's eldest son, Vishwasrao, had died in the battle of Panipat, as also the Peshwa's brother, Sadashivrao Bhau. On Nanasaheb Peshwa's death, his sixteen-year-old son, Madhavrao, succeeded him.

I knew, of course, of the Peshwas; how could I not with their palace, Shaniwar Wada, still standing in Pune, and the pride that the Pune Brahmins (including my mother's family) took in them? They were the Prime Ministers of the Maratha kings and later gained power in their own right. I saw the Marathi play *Swami*, based on the novel by Ranjit Desai, in which the hero was Madhavrao Peshwa, of whom it was said that, if he had not died so young, the history of India would have been different. After I saw the play, I became an admirer of Madhavrao, who was shown as a gentle and sensitive man, as also a great warrior. His wife, Ramabai's act of committing sati after her husband died, had filled me with both horror and compassion.

But however much I admired these characters, I would not be writing about them. I am not a historical novelist. I write of ordinary people whose lives are affected by historical events. I am more interested in the tangential connection between historical events and people's lives, than in the history itself. My novel was connected to the fact that Madhavrao travelled South and repeatedly invaded Haidar Ali's territories. It was a period of ding-dong battles between the Nizam, the Peshwa and Haider, and after him his son Tipu. Madhavrao, after one of his raids, left behind some of his people to administer the territories he had conquered. One such man, a Brahmin, who was to collect taxes and keep accounts, would be the ancestor of the family I was going to write about. This was the first novel in which I would be looking at the impact of history on individual lives.

In fact, this was a novel of many firsts. After twenty years of living there, it was in this novel that I moved to Bangalore, locating my story in the city. It was the first time that I moved away from a first person narrative to a third person narrative. It was not a conscious decision. The novel came to me in the third person, because it needed a larger, broader perspective; a tunnel view would not do. It was the first time that I got into a man's mind; the few first-person passages in the novel belonged to a man, Gopal. This was the first time the authorial voice appeared in my novel. I have no idea how or why it slipped in. But there it was, and it led me to another novel in which these characters returned, a novel that came nearly twenty years after this one.

It was also the first time since *That Long Silence* that I was so immersed in my novel, in the characters. Gustave Flaubert is supposed to have said, 'I am Emma Bovary.' I could have said, 'I am Sumi, I am Kalyani, I am Aru, I am Gopal.' All these characters whirled in my mind like the colours in a kaleidoscope. While writing this novel, even the minor characters possessed me: Charu, Seema, Hrishi, Goda, Devaki, Rohit, Surekha. Strangely, considering the fact that the novel has two failed marriages, a bustling happy family life is very much a part of it, leading to some inner truths of human relationships. And this was the first novel which had a launch. No, launch is not the right word. Four women came home sometime after the book was out. I knew three of them: Arundhati Rao, the actor who changed Bangalore's theatre world by getting the wonderful theatre Ranga Shankara built, Vanamala Vishwanath, translator and a teacher in the university, and Pratibha Nandakumar, the poet who had written Mira's verses for me. The fourth young woman was opening a store, a boutique store. They asked me: could they read out some passages from my novel for the opening? *Could they?* Indeed they could, most certainly they could. It would be an honour to have these women read out from my novel.

It is with a certain kind of launch, where the publisher is visibly present, that a writer becomes 'An Author'. But launches were not much known at the time; publishers organised them only for a select few. In any case, this reading from *A Matter of Time* was scarcely a launch. It was not a commercial event; I don't think the publisher was involved, or that books were kept for sale. I don't remember signing books, either. It was a joyous occasion, an unstructured, spontaneous, informal event. I think it was Basant Panchami day and there had been a suggestion that women wear yellow. Many did. I remember the colour, the smell of mogra flowers, the pin drop silence when the reading started. I have had many launches since then, some in bookshops, one or two in five-star hotels. But none have given me the pleasure that this one did. I was surrounded by friends and there was an air of excitement, a sense of celebration, of rejoicing all around.

Launches are difficult occasions for writers. A launch should be a moment of celebration after years of solitary hard work, a celebration before the spoilsport reviews start coming. But it can also be a tension-filled affair. Many things have to be done: the venue to be found, the programme to be planned, the invitations sent, the right person approached to launch the book. Margaret Atwood's essay, *Travels Back*, gives a fascinating picture of her on a book tour, trudging a mile, dragging two suitcases of her books behind her, 'because there may not be any bookstores' in that town. I've never had to do such a thing; I always left it to the publisher to bring the books. Of course, there was that time in Australia, when the publisher didn't send a single book of mine to the Melbourne Festival. So there I was, hanging about, when the other authors were busily signing their books for readers. I was both embarrassed and furious! However, making up the guest list is often mainly the author's job, and I find this difficult; who, and how many the guests are, can make or mar the occasion. Too often, the guest-list consists primarily of family and friends. Since we don't have much family in Bangalore, I could not depend on filling up the hall with family. And I rarely invite the family for launches, anyway, unless they are interested in books and reading. Why make them submit to an hour or so of boredom?

There was one launch, however, when I had almost my entire family with me. Both our sons and their wives were there, apart from nieces, nephews and their spouses. I was happy about this, but even happier that the family constituted only a small part of the audience. My little grandson launched the book – he did it by holding it high above his head, like the Wimbledon winner holding her/his trophy. Unforgettable. It was a great occasion for me. I must admit, I have been lucky in Bangalore; I have always had a good crowd, people who have read me and are with me. I can feel the affection. But there is always apprehension, there are always fears. What if there is a sudden strike and no one comes? What if I am suddenly unwell on the day? What if no one comes because no one is interested? Once, in Chennai, a cloudburst and a political 'human chain' prevented most guests from coming. It was devastating. I still feel guilty when I meet the generous organiser who had so meticulously planned everything.

Ann Patchett's essay on book tours and launches, 'My Life in Sales', should be a must-read for all young writers. According to her, launches began with Julia Child (famous for her cookbooks), whose publisher's publicist thought of organising a signing of Julia's book on French cooking, along with demonstrations, in a local departmental store, linking this event with the local TV stations. The experience was a huge success, and the books sold like, yes, hot cakes. And so began the era of publicity and promotion of books. Ann Patchett says that a fellow writer once told her, 'The only thing worse than a book tour is no book tour.' She chanted this line like a mantra when she was going through her first book tour. The publishers offered to organise it themselves, or, alternatively, they would give her a certain sum and she could do it on her own. She chose the latter. Brave woman! She drove from town to town, reaching just in time to freshen up at a McDonald's rest room (whatever the quality of their food, she writes, their rest rooms are excellent). At times, there would be a few people, sometimes it was just her and the girl at the desk in the store.

This is an author's worst nightmare. I'm terrified of empty chairs, of half-empty rooms. I remember my first big event, a talk in Delhi organised by the Sahitya Akademi. I was utterly cast down by the small crowd, until another writer, a poet, told me it could have been worse. 'Poets have scarcely twenty or twenty-five people in the audience,' he told me. On the other hand, it did my morale no good when someone else told me, 'You should have seen how it was when Kamala Das was here. The hall was full, people were sitting in the aisles, standing along the walls.' Really?

I don't remember how I responded, but I remember how murderous I felt. Why tell me this? In fact, Kamala Das was mentioned to me once again when I was in Calcutta, the organiser waving an expansive hand all around to show me what a crowd they had had at her event. By then, I no longer felt bad about it. Kamala Das was, well, Kamala Das. There was no way I could even think of competing with her; she was a very interesting woman who had led a very colourful life – at least her autobiography made it seem so! And there was her amazing turnaround when she became a Muslim. I met her once when she invited me to visit her in Bangalore. She came out to meet me, wearing a burqa, hugged me, then drew back and asked, 'You don't mind meeting me?' I was amazed at the question. 'Why should I?' I asked. 'Because of this,' she said, pointing to her burqa. It made me realise what she must have gone through after her conversion. Kerala is often wrongly called a matriarchal place. It is not; it is matrilineal. And as patriarchal as anywhere in the world.

A launch that really had all twenty-two feet of my colon in knots was the one for *Moving On*. There was an event for Naipaul's new novel in a bookstore on the same day and at the same time. A local paper played up a fairly recent fracas at a conference between Naipaul and me (why do I say 'between'? He scarcely knew I existed). He had lost that famous temper of his and got into a tantrum at something I had said during a discussion at which he was present. Now, the newspaper brought this back, and asked: who will have the larger audience? I had no doubts that he, a Nobel Prize winner, a world-famous author, and a MAN, would have the bigger crowd. In fact, I wondered whether anyone would come to my event at all. When we went to the store I refused to enter, I was sure it would be empty. Pushed and chivvied into going, I went in and found a respectable crowd; by the time we began, the room was packed. Naipaul's event was very well attended as well. So much for the media's attempts to start controversies!

A Matter of Time is memorable to me for the most vicious review I have ever had. I had earlier had bad reviews and would continue to have them; no author is exempt from these. Most 'bad' reviews come out of the reviewer's ignorance of the author's entire oeuvre, out of a desire to show off the reviewer's own cleverness and often a lack of understanding of what a review should do (they do come out of bad books as well!). I blame the choice of the reviewer for most of the bad reviews. I myself do not review a book if I have not read at least some of the author's other works. I also won't review a book when I find my response to the book totally negative (I did it twice, though, something I deeply regret).

But this particular review of my novel was vicious, spiked with malice and a desire to hurt. Nothing in the novel was spared – neither the language, nor the characters, nor the narrative style; everything was condemned, even the metaphors. In spite of family and friends telling me I shouldn't bother about such reviews, it hurt me deeply, mainly because of the malice I sensed behind it. How could I remain unaffected? I'd read of Virginia Woolf anxiously waiting for reviews, her entire mood depending on what they said. 'I am publicly demolished,' she wrote once. 'Nothing is left of me in Oxford and Cambridge and places where the young read Wyndham Lewis (the reviewer).' If Virginia Woolf felt this way …

All writers are sensitive to reviews. Despite knowing that, generally, good reviewers can be counted on the fingers of one hand, we are elated or downcast depending on whether the reviews are good or bad. And we feel ignored, erased out of existence, when there are no reviews. This is because there is no other feedback for a writer. Actors, musicians, dancers at least get an instant response from their audience. For authors, until the reviews come out, there is nothing. Without reviews, one is left feeling completely at sea about one's work. Writers, like all artistes, veer between confidence and insecurity. A few favourable words about their work and their confidence shoots up, like the temperature of a malaria patient. A bad review, and the same confidence plummets down, like a bird shot in mid flight.

And yet, despite the nasty criticism of *A Matter of Time*, I knew it was a good book; I had enough confidence in myself by then. And I was justified. The book was later published by the Feminist Press (with an Afterword by Ritu Menon, which I consider one of the best critiques of my entire work, not just of this one novel), and it got many excellent reviews and was talked about. And, the same reviewer who had demolished *A Matter of Time*, later reviewed

Small Remedies, and said I was improving. Boy, was I glad to hear that! I'd never have known it otherwise.

I always have a book to dip into when I am working on a novel — *The Golden Notebook* once, Dickens' *Bleak House*, to me the best of his novels, at another time. For *A Matter of Time*, it was the Upanishads in Dr Radhakrishnan's translation. The three epigraphs, which introduce the three parts of the novel, are from the Upanishads. They lead away from the story, but they also led me back into it, signposts, pointing out the road I had to take. I was constantly going to the Upanishads at the time of writing *A Matter of Time*, and I was astounded, I remember, at the wisdom in it, at the understanding of life, at the questions asked in it. Much of it is repetitive, like the constant references to the long line of teachers and students. At times, it is sublime, at other times, gross; or perhaps earthy is a better word. (I would like those who speak of 'our culture' and 'our ancient past' to read the part about how to be sure to conceive a male child. Explicit! No holds barred. This too is part of our culture.) But this is how we are, this duality is part of all humans, made up as we are of spirit and matter. Reading the Upanishads, not all of them, of course, mainly the Brhadaranyaka Upanishad, and only the parts of it that interested me, filled me with awe for our ancestors' understanding of life, for the questions that were ceaselessly asked. Asking questions is the beginning of understanding; once we stop asking questions, we will remain mired in ignorance. The verses in the Rig Veda, 'To The Unknown God', in which each stanza ends with, 'To Which God shall we offer Worship?' gave me an epigraph for *Small Remedies*. It is a question humans are still grappling with. The doubts, the uncertainty, the questions gave me a sense of a wisdom of great depth.

Two questions are often asked about *A Matter of Time*: why does Sumi die and why does Gopal walk out on his family. The answer to Sumi's death is in the book itself, in the final epigraph, where

Yama, the God of death, tells the wonder boy Nachiket, 'Ask me anything but don't ask me about death.' Death is an unanswerable question, death is an ending which closes all doors. On a more mundane level, as soon as I had written about Sumi's death, I was startled, I was aghast. What had I done? How could I have killed her just when she was beginning to flower? I was full of grief myself. I tried to rewrite it, without Sumi dying, but it would not work. Sumi had to die.

Gopal's walking out on his family remains a kind of mystery through the novel. The truth is that Gopal himself is not clear on why he can no longer live with his wife and daughters. The talk of *vairagya* (renunciation) is a red herring. Sumi, though she does not know the reason, understands that he has to go, that they can no longer live together. Which gives her an understanding, a clarity, the others lack. However, I, the author, had to know the motives for Gopal abandoning his family. The revelation of motives may come to the character gradually, but the author has to be clear from the beginning about the 'why?' of a character's actions. I knew why Gopal had to go, but the explanation came only when I wrote *Shadow Play*, a novel about the same people, the same family, nearly two decades later.

I don't remember whether I sent *A Matter of Time* to Virago. Things had changed by then, Virago had become a part of the Little Brown group and Ruth Petrie had left. However, I do distinctly remember that I sent the manuscript to an agent who responded with a suggestion: I would have to remove the entire opening chapter of the second part of the novel, The Family, the part which described the background of the family and how and why they came to be where they were. The message sent to the old Peshwa, Nanasaheb, in Pune after their disastrous defeat, and the death of their best men at Panipat, had left a deep impression on me. 'Two pearls have been dissolved, seven gold mohurs have been lost and of the silver and copper the total cannot be cast up.'

This coded message, which told the Peshwa that his eldest son was dead, and so was his brother and some of their best generals and innumerable soldiers, almost killed the old man. These things were, to me, very much a part of the novel, or at least the background to it. Now the agent was telling me to remove this entire chapter. I remember Margaret Drabble telling us during her session in Cambridge, that her American publisher had wanted her to change something for the American edition. And did she, someone had asked. Yes, she said simply. But perhaps what she changed was a minor matter. This deletion of an entire chapter was not. I did understand the agent's motive: she thought this would mean nothing to an English reader. But I had not written my novel for an English or American readership.

I never think of a readership when I write a novel; one never does. The question of readership is a matter of concern to the publisher, not to the writer. For the author, readers emerge only after the book has been published. Or so I believe. I only knew I could not change anything in my novel for the illusory advantage of getting more readers. If people outside India read my book, I would be very happy. Some did, a few responded. An Italian woman wrote to me after reading *A Matter of Time* in Italian, saying, 'I think you have written my story, it is about my life.' A man in the USA wrote about the book in words that warmed my heart. But, primarily, if it had to be for any readers at all, the book was for Indian readers who would get more out of it, because of their understanding of the context, than others could. No, I was not going to change anything, I was not going to add explanations, either. An Australian writer told me that an American publisher asked her after reading her novel, 'Where are the kangaroos?' I guess in the same way a foreign publisher could want symbolic elephants in mine. But the elephant would come into my novel only if it had some purpose there. (Actually, an elephant is as exotic to me as it would be to a foreign reader.)

I told the agent that I would not change anything and we parted ways. I think it was here that I realised I would not write anything except what I wanted to; the moment when I knew that I would not chase a market. An exercise that can be quite futile, because you never know what different readers want. And the market is famously fickle. I needed good editors, of course, and with *A Matter of Time* I got a young, enthusiastic and excellent editor with whom I could work very well, an editor whom I began to trust completely. This editor, Karthika, edited three more novels for me after that, and it was always a pleasure to work with her. But to change things for some unknown readers, because they might not understand what I had written – no, I wouldn't do that. Even publishers don't really know what readers want. Which is why readers are manipulated into believing that a novel which is highly publicised is what they would like to read.

A Matter of Time gave me what I had always hoped to get: the sense of being regarded as a serious writer. My writing, I thought, was finally being taken seriously. I was also very pleased about the way the novel had come together. The hardest thing about it was, actually, the title. Even after it was complete, I just could not find a title. It came to me, at last, when we were in Portugal. I had been invited to Oviedo, Spain for an academic conference. As always with conferences, my memory fails me when it comes to the actual sessions and papers presented. What I do remember is Gayatri Spivak's lecture. Though most of her talk went over my head, I think I learnt about the importance of scholars and critics then. The way Spivak's talk was received by the audience told me what she meant to the academics. She had made Mahasweta Devi available to the world, just as Ramanujan had made U.R. Ananthamurthy a part of world literature by translating his *Samskara*. I realised the power of academics to keep a book alive. I remember, too, the beautiful girl students who hovered about us; a picture of me in the midst of these lovely young students is one of my favourite pictures. The beauty of the young women seems to have shed a glow on me. The best of Spain was Madrid, one of the most beautiful cities I have seen, and the Prado. I had long admired Goya and Velásquez, and when we were in Madrid, there was a special exhibition of Goya's paintings going on. But the queues for this were so long, we knew we could never hope to get in. However, I got my compensation in Toledo where I discovered El Greco. I find his crowd pictures fascinating, especially the way he puts himself somewhere in the crowd. I have in my bedroom a copy of his painting of a Spanish nobleman, which I think is exquisite.

For us 'early to bed, early to rise' people, Spain presented a strange problem. For one thing, there was no sign of dinner in hotels even as late as ten, which was our bedtime. And, for me, there was the even more serious problem of what to eat. I had become a total vegetarian – not even eggs – sometime after we went to Bangalore. Spain was tough for a vegetarian. In Oviedo, on the first day, I'd got one of the students to write *No meat, no fish, no eggs* on a piece of paper. I would show it to the waiter, whose eyebrows would climb up to his hairline and he would throw up his hands, the universal gesture of despair, asking, 'What do we give you, then?' What, indeed! Bread and cheese were not always available everywhere, and I soon got sick of eating slices of cucumber and tomatoes as a substitute for a meal. Nothing in Spain was free of ham, not even what had seemed like rice pudding! *Kheer*, I had thought joyfully, before I saw some suspicious-looking bits floating on top. And slaughtered pigs decorated the entrance to restaurants. A dreadful sight for a vegetarian, especially someone like me who had turned vegetarian in a moment at the sight of the carcass of a slaughtered sheep in a butcher's shop in Bangalore.

From Spain we went on to Portugal. There, I thought of all my Christian friends in school, many of whom had come from Goa, and who, in those early days, spoke of their connection with Portugal with pride. I remembered, too, my march in Mumbai shouting slogans against Salazar. However, by the time of our visit, Portugal had moved a long distance from its Colonial past; there were few signs that Goa had been a treasured colony. It was in Lisbon that, one early morning, when I woke up to the melodious chimes of church bells, the title 'A Matter of Time' suddenly came into my mind. It seemed just right. *Kalosmi*, says Krishna in the Gita. I am Time, controlling the world, subduing the world. In my novel, too, there was the idea of Time as a powerful factor. And so *A Matter of Time* it was.

With my next novel *Small Remedies*, I took, it seems so now, a great risk: I wrote about a musician, a classical Hindustani singer, Savitribai Indorekar of the Gwalior gharana. This was going to be hard enough; what did I know about music? I was, at best, a desultory and appreciative listener. I could not even identify the ragas when I heard them. And to write in English about Indian music is a daunting task. Fortunately, when I began, I did not know, or rather, I did not think of these things; I solved the problems as they arose, I unknotted the tangles when I came upon them.

For some reason, I am never very sure how many novels I have written. Not that I have a great many; but somehow, perhaps because I sometimes include, and at other times exclude, my crime novels, the figure seems to move up and down. I have to count each time (on my fingers) to get the right figure. By this process, I now know that I have written ten major novels. Or eleven, if I include one crime novel (there I go again!). And I have to add that there are also two crime novellas, but I close my eyes to them, not only because I think they are slightly flawed, or rather amateurish, but also because it would make the total thirteen. My superstitiousness (I am tremendously superstitious as far as my work is concerned) puts me on the alert about this. The point I am trying to get to is that, even today, I rarely read a novel of mine after it has been published, except for the first hasty skim to see that everything is all right. This is because I don't enjoy reading my own novels. I guess that most authors, after reading the text over and over again, checking for errors, looking for weak connections, disjointedness and repetitions, are so sick of it that they don't want to look at the book, leave alone read it – not for a long time, anyway.

However, there are times when one has to do a public reading, something I find both embarrassing and uncomfortable. I think prose passages are not meant to be read aloud and that excerpts, read out of context, are quite meaningless. But there are even worse problems. When I read, if I have to, the bad parts obtrude themselves on my notice and I squirm; I think, how could I have written this? The good parts are equally problematic, because I think with disbelief: did *I* write this? And then: I will never be able to write like this again. I know a writer who confessed that she went any place she was invited to only to read her own writing, that she waited for the time of her session and was disinterested in everything else, before and after that. I thought she was a brave woman to make such a confession; or, perhaps, this, too, was a part of her self-centeredness.

There have been occasions when the reading from my novel has been done by an actor who is so good that I can distance myself from my own words and listen with an objective enjoyment. Arundhati Rao reading from *Shadow Play*, an amateur actor reading some passages from *In the Country of Deceit*, a reading of a passage from *A Matter of Time* in French in Lille, France. Of course, I could not understand the language, but the rapt silence of the audience and the little smile on the face of the French translator, Simone Manceau, sitting beside me, told me that the reading, and the translation too, I think, was very good.

Sometime back, I decided to reorganise the files of my novels on my hard disk, which had been filed in any which way. My mother, in her last years, used to constantly tidy up her possessions, saying she did not want my sister and me to have any trouble after she had gone (concealing her jewellery, each time in a new place, in an attempt to deceive any thieves, if they came). I guess it was the same thought that made me decide to put my work in order, though why I imagine anyone will want to do anything with my novels after I'm gone is a mystery, even to me. I did not read the files as I moved from novel to novel, just swiftly glanced at the page numbers and the file names. But when I came to *Small Remedies*, for some reason, I don't know why, I found myself reading the text. I went on to read the entire novel on the computer, which was strange because I don't like to read on the computer, my eyes are now not up to the task. And, in fact, I could have stretched out a hand, picked up a copy of the novel and read it. Equally strangely, when I came to the point where Madhu talks of her son's death, I found tears running down my cheeks, even as I went on unconsciously checking the page numbers. It is true that, 'there is a splinter of ice in the heart of a writer,' (Graham Greene, *A Sort of Life*) but I am sometimes overcome by emotions when writing, like I was when writing of Sumi's death in *A Matter of Time*. But the emotion that overtook me when I was doing what I had thought was a business-like reading, took me by total surprise.

Later, I thought – of course, this novel is so imbued with the *shoka rasa*, it had to bring out grief in me. But no, there is no such thing as the *shoka rasa*, the Natya Shastra does not mention it as one of the nine rasas. Only that *shoka*, or grief, leads to compassion – the *karuna rasa*. 'Out of *shoka* came *shloka* (a verse),' so says the Ramayana about its beginning. Valmiki, out of his grief at seeing a bird die of a hunter's arrow, out of his compassion for the bird's companion's piteous wailing, began chanting the Ramayana. No wonder the epic is so imbued with sadness. My tears had come out of compassion for Madhu's grief. Truly, it was a strange, inexplicable experience, sobbing over a novel I had written nearly twenty years ago, a novel which I thought was out of my system, my tears falling on the keyboard with fat plops as I wept, experiencing the book as if it had been written by someone else. Now, as I look back, I wonder whether it was some kind of a dreadful prescience which was alerting me through these tears that came out of a mother's grief for her son.

Small Remedies was the last of the three novels that had presented themselves to me after I was done with *That Long Silence*. I began writing it nearly ten years after the seed was planted in me. Actually, it's beginning went a much longer way back. It began, as I've said earlier, in a voice I had heard in Dharwad as a child, a voice that emerged from a small shabby tile-roofed house which we walked past every morning on our way to school. It's such a hazy memory, yet I remember it was a woman's voice, a woman about whom people spoke in a way which, I could recognise even then, was odd, but the nuances of which I could not understand at the time. The real beginning however came when I was once again in Dharwad, decades later. I was invited to give a lecture in the university and I was staying with the Professor who had invited me and had organised my lecture. The morning after I got there, I woke up to a chorus of approaching voices. I sat up and looked through the window, but the tall humped compound wall prevented me from seeing the road, or anyone on it. I could not see even the tops of people's heads. There were just the voices raised in song. For some reason, it entered into me and stayed with me; it was an unforgettable experience. I did not speak to my hostess about it, nor did I ask her any questions. I never came to know who the singers were. At times, I wonder, did I really hear it, or was it an early morning dream? I don't think it was. Whatever the case, it was here that *Small Remedies* began.

This, too, was a novel with women as the main characters. It was the story of the singer Savitribai Indorekar; of Madhu, who was to be her biographer; of Madhu's aunt Leela and of Munni, Savitribai's daughter. These women occupied most of the space in my novel and my mind, in the years I wrote it. No, not quite all my mind, because once again there were minor characters with whom I got involved, much more so than I had with the minor characters in *A Matter of Time*. There was Joe, the doctor who married Leela, and took Madhu, her niece, into his home without a second thought when she lost her father. And Tony, who grew up only after his father's death, and who learnt what love was in his relationships with Rekha, his wife, with Leela, his stepmother, with Madhu, who was his — what? Stepsister? No, the two of them emphatically denied any sibling-like relationship. 'Brother and sister, indeed!' Tony says once, quoting Mr Knightley's words in *Emma*. (Like Hitchcock suddenly popping up in his movies, like El Greco coming into his own paintings, Jane Austen makes an appearance in most of my novels.)

And there were Hari and Lata, a young couple, Madhu's hosts when she went to live in Bhavanipur, while she wrote her commissioned biography of Savitribai; Hari and Lata who firmly told me that they were part of the story. 'I've fallen in love with your Lata,' an American man told me after he'd read *Small Remedies*. Me too, I wanted to say, but modestly didn't. Yes, Lata was one of those characters who developed in a way I'd never expected her to. Warm, impulsive, impetuous, seemingly light-hearted, yet capable of great love, she was, in spite of her slapdash ways, a great delight. And, of course, there was Munni, Savitribai's daughter and Madhu's childhood friend. Munni, who refused to accept the realities of her life, denied the fact that she was Savitribai's daughter by Ghulam Saab, the tabalji with whom Savitribai had walked out of her marriage. Munni resolutely lived out the fantasy life she created for herself, as the legitimate daughter of her mother and the wealthy Brahmin man Savitribai had walked out on. At times I wondered whether the novel was too crowded. But I knew, or rather sensed, that as long as everything blended into a whole, as long as the central thread remained intact, it would be all right. I have never had such a sense of harmony about a novel as I did about this one.

When a review spoke of *Small Remedies* as being a novel about middle-class women, I was enraged. Leela, who, after her husband's death taught in a municipal school in Bombay (one of the worst paid jobs then, perhaps even now); Leela who lived in a chawl, which meant an almost communal living, with communal toilets; Leela who became a trade unionist and worked among the factory workers in Bombay and was deeply involved with women of the working class; Leela, a Hindu widow who married Joe, a Christian – could this woman's identity be encapsulated into the term 'middle class'? And Savitribai, with her passion for music, a passion so great that she, a Brahmin woman, walked away from her marriage and with her Muslim tabalji, and single-mindedly pursued a career as a professional Hindustani classical singer – was she only a middle-class woman? Both these women were rebels, both ahead of their times, both of them uncaring of the world's mores, or what the world would say – can they be defined only as middle-class women? And there was Madhu, Leela's niece, to a great extent shaped by her, Madhu who was devastated by the death of her only son, Madhu who was writing a biography of Savitribai – was she only a middle-class woman? Was a woman to be defined only by the social class she belonged to? I have rarely, or maybe never, heard of anyone speaking of a male character in a man's novel as only 'a middle-class man'.

I have never lived so intensely in a novel as I did this one. I was wholly submerged in it. Many things happened, life went on, but nothing remains. Perhaps it was a compliment when a reviewer reviewed it as if it was the biography of a real musician. But when she asked, in the review, why I had not included some pictures of the singer, Savitribai, in the book, I was embarrassed for her. How could she not know it was a novel? Clearly, she had not read the book. Yes, there are pictures of Savitribai, I could have told her, but only in my head. I can see her, taanpura in hand, a small-made woman, very fair, dark sleek hair parted in the centre, a beautiful Chanderi sari, pearls round her neck.

This was a hard novel to write. Madhu's grief seeped into the novel, and sometimes, it seemed, even into me. Yet there were other characters, all of whom, even Savitribai's accompanists, the twins, saved me from the burden of grief. It was a novel of joy as well – joy in friendship, joy in love, in families and in music. When I came to the end, with Hasina singing a *vachana* (a devotional song) of Akka Mahadevi, a woman who lived centuries ago, for whom love meant love of God, it was as if I was laying down, not only Madhu's grief, but my own as well. The lines from the Upanishad, coming at the end of the novel, which told Madhu not to reject memory, but to embrace it, were life-affirming and a solace, not only to Madhu, but to me as well. I had travelled a long way from that single voice I had heard as a child going to school, to this end of a group of people responding to devotional music. A long way from the moment when I had, with great temerity, begun to write a story of passion – passion for music, passion for a son.

A few weeks ago, I was asked to speak to a group of senior citizens in a retirement home. At the end of my talk, a woman asked me: is it possible to inculcate compassion in the young? It is a quality that seems to be disappearing, living as we do extremely self-absorbed lives, the selfie being a symbol of it. I don't think, I said, that the quality needs to be cultivated; it is a part of us. It is because of our compassion for one another that humankind has survived so long on this planet. I have often thought of the kindness of strangers — something we experience in our lives at unexpected times and in unexpected ways — and how much it means. I remember how my husband was suddenly taken ill on a flight to Australia once, and how the woman seated behind me continually stroked my back, something which gave me much comfort at the time.

Compassion surrounds Madhu after her father and her son's deaths. In Bhavanipur, she finds her way out of her grief because of Lata and Hari, people she did not know when she came to live in their home. Lata breaks through Madhu's carapace of sorrow with her artless sincere affection and Hari brings Leela back into Madhu's life with his need to know more of his rebel aunt. And there is Tony, trying to pull Madhu back into the world with his great affection for her. Yes, there is compassion in the world in spite of the cruelty we see around us. And, ultimately, it is Madhu's own compassion for another, the widowed mother of the little boy she sees in a temple, which helps her come to terms with her grief. It is her memory of Joe, trying to comfort her after her father's death, that brings her back into life once again.

One of the reasons I had put off writing *Small Remedies* for so long was because I had to know something about music before I dared to write the novel. I had to learn enough of it to be able to write about Savitribai, for music was her passion and her world. In other words, I had to do some research, something I was, and still am, averse to doing.

> '...and indeed the recital of Events (except what I make myself) is uninteresting to me.'

Jane Austen's words. Fay Weldon, quoting them in *Letters to Alice*, exclaims, 'You see! The born novelist.' But Jane was only fifteen when she made this rather exaggerated statement. The novelist that she became knew better. She knew (or I suppose she knew) that you can't write a novel, or any other piece of creative writing, without taking facts into account. And therefore, in her novels, she wrote about the things she knew best – about the reality of the lives of spinsters (Miss Bates in *Emma*), of women's fears of remaining unmarried (the reason for Charlotte's acceptance of Mr Collins in *Pride and Prejudice*), of the thin line between a life of want and one of prosperity, which women can cross over only with a good marriage, which Fanny Price's aunt, Lady Bertram, in *Mansfield Park* did, while Fanny's mother got left behind in a life of want. And she wrote, as no writer of her time did, of incompatible marriages (the Bennets in *Pride and Prejudice*, Sir Thomas Bertram and his wife in *Mansfield Park* and, to a smaller extent, the Palmers in *Sense and Sensibility*). She knew the routine of country life very well and a little about London and Bath. And she stayed within the boundaries of her knowledge in her novels, which made them, not limited, but deeper and richer. She advised her niece, Anna, against venturing into unknown areas in the novel Anna was working on: 'We think you had better not leave England. Let the Portmans go to Ireland, but as you know nothing of the manners there, you had better not go with them. You will be in danger of giving false representations. Stick to Bath & the Foresters. There you will be quite at home.' Sensible advice which she followed herself. As she famously wrote to Anna, '3 or 4 Families in a Country Village is the very thing to work on.'

I told myself, very grandly, that the word 'research' was incompatible with fiction writing, but the truth is that I don't enjoy the thought of chasing facts. When I read the long list of acknowledgements at the beginning or end of a novel, I have a fleeting envy of writers who are able to talk to the right people and get the necessary information out of them. I find it hard to do this. I don't know how to ask anyone for information – I am incapable of small talk and it seems rude to immediately get down to business with someone who has been kind enough to make time for you. It is also very hard to let someone know what exactly it is you want, since you yourself do not know what that is. I can read up on any subject (and there's always Google now!), but quite often what one treasures are the little details that slip through in conversation. Luckily for me, my early novels needed very little of facts. But *Small Remedies* needed a good knowledge of music, Hindustani classical music, a very esoteric subject, full of technicalities, which a lay person cannot possibly know or understand. Since Savitribai was a musician, knowledge of music was important to me, her creator, for, without that I could not write about her. I have to know what my character knows, even if the knowledge is not used in the novel. And actually, very often, a large part of the information gathered is not used; it remains the foundation of the novel, the underpinning of it. Hemingway, who spoke of the principle of the iceberg also said, 'If a writer omits something because he does not know it, then there is a hole in the story.' And therefore research becomes necessary. But it is the part that should remain submerged.

To me, Georgette Heyer is a novelist who used the knowledge

she gathered for her fiction to perfection. Her husband pays a tribute to her meticulous and laborious research in an introduction to her last and incomplete novel, *My Lord John*. This is a novel about John Bedford, brother of Henry V, he who went wenching and taverning with Falstaff as the Prince of Wales in Shakespeare's play. The amount of facts she had to gather for this novel set in an earlier time must have been stupendous, yet at no time does the reader get a feeling that the novelist has researched. The facts are easily assimilated into the story. Whether it is her Regency romances, or historical novels like *An Infamous Army*, everything is just right – the clothes, the food, the habits, the houses and, above all, the language. For a reader to say, 'What excellent research!' means the writer has failed. The effort to acquire the knowledge and the knowledge itself must remain invisible.

For *Small Remedies*, I read up on music and musicians' lives, both in English and in Marathi (it was a revelation to see how few books there were on women musicians and how often they were just footnotes). I listened to music at home, I attended performances and I read reviews of programmes. I also listened to CDs that explained the basic concepts of Hindustani music, I bought dictionaries which explained musical terms. All this, until it seemed I was absorbing music through the very pores of my skin. I, who had run away from my music master once, now lived in the midst of music which filled my mind and ears as much as it did Savitribai's and her student, Hasina's life. It was through all this that Savitribai, who was becoming clearer as a ruthlessly ambitious, single-minded person, slowly evolved into Savitribai, the Gwalior gharana singer. In this novel I learnt the trick of research: to hold on tightly to the characters and to let the facts seep through them, through their lives. Never to introduce facts which are not relevant to the story. It is the rigorous logic of the novel that decides what has place in it. Facts are always subservient to this logic.

'A Damned Mob of Scribbling Women'

... this attempt on my part assumed that the filter which is a woman's way of looking at life has the same validity as the filter which is a man's way.

Doris Lessing, Introduction to *The Golden Notebook*

We are all very early risers in our family. For this reason, and also because in those days telephone calls were cheaper late at night and in the early hours, my sister and I had got into the habit of speaking to each other as soon as we woke up. Therefore, I knew when the phone rang one morning even before we had had our early morning tea that it was my sister, though, perhaps, it was a little earlier than usual. Her voice, too, was different and she began abruptly without any preliminaries.

'She's gone,' she said.

I didn't need to ask whom she meant, because we'd been talking a great deal about her the past few days.

'When?'

'Three in the morning,' she said and put down the phone. I knew she could not talk any more because she was crying. So was

I. Why did this young woman's death hit us, and so many others, so hard? For days we had watched the protests and the demonstrations on TV – women, men, girls, boys, young and old, all coming together on behalf of this dying girl. After her death, the protests intensified, the anger could barely be controlled, though the crowds were never violent. The police, however, didn't hesitate to attack the protestors with lathis and water jets. An indelible image of those days for me, is of a young woman being knocked down by a policewoman and lying still on the ground for a moment, her face registering her shock and disbelief. And then, springing up, and throwing herself at her attacker with a ferocity that took the policewoman by complete surprise.

What had brought about this upsurge of support for one young woman from so many people all over the country? Except for Anna Hazare's anti-corruption movement, which sadly fizzled out, I could think of no people's movement that had been as spontaneous and powerful, in the last few years. One of the reasons was, perhaps, the ugliness of the crime committed against her. It was not just rape, but gang rape, accompanied by an indescribable bestial cruelty. The girl's friend had been forced to watch what was being done to her, and after the four men were done with both of them, they had been thrown out of the moving bus, in which all this had happened. Thrown out on the road, as if they were trash for which these men no longer had any use. Part of the huge sympathy for the girl also came out of admiration; she had fought back fiercely, she had not given in. Even afterwards, when she was in hospital, she gave her dying declaration to the authorities, twice, in spite of the terrible state she was in. The sympathy partly came out of the persona of the girl herself, a girl who came from a rural area, from a family in very modest circumstances, and who was, with her own efforts and her parents' support, trying to move into a career and a better life, both for herself and her family.

But let me call the young woman who died by her name: Jyoti Singh. The media, in accordance with the policy of not naming a rape victim, spoke of her as Nirbhaya. They continued to call her Nirbhaya a year after her death, when Jyoti's parents and many others were agitating for a quick trial and maximum punishment for the rapists. It was then that Jyoti's mother, a woman of great dignity and courage, said, in response to a journalist who spoke of her daughter as Nirbhaya, 'My daughter's name is not Nirbhaya. Her name is Jyoti Singh.'

It was, so I think, a moment of great significance that marked the end of an era. An era, which considered that rape shamed the woman, not the rapist. More than two decades earlier I had written *The Binding Vine*, a novel that had come out of another rape, the rape of a young nurse, which had also sparked off public outrage. In my novel, the mother of Kalpana, the rape victim, insisted on not letting the world know that her daughter had been raped. And now, here was this woman saying, 'My daughter is Jyoti Singh.' I felt the goose bumps come up on me when I heard those words.

I have always considered rape to be one of the worst crimes that a human can commit against another. Lust-driven, yes; a violation of a woman's right to her body, yes; an assertion of male power, yes; of a male's right to possess the female body, yes. But more than these, and above all these, it is an expression of contempt and hatred for all women. The barbaric and savage things that had been done to Jyoti had filled everyone with horror and anger. This most intimate act between two humans – an act that expresses love and tenderness, and a desire for a complete union with another human being – how could it become an act of such violence and cruelty? How could anger and hate fuel an act that is supposed to be driven by love and desire? Rape can also be, and often is, a political act. I can never forget how shaken I was by a hard-hitting poem, written by a Marathi poet Neeraja, about two rapes. One, a rape of two Dalit women, a mother and daughter, who dared to stand up against upper caste pressures. The rapists were Maratha (upper caste) men. And the other, a rape by Dalit men of a young Maratha girl. Both the rapes were later used by the victims' communities for their own political purposes, used to show their strength, their power. As Neeraja's poem *From Khairlanji to Kopardi* says:

> 'You have pushed your political ambitions into her body/ fought battles and defeated your enemies/by playing the game between her thighs.'

Equally bad were the comments that came, after the outcry against Jyoti Singh's rape, from males from all over the country, especially politicians and those in responsible positions, blaming women themselves for rape, saying that women sent the wrong signals by the way they dressed/behaved/went out in the evenings/ spoke on mobile phones, etc. And therefore, when he was so provoked to lust by these things, what could a poor man do? 'Boys will be boys,' one national politician famously, or rather infamously, said. These statements too smacked of hatred of women. Men spend some of the best moments of their lives, some of the most tender moments of their lives, with women. So, where do these statements come from? Where does the hatred come from? And how can we expect men, whose minds are dark pits of such ideas and thoughts about women, to pass any laws which benefit women? Why would they pass a law which would allow women a proportional representation in Parliament? And I thought, a bleak thought, if neither laws nor society changed, what hope was there for women?

As a child, I had been blissfully unaware that being a girl made me a lesser person. Girls and boys were different; that was all. But, as I grew up, I saw that to be a female marked you out for a certain role in life, it meant that you lived within certain boundaries. I can still remember how, as a child, I had written my name in the gravel on the college grounds, enjoying the act of writing, of shaping my letters. Later, someone came and told my parents about it and I was chastised by my mother. How could I make my name public? I was bewildered. What was wrong with writing my name? In time, I began to realise the restrictions that hedged in females. Don't wear that dress, cover yourself properly, don't talk/laugh so loudly in public, don't sit that way with your legs apart, don't draw attention to yourself, don't argue so much, don't talk back, don't stay out late in the evenings, don't let boys touch you … The 'don'ts' were endless. A little less in some families, a little more in others, but the restrictions were always there. Even my sister and I, left so free otherwise, were firmly told that we had to be home before seven in the evening. I remember us running home, our hearts thudding in our chests, as the college clock in the tower marked the hour with seven loud booms. But the first time that being a female really impacted on my life was when my mother spoke of marriage and I understood that marriage was the necessary next step in life. Of course, families in India make the demand of marriage even of sons, but unmarried sons are not looked at the way unmarried daughters are. Unmarried girls are not only a burden on the family, they are a source of shame and humiliation, they are scorned, pitied. In my case, however, marriage loomed on the horizon mainly because I was clueless about what I would do with my life otherwise. And so I got married. Fortunately, my marriage was one of equals, of companionship, not of authority and subservience. (Though sometimes, rarely, I had to make this clear.)

Once having entered the married state, once having entered the circle of married women, my vision changed. I saw women's lives differently – women whom I had lived with and among, women whose lives I had taken for granted. I remembered an aunt who had been brought home when she was widowed two years after her marriage and who stayed within the house for a whole year. The first time she went out, she told me, she was so blinded by the bright light outdoors, she stumbled across the high threshold and fell, hurting herself so badly that she bled profusely. I don't remember why or when she told me this, but I remember how matter-of-fact she was when she said these things. And there was another aunt, who also came home as a widow, but with two children. A good-looking woman with sharp features and intelligent eyes, she, I was told, rumpled her hair after combing it, so that it would not look as if she cared about her appearance. I remember her as a bitter angry woman, taking her anger out on her son.

And there were two of my mother's aunts, both widowed as children. One was taken to Kashi to have her head shaven when she was only twelve, whereas the other escaped this dreadful fate, because her natal family stood up against this barbaric custom. Both these women were workhorses in the family, they lived all their lives in the service of the family. I remember one of these aunts had the duty of making early morning tea for the family. She sat patiently before the hissing Primus stove from early morning, making fresh tea for each person who came and sat down before her. It went on for nearly two hours. Fresh tea each time, even for us children. (Milky and sweet; surely nectar must have tasted like this?) And for herself, nothing. Certainly no tea. As a widow, she could not drink tea, one of the innumerable prohibitions she had to live with. I never thought of this then, but I do think of it now.

I also remember how both these aunts were sent to married daughters' homes, to help with deliveries. They looked after the mothers and newborns, knowing all the while that they themselves would never have a child. That they were much loved and cherished made some difference; yet the fact that their lives were bereft of any kind of enjoyment, and that they lived only for others, could not be escaped.

As with women, so with their writing. I consider it one of the strange ironies of my writing life that, when I began writing, I wrote what was in me, I wrote what came to me. And I did not think that I was writing about women, that my writing came out of the lives of women. In time, however, I became conscious that my writing was looked at in the same way that the women, about whom I was writing, were. They, and their lives, were less important because they were women. So, too, was my writing less important because of my gender, and because of the gender of my main characters. I was not just a writer, I was a *woman writer*, a woman writer who wrote about women. Perhaps the fact that most of my early writing was published in women's magazines slotted me further as a 'women's writer'. Why had I sent my stories to women's magazines? Had I unconsciously imbibed the truth that only these magazines would accept my stories? Whatever it was, being published in these magazines did me much good initially. They published almost all the stories I sent them. I am grateful to them, because they gave me a readership, which was to stand me in good stead in the years to come when I became a novelist. Being published also helped me to grow as a writer. I strongly believe that one has to be published and read before one can think of oneself as a writer. You see your own writing differently when it is in print. To put your work away in a drawer, to think of yourself as a genius, perhaps a misunderstood genius, can only stunt you as a writer.

But after some years of writing for women's magazines, I found myself getting restless, claustrophobic. My identity as a woman who wrote for *Femina* and *Eve's Weekly* seemed to stifle me. I wanted to move out, to get into the larger space outside. As a part of this attempt, I went to meet the editor of the magazine section of a Sunday newspaper (yes, they published stories at the time). I was accompanied by a neighbour who knew the editor well. While they conversed, the editor just flipped through the typed pages of my manuscript, scarcely glancing at them, and then asked me, 'Why don't you give this to a women's magazine?'

I don't remember what I said; I am sure I was polite, out of regard for my neighbour who had taken the trouble to arrange this meeting. But within me, I was raging, I was arguing with the editor: *I am being published in women's magazines, it is because I want to move out of them that I came here. How can you decide without even reading my story that it is fit only for a women's magazine? Is your newspaper only for men? Are your readers only men?*

Well, that was a long time ago, but I have never forgotten the incident. Never forgotten, either, what happened to another story of mine – the story about Amba, Princess of Kashi, which came to me after reading Irawati Karve's *Yuganta*, a brilliant analysis of the characters of the Mahabharata. I remember my father often said there were only two heroes in the Mahabharata: one, an old man, Bhishma, the patriarch of the Pandavas and the Kauravas, and the other a boy, Abhimanyu, Arjuna's young son. But Irawati Karve read Bhishma's character otherwise. To her, he was no hero, he was a man who had been callous towards women. Not deliberately cruel, but worse – indifferent to his own cruelty, almost unaware of it. Irawati lists the women whose lives he ruined: Gandhari, Kunti, Madri and the princesses of Kashi – Amba, Ambika and Ambalika. After reading Irawati Karve's version of Bhishma, I wrote a story about Amba. A spirited girl, Amba was in love with a prince, Salva, when she, with her two sisters, was abducted by Bhishma to marry his sickly younger brother, King Vichitravirya. When she told Bhishma about her love for Salva, he let her go. But Salva refused to accept her. He had fought

Bhishma after the abduction and had been defeated by him. Amba, he said to her, now belonged to Bhishma. Hearing of her love for Salva, Vichitravirya refused to marry her. In desperation, she asked Bhishma to marry her. He refused, saying he had taken a vow of celibacy. Three very honourable men indeed, but what about Amba? For her, there was nothing left but disgrace. And so she killed herself. In the Mahabharata she was reborn as Shikhandi, the man/woman who was destined to fatally injure Bhishma, because Bhishma would never fight with a woman, not even a 'half-woman'. This had no place in my story. In my story, Amba's act of killing herself was her final attempt to have some control over her own life.

It was with this story that I began to think of how words could mean entirely different things to different people, how language had been shaped by men to their needs, their ideas. It was a man's idea of honour that made Bhishma reject Amba when she asked him to marry her, and a man's idea of honour that made Salva reject her because he had been defeated by Bhishma. When I look back, I see that it has always been this concept of 'honour' that led to tragedies. A man's idea of honour made King Dasharath give in to his wife Kaikeyi's demand that Rama be exiled, a man's idea of honour that made Rama accept his father's diktat, a man's idea of honour that made Yudhishtira agree to gambling with Shakuni, which led to his losing himself, his brothers and his wife Draupadi in the course of the game. The splendid resistance by Draupadi, which we girls had so admired in school, was futile. A man had a right to do whatever he wanted with his wife.

Two magazines rejected my Amba story, one of them saying that readers would not know who any of these characters were (strange to think that books about mythology are now bestsellers). Finally, a journalist who believed that the story mattered, and who was working for a reasonably progressive newspaper, said she would use it, but only in the special women's page which came out once a week. I have problems with women's pages, women's hour on radio, or on TV (but not women's magazines, some might say. Ah, but I had no choice). Reluctantly, I agreed. When my story appeared, it was in such fine print it was almost unreadable. The journalist apologised to me, saying, that was all the space she had; and neither she nor I wanted to edit the story. So there it was, dwarfed and diminished – symbolic, I think now, of the place allotted to women's writing in the literary world.

I must have been naïve, indeed, not to have expected this, not to understand that, since women were less important, so was their writing, so was writing about them. From Dr Johnson, who compared a woman's preaching to a dog walking on its hind legs, to Nathaniel Hawthorne, who spoke derisively of 'a damned mob of scribbling women', to Walter Scott, who spoke slightingly, condescendingly, of the 'calculating prudence' of Austen's heroines, and the Nobel Prize winner, Sir Vidia Naipaul, who spoke of women's sentimentality and narrow view of the world, there never has been a shortage of males criticising women's writing. And, of course, there was the Donald Trump of American literature, Norman Mailer, who said, 'I doubt if there will be a really exciting woman writer until the first whore becomes a call girl and tells her tale.' (The implied comment, that the only story written by women which *he* would find exciting was a story written about women who provide men with sex, is very revealing!) He also said, 'A good novelist can do without everything but the remnant of his balls,' which a woman critic called a 'testicular definition of talent'! Enough women writers in the USA took him on, but did it make any difference to the thinking, the attitudes, I wonder. No, I am sure it didn't.

Writers are often asked the question: why do you write? They can only fumble and mumble when they have to give an answer.

But with a pen in their hand, they are able to give clearer and more explicit replies. According to Joyce Carol Oates, social injustice is one of the sources of the artist's work. A great many writers have echoed these words. But I don't think there is such a clear and direct connection; in fact, writing never comes out of clear and logical reasons. Writing emerges out of chaos, out of confusion, out of a troubled mind. I can bring up Max Müller's words about the need for a 'passion in life' and say that it is this passion which is the real driving force. I could say that I had a passion for justice, but it sounds too pompous and gives me a role larger than the one I have played. But I know that I was troubled by a feeling of a wrongness in the world about the way women were perceived, about the way they had to live their lives, about the way they were never given their due as thinking, independent human beings. This, along with my love of language, of words, of stories, of my interest in people's lives, led me to writing.

Later, I woke up to greater cruelties, like thoughtless and persistent violence, like coercion, like rape; these entered into my stories, into my novels, as much as the affection between men and women and the support they give each other did. Yet, it seemed there was something odd about writing about women and their lives, for all my writing life I have been asked, 'Why do you write about women?' I have been asked, 'Is your next novel also about women?' As if it is a vice, or a bad habit, which I will be able to shake off eventually.

An interviewer, questioning me as a part of the documentary he was making on me, went on with these questions, making me feel I was in the dock. Until I stormed out, tearing off my mike, and refused to go on with the interview. Behaving badly for, perhaps, the first time in my public life. And glad I was doing so. 'I was only trying to provoke you into saying more,' the man said. Damn it, I want to say to all those who ask these questions, writers write about people they know best, they write about things that trouble them. And so do I. It just so happens that, in my case, these people happen to be women, it just so happens that what troubles me are *their* lives. And there is one question of mine no one has ever answered: do you ask a male writer why his protagonists are almost always male? And why, when he writes about women, is he lauded for that fact?

Queen Mary of England (daughter of that famous wife-killer, Henry VIII) is supposed to have said that if they opened her up after her death, they would find the word 'Calais' written on her heart. She had felt the loss of Calais, the last bit of English territory left on French soil, so badly. There is one experience just as indelibly inscribed on my mind. A journalist from a national weekly was interviewing me when our little grandson, who was staying with us at the time, came in. Soon he got bored and walked out and the journalist and I resumed our talk. I thought we had had a serious conversation about writing and literature, but when the piece appeared in the magazine, it was headlined, 'Grandmother writes old fashioned way'. I'd said that I write my first drafts by hand, with a fountain pen. Something I still do. I have a great love of fountain pens and, at one time, had a collection of some of the finest pens – my one luxury. And this is what was made of the two things, of my having a grandson and of writing by hand: that I was a grandmother who wrote the 'old-fashioned way'. Was this all that I was?

I was angrier than I have ever been in my life, I was furious, I was livid. I wrote an angry letter to the magazine. (By the way, the magazine was *India Today*, at the time the most sold Indian magazine.) They wrote back, the usual response full of banalities, saying that they didn't mean any disrespect and so on. But the words that headed the piece were loaded with disrespect, they were insulting. And it was a professional slight, something I could never forgive. To bring a personal identity, the way they had, into a professional interview was just not done. Even more offensive was the fact that they didn't seem to understand, or perhaps pretended not to, that they wrote this insulting headline only because I was a woman. Writers, like all other humans, play their roles in life. Why are these roles emphasised in a professional context only when the subject is a woman? Would they have called a senior writer a grandfather, would they have headed an interview with him calling him a grandfather? I asked this question in my protest letter, a question they just ignored. In fact, some years later, when Doris Lessing won the Nobel Prize, a friend told me that a local paper had given the news item the headline: 'Nobel for a grandmother'!

There is, in my mind at least, no doubt that the word 'grandmother', when used in a professional context, is reductive of a woman's work. It takes away everything from her but the quality of 'grandmotherliness', evoking images of knitting, cooking, cuddling the kids, telling them stories and so on. Even if a woman does all these things, does it take away her intelligence, her capacity to think, to write? In fact, I have seen that women, as they grow older, begin to learn their strengths, to exercise their power. Gloria Steinem once said in a TV interview (these are not her actual words, just a gist of what she said) that, for women, to age is to be set free. That the feisty self, which women remember in the girls they were, comes back after their reproductive age is over. I think she got it absolutely right. Besides, to speak of my writing by hand was to make me seem a quaint old-timer, scribbling away, not a serious writer. I had clearly told the journalist that I did use the computer for the final drafts, but writing the first drafts by hand was what I liked, because I love the almost sensuous feel of a smooth thick nib gliding over smooth paper.

I am certain though – and this is a cheerful thought – that this will never happen to a writer who happens to be a woman today.

(Even the magazine which so belittled me now projects women's achievements!) Perhaps, because we have moved on, possibly, because women have become more savvy and made themselves unobtrusive by moving into writing genre books: crime fiction and romances. Or, even more possibly, because the generation after me lives in a world in which such things can no longer be blatantly said without a severe backlash. I am writing this at a time when women all over the world, specially in the USA, are coming out with stories of sexual assault, of sexual harassment from men who had power over them. Men in positions of power are falling like ninepins because of these accusations. A Minister in the British Cabinet (I think) gave an honest apology, saying that he was sorry, but at the time it happened, he had no clue that what he was doing was wrong. It shows how men, who had power over women, thought it quite okay to paw a woman, to make lewd comments, to demand sexual favours. All these things were acceptable. Hopefully, men will now be more careful and women will no longer remain silent.

I remember when I was in hospital after my first son's birth, I was alone for a brief time in my room. A man appeared at the door, mumbling something, asking, I thought, for another room, another patient. But his blank face seemed to force my eyes lower, to see what his hand was doing. I screamed and rang the bell. By the time someone came, he had escaped. I remember how, along with fear, there was a kind of shame, I felt soiled; I could not talk to my parents about it. Now women are talking. #Metoo has brought out innumerable stories of women sexually assaulted by powerful men, specially in Hollywood. When I think of it, it seems absolutely amazing that a great movement against the physical and emotional abuse of women has come from Hollywood, the home, supposedly, of 'dumb blondes' and casting couches. The casting couches, we see now, were real, but dumb blondes the women are certainly not. For, women actors have suddenly opened up, they have begun making public their stories of being abused. *Time* magazine has named these women, 'Persons of the Year'. It will be a great step forward if men understand that it is no longer okay to take any liberties with women. I have seen a man casually put an arm round a woman's shoulder, I have seen the woman flinch, but say nothing. I want to scream, for God's sake don't touch her, for God's sake, push him away, shout at him. But I don't. The rules of civilised society stop me. And so many of us. Not much longer, I hope. It is indeed progress if what was looked at as being quite permissible has been shown up to be an ugly misuse of power.

Going back to literature and the literary world, I remember what a fellow jury member said, many years ago, during the course of our discussion on the short-listed books given to us. Speaking of a book of short stories, he said they were, 'women's magazines stories', his words and tone showing his contempt (by the way, they were good stories). 'I beg your pardon,' I could not help saying, 'I began my writing with stories in women's magazines.' It put him on the defensive and he tried to excuse himself, but he had said what he really thought. Today, political correctness will not allow anyone to say such things. A happy thought is that perhaps I am a fossil now, a relic of those bad old times when a woman who wrote could be called 'woman writer' and thus disposed of – like William James' crab. A favourite quote of mine, this one. 'A crab,' William James says, 'would be outraged if it could hear us class it, without ado or apology, as a crustacean and thus dispose of it. *I am no such thing*, it would say. *I am myself, myself alone.*' (Italics mine.) I hope that there are no longer writers designated as 'women writers' as I once was. So is it time then to 'stop moaning', as a friend told me sharply once?

But if I am moaning, there are a great many moaners in the literary world. Why, otherwise, do I read so many articles by women writers and journalists about the attitude to women's writing? And this, not in India, but in the Western world. In India, we put up with it. I don't know how many women 'gnash their teeth and ball their fists' (the words of Gauri Deshpande) in private, but few talk or write about it. Kamila Shamsie, the Pakistani writer, speaking of a discussion she attended on 'The Crisis in American Fiction' (with only one token woman on the panel), says that no woman writer was mentioned throughout the discussion, except Eudora Welty – and she, only once. Annie Proulx, Marilynne Robinson, Anne Tyler, Joyce Carol Oates, Donna Tartt were ignored as if they did not exist. 'The crisis in American fiction,' Shamsie adds tartly, 'is that there are no women in it.'

Hilary Mantel, in an article on the writer Elizabeth Jane Howard, comments on how Howard's husband's work was privileged, while hers was incidental, 'to be fitted around a wife's natural domestic obligations'. Her husband was the very famous British writer Kingsley Amis, of *Lucky Jim* fame. But Howard was no mean novelist herself. Yet, she is almost forgotten. 'The real reason why her books are underestimated – let's be blunt – is that they are by a woman,' says Hilary Mantel. Even more damning to me was the comment of an Orange Prize judge that men don't read women's writing because they are about 'small domestic issues'. (The Orange Prize, a women-only literary prize, has changed sponsors and names so many times, it reminds me, yet again, of Virginia Woolf's comments on men's colleges and women's colleges – on the wealth of one and the poverty of the other. Now the prize is called the Women's Prize for Fiction.)

Speaking of small and big themes, I must bring in Walter Scott who, after Jane Austen's death, wrote about her, saying, 'The Big Bow-Wow strain I can do myself like any now going; but the exquisite touch, which renders ordinary commonplace things and characters interesting, from the truth of the description and the sentiment is denied to me.' A very honest admission. And this, after his earlier patronising comments on *Emma*, written at the publisher's behest. But perhaps Scott was at that time influenced by the publisher, Murray's, gratuitous statement in his request letter that *Emma* 'wants incident and romance, does it not?' (According to Austen's biographer, Claire Tomalin, this remark consigns Murray 'to that circle of the Inferno reserved for disloyal publishers'!) However boring I think Walter Scott's novels were, however much he had annoyed me with his comment on Jane Austen's *Emma*, I love his phrase 'the Big Bow-Wow strain'. Puts the idea of 'big theme' in its place. There is also a prevalent idea that writing about the family, or rather, setting your story or novel within the family, automatically makes it a novel about 'small domestic issues'. Whereas, in my opinion, the family is the greatest influence in our lives, in all human life, because it is here we begin to see the world and learn about it. It is in the family that we learn about love and affection, about envy, hostility and hatred, about winning and losing, about sharing and generosity and meanness. Anne Enright, a Booker Prize winner, calls the family 'a hugely interesting place, a place where stories happen'. But when it comes to literature, this is not how the family is looked at. Though, it seems that when a man writes of family, it becomes 'microhistory'! The words of reviewer, Sam Tanenhaus, on Jonathan Franzen's *Freedom*.

Putting aside the matter of small and big issues, which has been so much debated (though one would have thought Virginia Woolf's *A Room of One's Own* had successfully put an end to all arguments on this subject), I have to say that I know from my own experience that it is true that men generally don't read books written by women. So many men have come to me with a book to sign, saying, 'This is for my mother/wife/sister/daughter/friend.' This hurts, because it means that I lose one half of my readers at one stroke. It hurts because this has nothing to do with my writing, but only with my gender, with the gender of my characters. These doom me, it seems, to being regarded as a less significant writer.

Many years ago, I wrote an article which I rather mischievously titled, in a parody of academic papers, 'How to Read, or Rather, How Not to Read the Writing of Women'. The problem is that, brainwashed by ages of thinking of women as lesser humans, of their lives as less significant, consisting as they do of 'trifles' like family, love and romance, of regarding women's thinking as emotional and less rational, men are unable to read women's writing the way they should. The truth is that men, as well as women, use both their intellect and their emotions when they write; to write fiction, you need both.

When I read Naipaul's words that Jane Austen wrote sentimental rubbish, I was sure he had never read her. He accepted the contemporary idea of her, of what TV serials and films have made of her — a romantic writer, because the romance is highlighted in the serials and movies based on her novels. But the lady was a hard-headed practical woman. Look at the openings of two of her novels:

Pride and Prejudice: 'It is a truth universally acknowledged, that a single man in possession of a good fortune must be in want of a wife.'

Emma: 'Emma Woodhouse, handsome, clever, and rich, with a comfortable home and happy disposition, seemed to unite some of the best blessings of existence ...'

Jane Austen wrote about money, because she knew how important money was. She wrote of marriage because it was the only career open to women then. It was not sentimental women's romance stuff at all. Clearly Sir Vidia had not read her.

Novel after novel, I kept hoping that my work would be recognised, not as being about women, but about the predicament of human beings. It never seemed to happen. With *Small Remedies,*

I was more hopeful. It was a novel about human beings daring to find their place in the world according to their inclinations and talent, not according to the role allotted to them. The book got some very good reviews and I also got a lot of personal appreciation from readers who knew me and many who didn't. It then got on the shortlist of a newly instituted Indian literary award. The sponsor persuaded me to go to the final event, where the winner would be announced. I don't like these things; competition always makes me uncomfortable. But I was persuaded to go. The organisers/sponsors were keen on making the event a big one, they hoped the award would be an Indian version of the Booker. It was a well organised function and there was quite a satisfactory buzz in the hall when I got there. There was also a great deal of security, because the ex-Prime Minister, Narasimha Rao, was to come. Perhaps, his book was on a shortlist; I have no idea why he was there. As I was entering the hall, a journalist asked me, 'Who do you think will get the award?' Instinctively, unthinkingly, I said, 'Amitav Ghosh', whose *The Glass Palace* was on the shortlist. I wonder why I said that. It was not a modest disclaimer of my own chances, it was what I truly felt. His was a historical novel, a novel on a large canvas; I knew that this novel would be considered more prize-worthy. Ultimately it didn't get the award; I don't remember which book did. *Small Remedies*, of course, didn't. I thought then, and still do, that this was because it centred round women's lives. One of the three judges wrote to me later, to tell me that he thought my novel should have got the prize, but … A jury member of another prize also came to me to tell me that he felt my novel should have got the award, but …

Yes, *but* …

Having been on juries myself, I know how it is. Prizes are quite often arrived at through a process of 'compromise and negotiation,' as Hilary Mantel said. I read a piece by her about a time before she got the Booker, in which she confessed to a tremendous lowness of spirits each time she was on a shortlist, for she never got the award. She did finally get the Man Booker Prize, not once, but twice, for *Wolf Hall* and *Bring Up the Bodies*. But as one article by Francine Prose pointed out, she had a man at the centre of her story: Thomas Cromwell. Write about a man if you want an award, the article said, adding, men have been at the centre of stories since Homer; they set the template. All very true and difficult to change. At least in the near future.

However, the world is changing. And I believe that this century will be the century of women. I hope so, anyway. The world has changed because of feminism. I hesitate to use the word, it is so loaded and carries such a baggage of negativities. But which other word can I use for all the various factors and agents that have brought about changes in women's perception of their own selves, their own lives. A great impetus to this change has been an easier and surer method of contraception: the little magic pill which women had been waiting for since, I imagine, the first woman dreamt of a life free of endless childbearing, free of the fear of dying during childbirth. I was lucky that the pill came into my life at the right time. The American writer Sara Paretsky says (in *Writing in an Age of Silence*), 'It was my good fortune to come of age when America became a land of great possibilities and opportunities.' I was also lucky I began writing at a time when feminism was just beginning to be acknowledged as a legitimate ideology, when it was acquiring, even if very slowly, a modicum of credibility.

It has not been a smooth journey. Progress for women has always been one step forward and two steps, or even three steps, backward. But one thing is certain: we can never go back to the point when the prejudices, the unfairness, the assumption of women's inferiority, were taken for granted. Winifred Holtby, an English writer, said she would be happy when the word feminism would no longer be used because it was no longer necessary. So, too, I hope that a time will come when 'women's day', 'women's page', 'women's hour' will become as extinct as an honest politician is today. It will mean that women are finally recognised as people. No more 'Thirty people, *including* ten women and children' kind of a headline. Why 'including', I've always wondered; doesn't 'people' include women? When, recently, I was invited to inaugurate a conference of women writers, I refused for many reasons. And I thought, invite me when you have a male writers' conference; invite me then and I will inaugurate it with pleasure.

And yet, even if I am glad that I have been a part of the chain of events that led to this point, some things still rankle. The greatest irony of my writing life has been that I, who hated stereotypes, because to me they spell mental laziness, I, who wanted to get rid of the stereotypes of women I saw in literature, have become a stereotype myself. A middle-class woman writing about other middle-class women. At times, I felt like I was carrying my identity of 'middle-class woman writer' like Sindbad, the sailor, carried the Old Man on his back. And now age has entered the stereotype. I have been asked, gently, so as not to hurt my delicate old-lady feelings, whether I am on email, whether I use the computer. (Evoking for me that deadly image of the grandmother who wrote the old-fashioned way.) I was using a computer when you were still in diapers, I want to say. But I refrain. I have learnt to ignore minor pinpricks. After all, these young people mean well.

A very happy memory is of a professor in a university in Sydney hosting four of us Indian writers, three of us women. As usual, we three women were offered orange juice, though glasses of wine were circulating. (This happens all the time in India as well. Seeing me – a woman of my age, and in a sari – soft drinks are invariably held out.) 'Thank you,' I said, when the orange juice came to me. 'I haven't come all the way to Australia to drink orange juice.' The professor took me in, all five feet of sari-clad, bindi-decorated woman and said, 'Bang! There goes a stereotype.' That's how stereotypes need to be dealt with! Recently, when an image of Indian women scientists in silk saris, with flowers in their hair, celebrating the successful launch of a satellite, went viral, I had the same thought as the Australian professor, 'Bang! There goes a stereotype!'

What is most troubling about the diminished valuation of women's writing is that it is possible for a writer to lose confidence in her own writing. To write, to write fiction specially, one needs immense confidence in oneself, in what one is saying. To write what may never find a publisher, or even if published, get lost in the crowded market place of the literary world, and therefore remain unread, unappreciated – this is what all fiction writers need to be prepared to cope with. But to know that what you write, because of your gender, because of the gender of your main characters, dooms you to being considered automatically a less significant writer, is even more damning. If men don't read my novels, I think in some of my worst moments, surely there is something wrong with my writing? Commonsense soon asserts itself and reminds me that there are so many novels by men I cannot read, not because they have been written by men, but because they are not *my* kind of novels. But how does one deal with a prejudice which judges the writing and slots it without even reading it? Confidence remains dented. And without this confidence, there can only be, in Orhan Pamuk's wonderfully true words, 'a troubled optimism scarred by the anger of being consigned to the margin.'

At times, I think of the short story writers and poets I read when I had just begun writing – women, whose writing I had enjoyed, some of whom I had admired. What happened to those writers? I never heard of them, or saw any writing by them, in later years. So many of them just disappeared, they vanished. What happened? Did they have only that much of writing in them? A limited talent? Or did they draw back from the total commitment which writing, or any art, demands? Did they feel that such a commitment would come in the way of their duties to their family? Because, for a woman to take any other work with seriousness, was a kind of threat to the family, to society itself, to the way it was organised. Or, were they forced to look at themselves, as mere amateurs, dilettantes, their writing only a hobby, if a good one? Easier to go along with the general idea than to go on fighting it. (I remember telling a newly married niece who wanted to take up a job, but was worried about her in-laws' reaction, 'Nobody is going to support you. If you do this, it will be in spite of others, not with their support. If you want it badly, go ahead and deal with the reactions later.') And, therefore, did they find it easier to succumb to the idea that women need hobbies, not commitments? In those days, the dreadful word 'hobby' hovered over all women's activities which were not part of their family duties. I wish I had counted the number of times I have been told that writing is a good hobby. Hobby? If I had wanted a hobby, I'd have chosen something else, not an activity which made such difficult demands on me.

Writing is hard work, steady work, disciplined work. There is an idea that writing comes out of inspiration, followed by quick and totally satisfying stints of writing. I wish it happened this way. It does happen, but very, very rarely. Brief flashes of illumination can't make an entire novel. The novel needs substance, body to hold these flashes together. This can only come through steady work, through constantly struggling to get where you want to. It means rewriting and rewriting *and* more rewriting, so that often you are sick of your own work. It means deleting, not only words, sentences and passages, but at times huge chunks you have worked hard at writing. But as far as I was concerned, it mattered to me to write, and as I later found out, it mattered to many of my readers to read what I wrote. In spite of all these things, that so many women did write, that they continued to write and to be published, in spite of knowing that their gender doomed them to being regarded as less important writers, shows a kind of courage which has to be admired.

Along with the curiosity about writing, there is a massive ignorance about it. 'Are you still writing?' I am often asked. As if it is something you can take up when you want and give up just as easily. You don't ever give it up, not until it gives you up. The first blurb of *That Long Silence* called Jaya a failed writer. I think she was not a failed writer, but a writer who never began. A writer who refused to take herself seriously. Who hid her talents, soft-pedalling, tiptoeing, whispering, so as not to hurt anyone. Deliberately giving her writing a touch that said, 'Don't take me seriously.' Which is infinitely worse than trying and failing. I had read Milton's *On His Blindness* in school, in which he speaks of 'that one talent which is death to hide/ lodged within me useless'. I now understand what Milton was saying. Yes, it is death to hide the talent you have. To silence yourself, for whatever reason. As Jaya did. As I never did.

This sounds too self-congratulatory, too smug, something I detest. What I am really saying is that I consider it my greatest achievement that I never gave up. All the putting down, the snubbing, the ignoring, the marginalising, the patronising, the slotting, did not stop me from going on with writing what I wanted to write. At times, I felt like Dickens' Dr Manette from *A Tale of Two Cities*, imprisoned in the Bastille of women's writing, women's issues, writing, supposedly, about suffering and victim women. (God help me!) Often, I am exasperated by the blindness to the fact that there are many feisty, spunky women among the galaxy of female characters I have created. There is Mira, whose wings were clipped, but who continued to sing, Leela and Savitribai, who went on to do what they wanted to do, uncaring of the world and its rules. I wrote of Jiji, to whom, as a girl, her family was the world, but who had the courage to break away from them when the time came, to stand on her own feet and remake and reshape her life. I wrote about Devayani, whose moral strength was tried to its utmost when she fell in love with a married man. There is Sumi, who quietly set about making a new life for herself and her daughters after her husband left her. And Kalyani, who emerged triumphantly out of her victimhood, surprising even me, her creator. I wrote of older women who challenged the stereotypes, like Belinda and Kasturi. Of younger women who did the same, like Aparna and Jyoti (in fact, I named Jyoti of *Strangers to Ourselves* after Jyoti Singh, a tribute to her). I wrote of thinking, questioning women like Jaya, Urmi, Aru, and so many more, women capable of fighting their own battles. I see none of them as victims, or as poor suffering women. Meenakshi Mukherjee, a critic whom IWE sorely misses, once wrote of how the critics had made me a 'champion of oppressed women', because they could find no other place for me in the post-*Midnight's Children* literature. Authors, to their chagrin but ultimately, as they realise, for their own good (it's a waste of energy), cannot respond to criticism. But if the characters in my books could respond, I am sure many of these women would stand up and ask: 'A victim? Who? Me?' And, perhaps, quote William James' words: 'I am myself, myself alone.'

After I had written *The Dark Holds No Terrors*, I realised that to write is to know the power in yourself, it is to defeat powerlessness. It is like Asterix drinking the magic potion: you can feel your muscles grow. Once having gained power, once having freed myself, so to say, there was no way I would renounce this power. I had to go on writing.

Inter Alia

The writer ... may not have realised on first putting pen to paper, where it would all end.

Fay Weldon, *Letters to Alice: On First Reading Jane Austen*

BY THE TIME *SMALL REMEDIES* came out, I was very tired. It had been a decade of a huge amount of work. Apart from three major novels, I had written some commissioned short stories and edited an English translation of my father's two books on the Gita (it had meant almost rewriting them). I had written many articles and essays for newspapers and I had given a number of lectures, which, as far as I am concerned, involve a lot of preparation and reading.

I had also done something I had never expected to do – I had written the script and the screenplay for a Hindi feature film. The well-known film director Govind Nihalani, after reading *The Dark Holds No Terrors*, thought I would be the right person to write the script and screenplay of a movie he was thinking of making. Which is how I got a phone call one day, and a strange voice asked me whether I was Shashi Deshpande, the novelist. And so the offer came to me. I accepted it, partly out of curiosity – could I work for this medium? – partly because of Govind Nihalani's reputation and my own regard for him as a film-maker and partly because, at the time, I was unable to write anything at all. It was a time when my husband had just undergone a cardiac bypass surgery. The procedure was in its infancy in India then and recovery was slow and painful. Our sons had come for the surgery, but had had to go back to their work and studies and I had to shoulder everything on my own. Obviously, writing took a back seat. To get back into writing was not going to be easy. Writing the film script did help; it also gave me the new experience of witnessing the shooting when we were in Bombay. It seemed incredibly tedious, the same line being said over and over again, because the actor who was speaking this line didn't get it quite right. Eventually, Dimple Kapadia, who was playing the main role and to whom this line was addressed, threw a minor tantrum. I saw Nihalani trying to placate her and encourage the other woman at the same time. I thought then that, of all the art forms, this must be the most difficult, since the director had to work out his idea, his vision, through so many people. Such a contrast to the solitariness of writing. One thing I knew when I had finished writing the script and screenplay, was that this work was not for me. Despite the fact that the movie, *Drishti*, won a National Award, I would never do this again. The clarity about what I could do and what I could not do has, thankfully, never deserted me.

Squeezed somewhere in the midst of all these activities were trips to Australia, the USA, South Africa and Italy. I would visit Australia twice more after this, to literary festivals in Melbourne and Adelaide, but this first visit was the most memorable because it was the worst organised (a trip which goes smoothly is rarely remembered). We were a delegation of four writers, writing in different languages: Bengali, Oriya, Tamil and English. We had been chosen to visit Australia as part of an India-Australia friendship project. We were to visit four cities – Brisbane, Sydney, Melbourne and Perth. Right from the word go, it was obvious that there was a major misunderstanding about who we were and why we were there. Not only were we put up separately in different Indian homes, the organisers had obviously not thought of what we would do when we got there. There were no literary events at all. Like all tourists, we saw kangaroos and listened to aboriginal music. This was not what we had come for! On our last day in Brisbane we rebelled and told the Australian gentleman who was escorting us that, unless we were put up in a hotel in Sydney, and unless we could attend literary events and meet Australian writers, we would fly back home. We'd just heard that the Indian cricket team was staying in one of the most expensive hotels in Sydney. Of course, as writers, we did not expect that kind of treatment, but certainly we could not be shunted off to people's homes. Our various hosts had been kind, but we had heard that they had been coerced into hosting us!

The organisers obliged and in Sydney we were finally put up together in a hotel. However, it was the weekend and we were left high and dry. In desperation, we rang up the Indian Consul, who responded splendidly. He sent us a car and a driver to tour the city, he had a party for us in the evening and, what was even better, got us our daily allowance, which had been withheld from us for some reason. I have found most of the Ambassadors and other Indian representatives I met in foreign countries to be very good. This one really saved our lives. But there were still no literary programmes for us. I had one radio interview, during which the interviewer asked me, in a very patronising manner, whether I did yoga and whether I cooked curry for my husband! That was the level of his knowledge about the person he was interviewing. And about India, as well. Even our Australian escort, who had been waiting outside and had heard the interview, was indignant on my behalf.

This was not all. We were supposed to visit an Indian fair, which was one more facet of the India-Australia bonhomie, of which our visit was a part. We were supposed to read there, competing, I think, with snake charmers and mehndi-appliers! I refused to read, but two of our group did. I thought it was very brave of them. On our last evening, we were taken to a café for a reading. We were told this was a place where reputed writers read, and that Vikram Seth had just done a reading here. We were very pleased. When we got there, our escort for the evening, a young man, left us at a table with huge glasses of wine and went around from table to table saying something. In a little while, most of the customers left, and we heard, to our horror, that people were supposed to pay for the 'privilege' of hearing us read. Obviously they all left, except two tables which sportingly stayed on, listened with interest, and even asked Mallika Sengupta, who read out her poetry in translation, to read the original Bengali. They loved it, it salvaged the evening. But it was our young escort (slightly alarmed when he found us walking unsteadily – no, it was NOT the wine!), who saved the rest of our Australia trip. We had come to know that he was the son of an Australian poet, Judith Rodriguez. She lived in Melbourne and he told her about us.

From then on, things changed. Judith took charge of us in Melbourne and we met writers, visited bookshops, colleges. She took us around Melbourne, a place she knew and loved. Judith is one of the greatest treasures I found during my visit to Australia, she is still in touch and as warm and generous as ever. Thanks to the literary grapevine, we met writers and had literary meetings, not only in Melbourne, but in Perth as well, where the writers had been told by Judith about our arrival. Our Australian visit had started off as a potential damp squib, but thanks to Judith, it turned out to be a visit where I had the most contact with writers, a place whose informality delighted me. I think this was the first time I realised that I belonged to the family of writers. Suddenly, when we met writers, we seemed to be among our kind, among people who spoke the same language. I was later invited to the Melbourne and the Adelaide festivals, and during my three visits I came to know how similar the Australian writers' problems were to ours – I mean, Indians who wrote in English. Their novels had to be published in the West to be truly appreciated, too! I had heard of Patrick White, though I found him tedious when I tried to read him. The only Australian book I had read was the best-seller *The Thorn Birds*. I knew nothing of many much better writers, who could not get foreign publishers, since there were 'no kangaroos' in their books. Perhaps we Indian writers were better off because India has a large readership at home. After my first visit, I came home with a collection of Australian short stories, one of poetry, and some crime novels, and I got a glimpse of a literature which deserved to be more known, more read. Sadly, all books don't travel. Only best-sellers do. No, that's not right. They become best-sellers because they travel. So there's something else that makes for their success. A kind of shaping for the global market, perhaps?

South Africa, when I visited it, was still a country with a troubled soul. We were horrified by the high crime rate in Johannesburg, by the electrified barbed wires surrounding houses of the wealthy, and the warning never to roll down the glass of the windows of our cars. This was, of course, not too long after apartheid had been done away with and perhaps things are better now. Cape Town, however, remains a vivid memory. A city in which I saw all the shades of colour that human beings can have. It made nonsense of race and colour prejudice; all the colours are beautiful. One had to admire whatever it was that had made such a variety of skin colours possible. Cape Town was a beautiful city; the two oceans, the dolphins, the Table Mountains in the background, the wonderful vineyards, and the wine made it absolute heaven! Of course, there was the slave-auction platform still left to remind people of the past, a dreadful memory, this one. Nevertheless, the thought that it was the past and that such a thing would not happen again was a cheering thought.

The USA visit was a lecture tour, the invitation for which came from Janet Powers, an American academic, who had been with her students in the American College in Madurai for an entire semester. She had heard me talk and she not only invited me, she made up the itinerary. It was a hectic tour, from the East Coast to the West Coast and then back again to Philadelphia, taking in universities all along the way: Berkeley, St John's, Gettysburg, Western Maryland, Franklin & Marshall, Rutgers and West Chester. We had a break for a few days in Detroit, where our younger son, Vikram, and his wife were then living. It was good to be home for a few days, but the city has left dreadful memories. The centre of the city was unoccupied, as if the core of it had been gouged out; our son told us that people had moved away to distant suburbs. He also said that the majority of cases which came to the hospital were of overdose of drugs, or of stab and gunshot wounds. Baltimore too had this kind of a ghost city centre. Baltimore was for me the city of Anne Tyler, one of my favourite American writers; it is the city in which all her novels are located. To me, it was populated with Anne Tyler's characters and it was sad to see it looking the way it did. In California I had seen people scrounging among trash bins, looking for leftovers in discarded pizza cartons – this was the underbelly of a most prosperous country. The ghost of Steinbeck's *The Grapes of Wrath* was still around, it seemed.

The lectures in the universities are all blurred now, they seem to dovetail into one another. I do remember, though, that where the teacher was good and enthusiastic, the students were eager and sharp. I was surprised by the informality of things. Students sat any which way during the lectures, some of them ate as they listened (I was told it was because they had sacrificed their lunch hour for this lecture), but they were receptive, curious and questioning. I rarely saw this in Indian students at that time; teachers had to coax them to talk, to ask questions. In Gettysburg, where Janet Powers taught, I would be lecturing to her students for a week. Best of all, they had given us a little place to live in for the week. It was a joy to live in this tiny 'home', even if it was only for a week, a home which, in spite of its size, had everything we needed. Gettysburg for me, like it is for everyone, was Abraham Lincoln. Recently an interviewer asked me who was the person I most admired. He was surprised when I said Lincoln. He had expected me to say Gandhi, I think.

Actually, there is much in common between the two men (both had a great sense of humour, for one), but Gandhi was surrounded by people who loved and admired him, whereas Lincoln had to face great hostility during his life. Both of them were assassinated. For me, Lincoln's Gettysburg address is one of the most remarkable pieces of writing; it has a Biblical simplicity and grandeur. Janet was a wonderful host and took us around the battlefields. She also took us to Washington. I remember she showed us the Pentagon, saying, this is where all the evil plots are hatched. I had to laugh. Janet was a pacifist and still continues to actively agitate against all wars, supporting the victims of war, wherever they may be, specially women. In Washington we saw the Arlington cemetery and the Vietnam Wall, a unique memorial which looks like a great plea against war, a cry against the loss of young lives.

I was exhausted when our trip was over. I had been unwell before leaving and had worked hard for nearly six months writing out all my lectures. Later, I had friends asking me why I took so much trouble; they told me that most people prepared one lecture and rehashed it in different ways for different places. I could not have done that. I have a very low boredom threshold, and to give the same lecture, even if slightly changed, in different places would have bored me to death. I had been very apprehensive about lecturing in so many places to unknown audiences. I always find public interaction a strain. It drains me, I have a strange feeling that I am losing bits of myself. I remember the first few times I had to talk to an audience, I had had to take something to calm myself, to reduce the anxiety. It must have been a tiny dose, because I don't remember ever falling asleep, head on table, during a meeting.

Fay Weldon, in her book on Jane Austen, *Letters to Alice* (one of the most unusual books on Jane Austen, and one I think all aspiring writers should read), says, 'The writer ... may not have realised, on first putting pen to paper, where it would all end.' So true. Had I ever imagined when I began writing that I would go all over the country, around the world, lecturing, meeting people, in fact having a kind of public life? 'Imagine Jane Austen talking at the Assembly Hall, Alton, on "Why I wrote Emma".' Fay Weldon again. Indeed, that was a simpler time which would have suited me better, because all that I wanted to do was to write and be published – and, hopefully, earn some money from my writing. And, when I began writing, I had absolutely no idea that I would have to interact with the public. How could I, who had run away as a child when I heard the sound of the gate, which meant a visitor, imagine myself coping with meeting strangers and interacting with them? Young writers of today are better prepared for such things, I think, and I envy them their confidence and blasé attitude. Though, for all I know, they too may be quaking inside. But I learnt, gradually, to cope with all these things. Still it never comes easy, no, not even today, when I am such a veteran.

There was one more stop waiting for us after our USA trip. I had a lecture in Zurich, another lecture organised through Janet. This talk was to be in the Zurich Museum and we would be staying with the organiser, Chandra Holm, in her home in Baden. Chandra, we came to know – one more coincidence to wonder about – was also from Bangalore. Her early life had been lived in Ramnagar, of *Sholay* fame, with the rocks among which Gabbar lived and where Hema Malini danced with bleeding feet. Married to Kurt, a physicist, Chandra was a mathematician, and worked closely with the Zurich Museum. She got Indian musicians, writers and Indian art historians invited to the place. We were very happy to be staying with her in Baden – another beautiful and serene little place, like Freiburg. My Zurich lecture was almost a catastrophe. I had lost the text of my speech for Zurich somewhere along the way. Once I realised this, Chandra settled me down with paper and pen and I tried to reconstruct the lecture I had written. I was still working on it the next day when, from the small room I had been shown into, I could hear the audience arriving. It was a large audience. Thankfully, my lecture, last-minute creation though it was, went off well. Later, it became the Afterword to my collection of short stories based on characters from the myths, *The Stone Women*, and, even later, became a text for some colleges.

I came back from the USA, sure I never wanted to see an airport or eat a flight meal, ever again. But even as I was coping with a mountain of unwashed clothes and piles of correspondence, I got a call from an unknown female voice with an accent I couldn't exactly identify, but which sounded like Sonia Gandhi's, and was therefore, I guessed (rightly) Italian. She told me she was a publisher and that she had published an Italian translation of *The Dark Holds No Terrors*, that it was being released in two months and would I go to Rome for it? I said no, but she was persuasive, too persuasive for me; I'd like anyone to say 'no' to this young woman, Marina, who bombarded me with phone calls, with faxes. One night I watched in disbelief as the fax machine kept spewing out an endless roll of paper. This was the contract for *That Long Silence*, which she would bring out soon after *The Dark Holds No Terrors*.

I went. It was an amazing visit, and the most amazing part of the visit was Marina herself. She was very sophisticated and much younger than I had imagined. I have never seen anyone as driven as she was. Obviously, she was just starting her career as a publisher and she was determined to succeed. She was on the move all the time, her stilettos going clickety-clack, her long, shapely legs moving as rapidly as a tailor's scissors. She had organised the kind of programme for me no publisher ever had, or has until now. There were interviews, photography sessions, visits to bookshops, lunches (one day with the Indian Ambassador), dinners and a big launch. She got a photographer, a fashion photographer from Milan (!), to take my pictures. I was taken to a kind of open market place, where flowers and vegetables were sold in the morning. The photographer kept darting from point to point, to get the best angle I suppose, saying 'bella, bella'. I knew the word was not for me, but for my sari, which fascinated him.

The launch of the book was in the Indian Embassy, the book released by the Ambassador. Marina had gone all the way for my novel, no, 'our' novel – she was so wholly involved. The launch/reception was a big affair. But I remember that there was little to eat at the launch, and whatever little there was, was finished by the time I was free of signing books and talking to people. We went back to Marina's home and her fridge was empty too, except for some bread. 'German bread,' her husband scoffed. 'Italy makes the best breads and my wife buys German bread.' Luckily, we found some little containers with vegetarian stuff; Marina's mother, with whom I had stayed the first two days, had, knowing her daughter, thoughtfully stocked her daughter's fridge with something for me to eat. Marina's parents lived in a large villa just outside Rome, whereas Marina's home was a tiny cubbyhole in the centre of old Rome. I am sure it cost the earth. It was a fascinating place, this part of the city, in which no cars were allowed, because traffic might damage the old buildings. The next morning – Marina's fridge still empty – she took me out, saying, 'Come, I will show you how Romans have their breakfast.' We went to a little stand-up coffee place, had some coffee (too strong and bitter for my South-Indian filter-coffee-with-milk tongue) and ate a biscuit kept on a little saucer at the counter. This was breakfast? Well, when in Rome, do as the Romans do!

I wonder how the book did after such a blaze of publicity and promotion. I never got to know. *That Long Silence* was to come out soon, Marina had told me, but it didn't. Instead, after some months, I got a letter telling me that the publishing house had changed hands and that they would be signing a new contract with me for *That Long Silence*. I was sorry that Marina had not been able to succeed, she had been so keen, so determined, so ambitious, so hard-working. In spite of her veneer of sophistication, I thought of her as a very vulnerable young woman; ambition makes a person vulnerable. I hope she did finally get what she wanted and I hope even more that she is happy. I think of her mother, a simple woman, looking at her daughter with bewilderment, amazement and love. Well, whatever it was, I was paid an advance once again for *That Long Silence*. This book has earned me more money than all my other books. There were two more books in Italian after that: *A Matter of Time* and *Small Remedies*. But nothing in the last two decades. Europe was not doing so well. Politics and economics also have an impact on publishing and literature, as I have learnt.

However, in spite of the adverse circumstances in the world at the time, I was invited to three literary festivals in Europe, a very novel experience for me. The invitees were writers, not celebrities. And, of course, they had to be writers whose work had been translated into the local language. By the end of the century, my novels had been translated into German, French, Italian, Dutch, Finnish and Danish. And therefore, the invitations. All the three festivals were large affairs and in all three India was the guest of honour. Lille was the smallest and the one with more young writers. Munich was the best organised, run with absolute German precision. Each one of us was given fifteen minutes for a presentation. Fifteen minutes to the second. I didn't have a problem, since I believe in brevity, and always rehearse and time myself before I speak in public. But I remember one author was cut off in mid-sentence, left with his mouth open, but speechless, because the mike was switched off. We Indians can never be so ruthless, though sometimes, listening to speakers going on and on, showing no signs of coming to an end, I wish we could just switch them off! To go back to Munich, the list of delegates was like a who's who of Indian literature, there were veterans from so many different languages: Dr Ananthamurthy, Nirmal Verma, Sunil Gangopadhyay, Nabaneeta Dev Sen, Ashokamitran, Keki Daruwalla, Dilip Chitre, Kiran Nagarkar, Gagan Gill and many more. Most of us there were ... well, let me only say that most of us were not very young. I remember Ashokamitran's gently murmured complaint, 'When I was young no one invited me, now I find it hard to travel and I get invitations!' I am sure this complaint was silently agreed to by many others. We were in Munich soon after the horror of the Gujarat killings. Obviously many questions were asked about what had happened there. There were also two papers on the troubled areas – Gujarat and Kashmir. The ghost of Gujarat seemed to follow us when we went abroad.

The Paris Literary Salon, which that year focussed on India, was a special pleasure for me because my French translator and friend Simone Manceau was there to let me feel the magic of Paris. I remember that there were posters on the Metro advertising the Paris Salon, and that my picture was prominent on one of the posters. It was strange to see my name (and face) so loudly visible. When it happens at home, I feel I have to go into hiding for a while, to avoid people telling me 'I saw your picture in …' But here, away from home, it was different. I was pleased. I did wonder why I was given so much prominence, then guessed it was because of Simone's translation of *A Matter of Time* and the go-getter publisher who had published it.

Ultimately, it is publishers who decide whether authors matter – or don't. If the publisher decides you are not important, nothing will make you known – as I once wrote to a publisher in a fit of pique! It was still a good time in Europe, though Simone pointed out places on the outskirts of Paris where there had been riots. The backlash of Colonial rule – surprising that it hadn't happened earlier. In another decade, refugees would stream in, creating a moral dilemma for Europe. Past wrongs seem to be coming back to haunt those who had once colonised the world.

If this was a decade of much work and much travelling, it was also, sadly, the decade of many deaths as well. I lost two good friends, both to cancer. My husband lost his mother, but the worst blow was the sudden and shocking death of his brother, to whom he had been very close; they had been friends, as much as brothers. One of my husband's sisters and two nephews also died untimely and painful deaths at this time. My husband's being a doctor meant an inevitable close involvement with the deaths. Not surprising that when *Small Remedies* came out (yes, I have a date for this, it was when the new millennium began), I said in an interview that, perhaps, *Small Remedies* would be my last novel. I was truly exhausted, but it was not only my physical state; for the first time since I began writing novels, I did not have the next novel in my mind when I had completed *Small Remedies*. And therefore, my rash statement. Rash, because I was confronted by the statement over and over again – 'But you said you wouldn't write any more novels,' a friend said when *Moving On* came out, with what I can swear seemed like disappointment.

Moving On took me by surprise, coming to me in the flash of a moment when it seemed I had no ideas for a new novel. It came out of the sale of my mother's house in Malleswaram – a beautiful part of Bangalore once – when she finally decided she could no longer live alone. It was also a novel that was triggered by the huge changes that had overcome Bangalore. 'It's a city where a middle-class man can live with dignity,' my husband's teacher had told us encouragingly when we decided to move to Bangalore. But this big, yet easy-to-live-in town, had suddenly turned into an international metropolis, it had become a glitzy and prosperous city, the software capital of India, the Silicon City of India. Areas where international software companies had congregated, Whitefield, for example, looked like a foreign country, not like the Bangalore we had known and lived in for years.

With a huge influx of people from outside the city, from outside the State, even from outside India, rents zoomed. Suddenly there was a bad feeling against 'outsiders', against non-Kannada people; suddenly there was a huge gap between the rich and the poor. People who had been easy-going and tolerant, became bitter and angry. It was not surprising that any little thing ignited a spark. I remember the anti-Tamil riots that happened after the trouble between Tamil Nadu and Karnataka over sharing the Kaveri river waters. As always, the slum-dwellers were targeted; many crossed the border and fled back into Tamil Nadu.

I remember, too, the violence that broke out in our peaceful bourgeois Jayanagar, over the death of a scooterist, who was run over by a bus in the crowded market place. This death was but one more of the many accidents which had happened at the same spot, where the road was both narrow and hazardous, because it was the entrance to the bus station. The Muslim body in charge of the ground adjacent to this road had refused to surrender any land to widen it. The violence threatened to turn into a Hindu-Muslim conflict, but luckily it was scotched in time, with the Muslims allowing the demolition of a part of the wall to enable the widening of the road. Both the demolition and the widening of the road were done during the course of one night, the work done as stealthily as if it was a criminal activity. Never has any government construction been done so rapidly!

And there was the strange incident of the kidnapping of a much-loved movie star, Rajkumar, by Veerappan, a sandalwood smuggler, who, with his trademark handlebar moustache, had achieved a kind of larger-than-life reputation. We had read of his ongoing battles with the police, of the villages he terrorised, so that the villagers never dared to speak against him or his gang and of the police officers he kidnapped and killed. And then he kidnapped Rajkumar. Rajkumar was not just an actor, he had attained the kind of iconic status that another film actor, MGR, had achieved in Tamil Nadu.

Rajkumar was in his farmhouse on the edge of the forest when the brigand walked in and asked the actor and his son-in-law to go with him. The two men quietly walked away, in a gentle drizzle, with Veerappan and his gang. It was an incident that lacked all the melodrama of the actor's movies, yet it was a dramatic moment, as everyone would soon realise. The media went wild, the government was thrown into confusion and fear. If anything happened to the actor, there would be violence and bloodshed, and the government would fall. The actor remained in the smuggler's custody for five, maybe six months. Clearly a great deal of negotiation went on between the government and the bandit and a huge ransom must have been paid before the actor was released. Many books have been written on the subject, but the real truth has never been revealed. The government survived (though this was the first shot that ultimately brought it down), violence had been averted, but it was still waiting to happen.

It broke out after Rajkumar's death, some years after the kidnapping. It was a natural death. Nevertheless, mobs came out on the street, they went berserk, damaging everything they could. Not a single glass-fronted building was spared. The police became the arch-villains. For two days, TV covered all that was happening on the roads. We watched a police van drive into Cubbon Park, ostensibly to control the rampaging mob. The van stood still, its windows barred, its door bolted. Then the door was cautiously opened, a policeman came out, was pushed out, rather, and the door closed immediately behind him. We learnt later that this very young man had just joined the police force. What happened to him remains for me a symbol of how people can turn into savages, of the mysterious alchemy that transforms men into killers. The policeman was chased, he was caught, and then – the scene mercifully hidden from us by the men – was beaten to a pulp. They killed him with their bare hands. These were not criminals, they were men who must have gone home to their families, back to their work the next day, just as usual.

Prosperity had brought in criminalisation as well as violence. Land prices had skyrocketed and criminals who had found Bombay too hot for them, with the top men either dead or having fled India, entered the real estate field in Bangalore. I got a glimpse of the criminal world in real estate when we decided to sell my mother's house. She had been living on her own since we moved into our own home in Jayanagar. I had engaged a woman to give her company at night, but I was constantly frightened for her; an unanswered phone, a call at night, or too early in the early morning, set my heart racing. My fears were not groundless. Her home had been broken into twice earlier, once when she was out of town. The intruder had tried to open the locked drawers of my father's writing table, obviously looking for documents. I later realised, to my horror, that my mother had labelled all the keys in the house (this was for our convenience, my sister's and mine, after her death, she told me) and kept them in an old school bag of my brother's, the bag casually placed on a stool in her bedroom. Obviously the intruder had either been illiterate, or he had not cared to look into a shabby bag so openly placed. Another time, she was at home when a man entered from the side door of the passage at the back of the house. She felt, rather than saw a presence, and went to investigate. The man rushed past her and ran to the front door. While he was struggling to unbolt it, she caught up with him and whacked him with a stick she had kept by the front door 'just in case'. Thankfully, he had opened the bolt by then and ran out without harming her. Clearly, whoever they were, they were trying to frighten her into moving out. Nothing more, because the man was, perhaps, more terrified of her than she was of him!

We suspected our neighbours, a family that had suddenly grown prosperous after getting into the real estate business. I told my mother that if someone broke into the house, she should give him her jewels, her money and anything else he asked for. 'Why should I?' she asked. 'I won't do it.' My mother was in her eighties then! A feisty old woman, but it only increased my anxiety. The idea of her battling with an armed robber was too terrifying for me even to think of. I always feared the worst when her phone went unanswered, imagining her lying on the floor, injured and unconscious. It was a great relief when she agreed to sell the house.

As soon as the news that the house was for sale got out, the lawyer, who was managing the sale for us, told us that he had been approached by someone who offered an unrealistically high price.

He warned us this was a ploy, and that most probably they were part of the land mafia, wanting the house at much lower than the market price. Soon after, I started getting blank calls, which were meant to frighten me and did. But there was no way my sister and I were going to allow criminals to get the house which my father had bought with his very hard-earned money, the house in which our parents had taken great pride. Then some burglars broke open the back door of the house and entered it, one afternoon. It was only a warning message, for the house was empty and there was nothing in it to steal. But they soiled it in the most disgusting way and I felt my parents' home had been desecrated. A burly thug was stationed in front of the house to scare off prospective buyers. At which point I approached a police officer, the nephew of one of my father's friends, who sent a policeman to guard the house. But he advised us to sell it quick, and luckily we found a good buyer and disposed of it, though at a much lower price than what we should have got.

    After this episode, Jiji came to me, a single woman living alone in a house in Bangalore, threatened by criminals. An entire world came along with her: her parents, her sister Malu, her uncles BK and RK, her aunts, and Raja, her cousin. If the criminalisation of Bangalore came into it, so did an earlier Bangalore, of large bungalows set in huge compounds. A Bangalore of leisure and charm, of fish and chips at Koshy's, of heavenly dosas at MTR, of strolling in Lal Bagh or Cubbon Park. Bombay came into it as well, a Bombay of mill workers, trade unions and criminals. There was, too, the medical college in which Jiji's father, the 'haddi doctor', worked, the hospital quarters in which they lived. And the world of Marathi women's magazines and the romantic stories they carried – stories which Mai, Jiji's mother wrote – entered into the novel as well. There was the movie world of which Shyam, Jiji's husband, was a part. With Lakshman, Jiji's uncle, I made my first foray into a criminal mind and life. Once again, I lived for all the time of writing this novel with my characters – Jiji, Malu, her father, her mother, the brothers RK and BK, and Gayatri, who was a good woman – a rarity, but such people do exist. And, of course, Raja, Jiji's persistent lover. *Moving On* was a novel with so many characters, so many complex layers and so many strands of different colours that it was hard to put together. Hilary Mantel speaks of the importance of 'placing the facts' in historical fiction. This is true of all fiction, in fact, even non-fiction. But it is more difficult in fiction because the facts have to be integrated into a story which has been created out of the imagination.

My mother died during the writing of this novel; it was a time when I was grappling with the usual 'I wish I'd done this' or 'I wish I hadn't done that' kind of futile regrets. Apart from the loss, I had to deal with some even more difficult feelings, for my mother had become strangely hostile to me in the last years of her life. Senility, perhaps, but it left me full of hurt, and grief, as well, for what she had become. *Moving On* was written in the midst of this tumult of feelings. In fact, the part about Jiji's mother's death was written immediately after my mother's death. When writing of Mai's death, it was the small wasted body of my mother that I saw. Was this writing a kind of catharsis? Or did it bring all my guilt and confused feelings back? I don't know. But I know that it helped that I was caught in a story of people whom I was getting to know well, that once again I was living most intensely among people who were of my making, yet not of my making.

Each time I wrote a novel, I found myself pushing the boundaries. With *Moving On*, I stretched myself in many ways and in many directions. This turned out to be my most philosophical novel in a way, mainly because of Jiji's father's ruminations. It was also a novel with many love stories: Jiji's father's love for his beautiful but frigid wife; Jiji and Shyam's love story; Gayatri and BK's love story; and Raja's Dobbin-like steadfast pursuit of Jiji. But, above all, this novel was Jiji's story. Jiji who, through the tragedies of her life, grew up from being a sheltered girl to a woman who takes full control of her life. A girl who, when the time comes, walks out of the family, which had been her entire world. A woman who, in spite of all that she has gone through, is able to laugh, to enjoy the small pleasures of life. Jiji remains, even today, one of my favourite characters. I was asked by a friend whether Jiji would ultimately accept Raja. I don't know, I said. I will have to write another novel about them to know what happens. I think their relationship is full of possibilities, but I don't think I can write about them any more; it's over as far as I am concerned.

This novel was different for another reason as well. There was a mystery at the heart of this novel which therefore required careful crafting. Meenakshi Mukherjee, who launched the book in Bangalore, made a very perceptive remark about the novel. 'This,' she said, 'is the mystery novel the author always wanted to write.' But, as always, it was dubbed a novel about women and left at that. There were some good reviews, but I think the complexity of the novel, the many strands and levels in it, were not really taken note of. Oh well, which writer has ever felt that reviewers have done justice to her/his novel? Like always I had to forget the fate of this novel and move on. After this, I did some translations, from which, thankfully, one is rather distant, if not detached, because the work is someone else's. The translator is the faceless, if not the nameless person, who conveys the work into another language.

I had always thought I would do something for my father as a part of his centenary. I had already translated a play of his, a playful spoof on modern drama and, before that, some bits from his autobiography for the *Deccan Herald*. Now I thought I would translate the entire autobiography as a tribute to him in his centenary year. However, I had to abandon the thought for many reasons. For one thing, I read Kannada very slowly and just to read the entire book would have taken me months. Besides, there was much in the book which would be of no interest to a non-Kannada reader. And then, while rooting through his books for some material to write an article on him, which the National School of Drama wanted, I came across a little book, a booklet rather (priced four annas – a quarter of a rupee, remember?), called *Nanna Natya Nenapagalu* (literally, My Theatre Memories). This material had later been included in his autobiography, from where I had picked up the passages I had earlier translated for the *Deccan Herald*. Delightful bits, I had thought them, about his first exposure to the Marathi theatre and his great admiration for two of the actors he saw, the chapter ending with the epiphanic words '… the revelation that I was a dramatist flashed upon me.' I thought that this book, thankfully a very small book, was crying out to be translated.

Strangely, one of the very first pieces of writing I had done had been a translation. For some reason, my father had sent me a short story by Shantinath Desai, a Kannada writer, when I had just begun writing and suggested that I translate it. It was a story with a commonplace theme – a relationship between a young Indian man in England and an English girl. I did translate it, but I don't think it was ever published. In fact, I don't remember whether I sent it anywhere, or whether I just let it lie in my drawer. Translating my father's book was an entirely different experience. It is also one of the experiences of my life that I greatly cherish. Not only because it was a filial duty, but because it became such a collaborative effort. It was entirely unlike all the writing I had done until then, specially my novels. Writing a novel is a secretive, solitary business; not so translation – at least the way I did it. My husband first read out my father's book to me in the serene surroundings of Protima Bedi's dance gurukul, Nrityagram, on the outskirts of Bangalore. Later, Pratibha Nandakumar (yes, she who wrote the poems for *The Binding Vine*), read it to me, with great feeling, more dramatically and with many pauses to laugh at the humour and to appreciate the writing. Now I knew the text well and could read it myself, fairly easily. Once I began the translation, we fell into a routine. At the end of a day I collected all the words, phrases, sentences and sayings I was not familiar with, or was not certain about. My husband and I discussed these over our morning cup of tea. The day was yet to dawn, it was still dark outside, more so because the street lights had been put out. I could see a bat swooping just outside the window as we tried to find the exact sense of a word.

Some words my husband could not help me with, he took with him on his morning walk to the park. Jayanagar has (or used to have, before the Metro came and the gardens were cruelly amputated) one of the most beautiful boulevards in the city (next only to M.G. Road), tree-lined and bordered by parks. The boulevard was at first commonly called the Rose Garden Road, which gives one an idea of what the gardens had been like. In a few years the rose gardens vanished, but the parks were still good, and played a big role in the communal life of Jayanagar. Social, political and cultural matters were discussed in the park; in fact, my husband and his co-walkers formed a cultural organisation, which is still active.

My husband's co-walkers at that time were a very distinguished group: a retired bureaucrat-cum-engineer who had begun learning Sanskrit and was reading scholarly books post-retirement; a bank officer who became a writer, a successful one, also after retirement; a retired English professor with a passion for reading both English and Kannada; a musician who ran a music school; a successful businessman who found the time to run charitable and cultural institutions; a couple who visited from Australia regularly, the husband, a professor of Mathematics and a self-taught *harikatha* exponent in English (telling stories from the Puranas, the narration interspersed with music), the wife, a teacher of English. And above all, there was GV, as he was affectionately known, G.Venkatsubbiah, doyen of the Kannada literary world, a lexicographer who had compiled innumerable dictionaries, whose memory, even as he neared his centenary, was phenomenal and whose knowledge of both Sanskrit and classical Kannada literature was amazing. I went to him for the exact wording of a verse from the Ramayana, which I wanted to use as an epigraph for *Shadow Play*. He recited the lines immediately without a pause! It is to this great scholar that my words and phrases went. Besides, once or twice I consulted Prof. Amur. I was extremely fortunate, privileged, in fact, to have had such help.

By this time, I was being recognised in the Kannada literary world, not only as Shriranga's (my father's pen name) daughter, but on my own account as a novelist in English. I was invited to a seminar on my father, held during his centenary year, by Rangayana, a theatre institution in Mysore. And B.V. Karanth, the well-known director who had invited me, insisted I should speak in Kannada. I was hesitant, knowing how difficult it was for me to get words off the cuff, but he would not let me off. I somehow managed to do it, which was reassuring, and it gave me the courage to speak in Kannada some more times after this. In the meantime, my other language, Marathi, was getting rusty; after my mother's death, there was no one in Bangalore with whom I could speak in Marathi. After *That Long Silence* had been translated into Marathi by a reputed Marathi writer, Saniya, I made some contact with the Marathi literary world as well. One of the consequences was that I was invited to an event organised in honour of Gauri Deshpande, bilingual poet, short story writer and novelist in Marathi, on the first anniversary of her death. Pune was not the place where I dared to speak in Marathi; its people are famous for their high standards and for looking down their noses at those who don't come up to those standards. Yet, when I was repeatedly asked, a little before the event began, 'Do you know Marathi?' I was indignant. Do I know Marathi? Why, it was the first language I had spoken as a child. It was only that, never having studied or read Marathi, knowing only the colloquial language, I was hesitant to speak it in public. But at the event in Pune, something made me suddenly abandon my English speech and I began speaking in Marathi, hesitantly at first, then with greater confidence. It felt wonderful. I had begun thinking that I would like to do something for my other language, Marathi, as well, and decided to translate a novel of Gauri Deshpande's.

Earlier, she had, with her usual generosity, sent me all her novels when I said I could not get them in Bangalore. This one, *Nirgathi*, had impressed me greatly, it was so harsh, so angry, so uncompromising in its honesty. The translation would be a kind of 'thank you' to Gauri. She had translated a story of mine for a Marathi magazine. I had been very impressed with the way she spotted a flaw in the story, a problem with the time sequence. She wrote to me about it, being, I thought, both stern and emphatic about the vagueness, the ambiguity. She translated the story only after I had corrected this little snag. I wonder how many translators would be so particular. Her novel was harder to translate than my father's memoirs. Once again I needed help and this time it was my brother-in-law, whose early education had been in Marathi and who read a great deal of Marathi, who helped. I also contacted Gauri's daughter Umi, who lived in the USA, for some clarifications. A very happy offshoot of this was that Umi, who had written a novel herself, years back, a kind of response to her mother's novel, now brought her own out, brushed it up and had it published.

I learnt a great deal in the course of doing these translations. I learnt that, in spite of my frequently affirmed belief that Indian writing in English was as valid as writing in any Indian language, there were some problems about certain kinds of writing in English. Writing about rural areas, for example. Or political novels, for the ethos of politics is inextricably linked with the local languages. A novel about caste would be difficult in English; caste, too, is closely connected to language. I came to know some positive things as well. That a reader of a translation can feel 'joyful and astonished' (Shama Futehally's words). This is exactly what happened to me when I read Ramanujan's translation of Tamil classical poetry. The 'what he said' and 'what she said' poems are remarkably contemporary and alive even today. I used one of them in *A Matter of Time*:

'And how
did you and I meet ever?'

It expressed so exactly Sumi's feelings about her relationship with her husband Gopal at the moment, it was as if the poem had been written to suit my purpose. I also learnt, in the process of translation, about the democracy among different languages – no language was richer or better than another, none superior to the others; each had its own plus points. I had thought English has a vast vocabulary; it does, yet I had to struggle to find equivalents for certain Kannada and Marathi words. I learnt about the shades and nuances of meaning in words and how important it was to get exactly the right shade of meaning, the exact nuanced word. I learnt that, while in creative writing there are no choices, in translation there are choices, starting with the book you translate. You can choose. Ramanujan, the great translator (he called himself the hyphen in Anglo-Indian writing), said, 'A translator has to believe, even irrationally, that everything is translatable, if it meets the right translator.' In fact, his words seemed to bear out my idea that some texts are untranslatable, for how often does a text meet the right translator? It is as long a shot as two people, who are perfectly suited to one another, finding each other. And how does one know whether one is the right translator? I remember beginning to translate a play of my father's, which was, like his plays often were, preceded by a devotional poem as an epigraph. This was a poem that addresses God, demanding, 'What can I ask you for?' From which it goes on to detailing a list of people who asked for something and got something quite different. Like, King Dhritarashtra asked for sons and he got Duryodhana and the rest of a wild, unruly brood of sons. The child Dhruva asked for a mother and what did he get? A cruel stepmother. And so it goes on, this devotional poem, slyly accusing God of not being able to fulfil human wishes. The translator Lakshmi Holmström, in her introduction to the short story collection *The Inner Courtyard*, says that such songs belong to the tradition of *ninda-stuti* (Censure and praise, or ironical praise).

One of the verses in the poem my father had used, spoke of Dyunamaka, who asked for a sati (the perfect wife). And I wondered: who was Dyunamaka? I had thought of translating this epigraphic poem, but I needed to know who Dyunamaka was. I went around asking people who I thought would know, but no one seemed to have an answer to my question. Finally I got the answer from a most unlikely source. My friend Chandra Holm, to whom I spoke of this, mentioned it to her mother, who knew her Puranas well, and was able to tell Chandra who Dyunamaka was. This is the story:

Dyunamaka was one of the eight Vasus (heavenly beings) who, in a weak moment, and at the instigation of his wife (of course, a woman had to be behind every bad deed), stole the sage Vashishta's divine cow, the Kamadhenu. The Vasus were caught and cursed by

Vashishta, the Rishis being famous for their bad and quick tempers. Not surprising, I guess, considering the kind of self-punishing lives they led! And yet surprising, considering how hard they worked to get the power to curse and give boons, that they should just fritter it away in a fit of petulant temper.

Anyway, Vashishta's curse was that the Vasus would have to descend on earth and live a human life. But like all Rishis, he too moderated his curse later, shortening the 'life sentence', saying that they would die as soon as they were born and so get released from a life on earth. Ganga undertook the job of giving birth to the Vasus and then releasing them from life. She married King Shantanu and each time a child was born, she drowned the child in the river. The King, who before marriage had promised Ganga that he would never ask her the reason for any of her actions, could no longer control himself when it came to the eighth child and asked her the reason for her cruelty. She told him the reason. And then, she left him. This was the penalty she had told him he would have to pay in case he broke his promise. And so, the last child lived.

This was Dyunamaka, the Vasu who had actually stolen the Kamadhenu (on his wife's insistence, let's not forget), and had to face the worst punishment; he had to go through a long human life. He became Bhishma, the man who was torn between those he loved, the Pandavas, and those he owed a duty to, the Kauravas, a man who lived a long and tortured life, finally lingering even on his deathbed, a bed of arrows, while the war went on and the family, for which he had sacrificed so much, destroyed itself. He lived a life of great rectitude which, however, in the end helped no one. I had met this Bhishma much earlier in Irawati Karve's *Yuganta*, after which I had written the story of Amba and Bhishma.

The discovery of Dyunamaka's identity was a fascinating end to an interesting search. However, once I came to this point, I knew I would not translate the poem; it would not work unless the references were understood by the reader. It would not work, either, if I provided long explanations, or footnotes. Perhaps, if I were to believe Ramanujan, I was the wrong translator for this particular poem. Actually, neither of the books I translated did very well; translated books rarely do. So the disappointment was expected, it was not too great. And the pleasure I had in doing the translation remained with me, it is still with me.

I don't believe in chasing writing, or in hunting it down; it has to come to me. I wait patiently until it does, I give it time to become less shadowy, more real, sometimes waiting as much as a year before writing a word. The novel that came to me after *Moving On* began, unusually, with a character who had appeared in an earlier novel. I had written a few crime stories for magazines and then a full-length crime novel, *Come Up and Be Dead*. I had let this novel die a quiet death (though it was revived much later), but the main character Devayani would not let me alone. She haunted me. She was a character who seems passive, but has great strength. I somehow felt I had not done her justice, that I had not explored her depths. At the end of *Come Up and Be Dead*, she goes back to her home town and I could see her there, in her own home, a different person altogether. Still quiet, but with a realisation of her own strength. And so *In the Country of Deceit*. This novel was located in a small town, one which was closer to Dharwad than any of the fictional small towns I had created so far.

This novel centred round Devayani. A woman of great courage, who was able to give up the man she loved because her conscience rebelled against having an affair with a man who was married and had a child. I remember how hard it was to write of her anguish when she sends him away. All the time I was struggling to write this,

I kept hearing a particular Pandit Jasraj bhajan; it was as if it had to be part of the scene. Yet, somehow, bringing it in was proving impossible. Finally I realised that the bhajan was in *my* mind, not Devayani's, and only then could I write that scene. And, finally, when the lawyer Iqbal comes to her and offers her a job, I felt Devayani would be at peace with herself. It felt good, that ending.

The next novel, *Shadow Play*, also, strangely enough, started with a character from an early novel, *A Matter of Time*. *A Matter of Time* had been in one sense the most philosophical of my novels; *Shadow Play* continued in the same strain. I consider it as a rumination on life, just as *A Matter of Time* questioned death. This, and the characters, connected the two novels. *Shadow Play* is not a sequel in the classic sense. Sequels are always a little difficult. There is Galsworthy's *The Forsyte Saga*, which goes on for too long. The first three volumes, especially the first book, *The Man of Property*, are extremely good. Later, the interest wears thin. And except for the character of Soames, who begins as a kind of villain in relation to his idealised, but tiresome wife, Irene, and who surprisingly becomes a man you sympathise with, specially when it comes to his love for his daughter, Fleur, none of the other characters grip the reader. But I find Trollope's novels in the Barsetshire series fascinating, the way they keep the spotlight moving on to different characters in different novels, the same people who were central characters in one novel, becoming minor characters in another. He does it brilliantly, giving a kaleidoscopic effect. And there's Marilynne Robinson's triptych of novels, *Gilead, Home* and *Lila*, not sequels chronologically, but three novels dealing with the same people, the same events, the same time, yet giving you completely different pictures.

Shadow Play was a sequel unlike these. It went back to the family that had been at the centre of *A Matter of Time*. In this novel, I had hinted at a possible future of Aru's, the oldest daughter in the family; it was almost like a promise to her. And I had to fulfil that promise. Aru's estranged father Gopal was back in their home, Aru still inimical to him. And Kasturi appeared on the scene, surprising me with her presence, surprising me even more with her growing closeness to Gopal. Kasturi brought along her friend Mira, Mira's sisters and her mother Belinda. It always remains a mystery: from where do these people come? But an author never asks herself such questions; they are best left alone.

As if it was a kind of relay, *Strangers to Ourselves*, which came later, began with a character from *Shadow Play*. The sulky young boy who is present at Aru and Rohit's wedding, assisting his grandfather, the priest, segued into a mature Shree Hari Pandit, ambitious, highly talented and passionate about music. And equally passionately in love with Aparna, the oncologist, whom he falls for in a moment. Like Savitribai of *Small Remedies*, Shree Hari came to me as a voice, a voice which I heard in a music shop – someone was trying out the CD I guess – singing the Raaga Patdeep. (Coincidentally, this singer was, I came to know, from Dharwad.) And so there he was, Shree Hari Pandit, lover of music and of Aparna. For this novel, which again required some knowledge of music, I was lucky that I had met an accomplished young musician, Bharathi Prathap. She gave me a lot of valuable insight and facts, though how well I have used them is anybody's guess. In any case I enjoyed getting to know Bharathi, enjoyed listening to her music even more.

Happily, when it came to medical facts I had many experts at home: my sister, her husband, my son, and of course, my husband. During our evening walks, people, seeing us in deep conversation as we walked, might have envied us for being able to be so engrossed in conversation with each other, even after so many decades of marriage. If they'd listened to us, they would have heard him giving me some gory information about a disease, about how, even after all the years, to see a disease under the microscope was to see a death sentence, and how frightening it was, even for a veteran like him. But for *Strangers to Ourselves*, I needed more specialised knowledge. I was also lucky in having a doctor, Rekha Kumar, who gave me a little understanding of cancer, of the treatment and the course of the disease – just enough for my purposes. Both these women, Bharathi and Rekha, were so kind, so happy to give me what I wanted, that, for the first time I felt that perhaps my writing did matter; it was because of my writing that they were so responsive, after all. Oh yes, I also read Siddhartha Mukherjee's wonderful book *The Emperor of All Maladies* before I wrote *Strangers to Ourselves*.

Strange that my last three novels have been love stories. In an introduction to an interview, a journalist spoke of the curious fact that *Strangers to Ourselves* was a love story written by an over-seventy-year-old woman. Has age anything to do with writing about love? Do we not, as we grow older, learn more about it? I remember that decades back, the editor of *Femina* had suggested I write a love story, and I wrote one which I knew was like any other love story. Later I wrote one or two romantic serials, but again I was unable to get out of the clichés and stereotypes of love. I did not take these stories seriously myself. I rewrote one of them and turned it into a novella, *Ships That Pass*, in which a deliberately light-hearted romance was mingled with a crime story. I thought that the love story came off as well as it could in a novel of this genre, but readers and critics took note only of the mystery angle, not the love story. I had to wait for decades before I could write about love without being mushy, without using worn-out, clichéd words and phrases, before I could write a serious love story.

I understood when I wrote *In the Country of Deceit* and *Strangers to Ourselves*, how difficult it was to write about love. Love is the most written-about emotion, romantic love, that is, and certain concepts, words, phrases cling to it like barnacles. To write without them is not easy. Why, even a writer like Dorothy Sayers went terribly wrong in a love scene between Peter Wimsey and Harriet in *Busman's Honeymoon*. This novel is, apart from the love scenes, one of the finest crime novels. It can be called a love story with crime in it, or a mystery novel containing a love story – whichever way you look at it. It also has some exquisite, almost Wodehousian comedy. But the love passages? One love scene begins with Wimsey saying, 'How can I find the words? Poets have taken them all and left me with nothing to say or do …' And then, unforgivably, goes on to use a language so heavy with literary quotations and allusions that the emotion is lost. It is one of the most embarrassing love scenes I've read, a close contender being the conversation between the lovers in Hemingway's *A Farewell to Arms* which is incredibly, impossibly inane. ('You have a lovely temperature!' Ouch!)

Yes, even the best writers can fall flat on their faces. The trouble is that love has been written about so much that, as any writer wanting to write about love realises, many of the words have become stale and shop-worn. No wonder clichés abound in the language of love! Silence can convey more than words ever can. But how do you use silence, which is so effective in movies, in literature? Literature ultimately needs words, even to speak of silence. And where does one find new words to speak of love? (Though in *Bardell v. Pickwick*, 'Chops and tomato sauce' were accepted as terms of endearment!) How does one convey what I can only call the 'real thing'? Specially when in real life, lovers' conversations are almost always inane? I once found myself, as a girl, sandwiched between two lovers, a friend and her boyfriend. I was a true *kabab-mein-haddi*. Their conversation consisted entirely of 'Yes, I do,' and 'No you don't.' I had been very uncomfortable when my friend forced me to go with her, I had told myself I would sit apart and not eavesdrop. But, in fact, I was bored. And disillusioned, because my ideas of love and lovers' talk came from books. And, like multitudes of young girls, my ideal of a lover was Rhett Butler, Mr Darcy, the Frenchman in *Frenchman's Creek* ...

For a writer, the problem is: what language do you use? The language of literature, or the language of real lovers and invite the charge of inanity? Or do lovers themselves use the words that literature has given them?

'It didn't matter whether you had an IQ of 170 or an IQ of 70 – you were brainwashed all the same. You longed to be annihilated by love.' (Erica Jong: *Fear of Flying*)

Brainwashed? Does that mean that if we had not read about love, we'd never experience the symptoms of a racing heart, a tumultuous pulse, never know 'fertile tears, with groans that thunder and sighs of fire?' (Shakespeare: *Twelfth Night*) Or, was the idea of love already with us, and have writers merely given words to our vague longings and emotions? It's too old a connection to disentangle now; however far back in time we go, we are sure to find a poem or a story of love between man and woman.

'Oh heart, there is no reality but her her her ...' (This by a seventh-century Sanskrit poet.)

'All I remember is/ I was in his arms,/ but who he was, and who I was/ and what we did/ – well ...' (A woman poet in Sanskrit of an unknown date. Both the translations are by P. Lal.)

Oh, well! One grows up and understands that the reality is different. But the magic of words never fades. The lovers of literature are immortal, eternal.

'What would you do (if you loved me)?' Olivia asks Viola in *Twelfth Night*.

'Make me a willow cabin at your gate/ And call upon my soul within the house,' Viola replies.

Unforgettable words. Shakespeare had the right words almost all the time. Look at what he says about lust: 'The expense of spirit in a waste of shame/Is lust in action.' A poem full of loathing of the emotion of lust. Why have these lines stayed with me through the years? And John Donne's beginning of a love poem: 'Busy old fool, unruly sun'? John Donne was a great love poet who invested love poetry with vigour and strength. And, perhaps, because he rarely used the usual words or phrases, what he says is often like a startling revelation. I came across him very late in life, and he was an amazing discovery. Darcy's proposal to Elizabeth in *Pride and Prejudice* is unforgettable, too, because of the jagged quality of surprise it conveys; both are surprised, he at making the proposal, she at receiving it. As a matter of fact, Jane Austen was perfect with her love scenes. Minimalist that she was, she kept an exquisite balance between the emotions and the words. Which is why Austen's *Persuasion* is one of the most accomplished love stories written. And there is Emma waking up to the fact that she loves Knightley: 'It darted through her, with the speed of an arrow, that Mr Knightley must marry no one but herself.' Such amazingly strong words. The problem is that love, in the hands of a poor writer, can easily slide into sentimentality, or a florid emotionalism; the more the words used, the worse it becomes. Oh well, perhaps there are as many ways of writing about love as there are writers.

What about erotic writing? Writing about sex has made great advances, but this is not necessarily erotic, for the erotic admits physicality without becoming a record of anatomical parts and bodily functions. Reading a comment about a Tamil book that it 'has more sex and violence than most English writing' – a statement that sounded, unfortunately, like a boast – I wondered whether we Indians have forgotten about the Shringara rasa, which produced wonderful erotic poetry like the *Gita Govind* and Bilhana's love poetry. I first read Bilhana's love poetry, believe it or not, in John Steinbeck's *Cannery Row*, which ends with an unforgettable scene, in which Doc (the main character, or the hero, as main characters used to be called) reads out this poetry to a crowd of people who have never read poetry, in fact many of whom have barely read anything at all. Prostitutes and pimps, small-time crooks and simple-minded people, all of them listen to the poetry in an awed silence. 'Even now …' each first line of a verse begins, followed by lines that are suffused with such love, longing, loss and regret that it sent shivers down my spine.

> 'Even now,
> I remember my love's face
> golden earrings
> grazing her cheeks
> as she strove
> to take the man's role …'

An amazingly beautiful poem written in the eleventh century, it is both a love poem and an erotic poem. Is there no longer any space for both love and the erotic? And what about women and their desires? I remember a reviewer who spoke approvingly of the fact that my novel *The Binding Vine* recognised a woman's sexual desire. It made me wonder whether this was so unusual as to be remarked upon. Indeed, women wrote of love, they wrote some great love poetry, but it was rarely erotic. Things have changed. Aparna in *Strangers to Ourselves* is deeply in love with Hari. A woman of today, she desires his body, and she is a passionate lover when they have sex.

In the same novel, there is a woman of an earlier era, of an earlier century, Ahalya, who is shocked when she stumbles upon her own erotic thoughts as she writes about her long-dead husband. The truth is that, whatever age we belong to, whatever the time we live in, we are, after all, human beings and cannot escape the basic urges that have been installed in us. And sex is one of the strongest urges. I wrote about both Aparna and Ahalya. Woman of the past and woman of today. Exploring the unsaid, breaking the silences, bringing out through words what has been lost or submerged, filling the blank spaces, the gaps, writing on the dotted lines – this is what writing is all about.

Confrontations

How odious all authors are, and how doubly so to each other!
Henry Edward Fox, *The Journal of Henry Edward Fox*

There had been a time – I must have been in my forties then – when I had wondered whether I would live to see the end of the century, whether I would be on this earth when a new millennium was ushered in. But I had not bargained for the great leaps that human longevity would take, nor for the genes I have inherited from both sides of the family. My father often joked that if someone in his family died at seventy, the survivors would cluck their tongues and say regretfully that he had died too young. My mother's family had an equally tenacious grip on life. So there I was, alive and working, if not kicking, when 1999 was coming to an end and the world was preparing to welcome a new century with enthusiasm.

I am sure the turn of a century has always been a momentous event for people living at the time. Now, the power and spread of the media created a kind of frantic excitement, verging on hysteria. And this, though we all knew that we would be doing the same things on that day and that nothing would be different, or, if different, only in the way that one day differs from another. The media rushed to the spot where the sun would first rise on earth, the place that would see the new century first. But to look back at the century that was over and see the changes was a more meaningful exercise. What could not be doubted was the way medical science had changed human lives. And technology that had brought about changes which were more radical and rapid than the world had ever seen before. It was this very technology that presented the world with a great problem as the century was coming to a close. Y2K, it was called, in the new shorthand we were all learning because of computers and mobiles. Y2K was an acronym (or a numeronym, which I believe is the word for it), which contained the question: how would computers cope with the change of date, or rather the change of the year? I am one of the most ignorant persons as far as gadgets, machines and technology are concerned, but from what I understood, it was the zeros at the end of 2000 that were the problem. The computer could not cope with these and therefore all computers would crash, and the world would come to a standstill. (So I had gathered.) Luckily, humans can meet most challenges (except when it comes to relationships between people or nations), and with hordes of software engineers all over the world working on the problem, they set it right. The world would not stop, planes would not crash in midair, as had been feared. But something else happened a little later which seemed just as dreadful, if entirely different from the earlier fears.

Once again we have condensed this great catastrophe into a few digits – it became 9/11. The 9th of September 2001. I so distinctly remember the day. We were watching the BBC news on TV, when suddenly the newsreader broke off and the camera showed us a plane flying straight, or so it seemed, towards one of the towers of the World Trade Centre in New York. Even as the news anchor kept saying it must be a mistake, a navigational error, the plane struck the building and plunged deep into it. It was hard to make sense of this, but there was fire and smoke coming out of the building where the plane had struck. Just as we were trying to take in the horror of this, a second plane appeared from nowhere and made straight for the second tower. Once again the smoke and the fire, and the even more horrifying sight of puppet-like figures, with flailing limbs, flinging themselves out of the inferno behind them on to the ground, filled our TV screens. In only a few moments the two towers collapsed into themselves and dust enveloped the area in such a thick haze nothing could be seen. We had watched something happening which was the stuff of nightmares.

The world changed irrevocably in those moments; nothing would ever be the same again. It was as if Pandora's box had been opened, releasing hatred and horror. Soon the USA went to war in Iraq and Afghanistan. For me, the indelible image of all the conflicts that followed is the picture I saw of an endless chain of men, prisoners of war, Iraqis taken prisoners by the ISIS I think, walking steadily along, each man with his hand on the shoulder of the man ahead of him, all of them looking down, all of them barely clothed. It was as if every attempt was made to humiliate these men, to take away their humanness. It is an image that still haunts me.

As the wars went on, I thought of the Iraqi student who had written me a letter in broken English about *The Dark Holds No Terrors,* which he had read and on which he had written an article. He sent me the journal containing the article; but, of course, I could not read it, I could only wonder how a man in a different country and such a different culture could respond to my novel. I also thought of the two gentlemen who had introduced themselves to me during a conference. They told me they were Kurds (they were Christians, they told me right away, as if it was the most important thing about them), and they too spoke of my novel and said that they were teaching it. I thought of how literature, any aspect of culture for that matter, links us and how wars destroy these links and in fact, destroy everything that has made us civilised beings, of how they take away every vestige of the dignity that culture and civilisation confer on us.

But strangely, as if in a kind of affirmation of the strength of literature, a new era of literary festivals began in India, festivals which were to be a celebration of literature, as well as a coming together of writers and readers. Literary festivals are now so much a part of the scene, they seem to have been around forever. I am sure younger writers, for whom literary festivals are an important aspect of their literary lives, of their calendars, will find it hard to believe that there was a time when there were no literary festivals in India. But, of course, before the culture of literary festivals in India, there were different kinds of events. And I did get a great many invitations, both local and outside Bangalore, mainly to colleges and universities, to lecture, or to take part in seminars and conferences.

There were also events which had nothing to do with literature, but to which I was invited because, my picture having appeared in the papers, I was considered a 'celebrity'. Something which irritates me. I'm a hard-working writer, I said, often, but nobody listened. Invitations from universities and English departments to talk to students were more to my taste, I have some interesting memories of these visits. One of my most memorable moments is of an all-girls' band striking up the moment I entered the college building, a wonderfully bracing rocking tune. I thought the girls and their music were amazingly good.

I remember well, too, a conference in Tirur, Kerala, organised yearly by the Malayalam writer, M.T. Vasudevan Nair. My friend Gita Krishnankutty was with me on this trip, always there to translate and tell me all about the place and its traditions. It was from her that I came to know that the men serving us our dinner were prominent people from the town. They looked upon it as an honour to serve literary guests at mealtimes. This was really giving literature its due! I also saw how M. T., as he was called, was surrounded by a crowd whenever he was spotted. Literature has obviously a special place in Kerala. I remember three girl students who came to visit me. Like the heroes in the film *Amar Akbar Anthony*, one of them was a Hindu, another a Christian and the third a Muslim; it was hard to tell the difference between the three. All three of them spoke of their problems with their parents who expected them to get married as soon as possible. They looked hopefully at Gita and me, as if we had an answer to this problem, but what could we tell them? Only that if they wanted to go on with their studies, they had to persuade their parents to let them do so. During a visit to another university, it was the teachers, three or four of them, who came to meet me. All of them had come from another part of India, they were far from home and living on their own. I was shocked when they began to tell me of the ordeal they faced in public places, in buses, on roads. Once again I had no answer to give them, except to tell them to stand up and fight for themselves. Looking at their faces, I knew this was easier said than done.

There are two literary meets in India, not academic ones, which I remember most clearly, because both of them were, in their own ways, unique. After *Small Remedies* came out, I was invited to become the chairperson of the jury for the Commonwealth Prize. The final judging and the event were to be held in India that year and tradition had it that a local person would chair the jury. And so I was asked. Why me? The question sprang to my mind (though I did not say it aloud), when I thought of how many literary heavyweights there were in Delhi. Writers much better known than I was. I came to know the answer by the end of the event, though it was never clearly spelt out. But of course I accepted; I thought it was a great honour. Such an honour that I agreed, in spite of having been invited to go to New York by the Feminist Press for an event at the same time. I accepted in spite of the fact that I don't like being on a jury; I dislike sitting in judgement on my fellow writers. I'd been on the Sahitya Akademi jury twice and had wondered whether I was doing the right thing; Indian writing in English was such a small world, everyone knew almost everyone else. I too had some friends. What if their books were on the list? How could I be sure I would not be biased towards them? There are also writers whom, for various reasons, I don't like very much. Wouldn't this affect my judgement? And what if a friend's book was on the shortlist? Obviously I would tell the other jury members about this, yet it would be awkward. But for the Commonwealth Prize, though there were two books on the shortlist by Indian writers, I did not know either of them. One was a first-time novelist, and the other a man who had become an international literary giant – Salman Rushdie. I had read this novel, *The Ground Beneath Her Feet*, earlier and hadn't thought very highly of it. Fortunately, now I had to judge it in the context of the other books on the shortlist, not absolutely. We would be looking at the best *among* the four books given to us.

But it was not going to be easy. Even in the sequestered jury room, as we were discussing the books, we kept hearing rumours that Rushdie was coming to Delhi for the final event. He was still in hiding, but he would somehow come. It sounded very adventurous and exciting and the rumour mills worked overtime. There was also a vague feeling floating around that since Rushdie was coming 'home', and at such a cost, it would be very fitting for him to get the prize. His book and Coetzee's *Disgrace* were the two main contenders, and after a huge amount of spirited, and sometimes heated discussions, Coetzee's book was chosen. Our choice was vindicated, I thought, when Coetzee got the Nobel Prize a little later.

Rushdie did come for the final evening. A short while before the event began, we heard that he had been smuggled into the hotel. The Press, which had been locked into a room till then, was let out and there was a stampede to get to Rushdie. I was almost knocked down by a frenzied photographer. I could feel the tension in the room when I got up to announce the prizes. After the First Book award, it was the turn of the best novel. I sensed the room collectively holding its breath. When I announced Coetzee's *Disgrace,* there was a tremendous applause. However, I am sure there were many admirers of Rushdie's who were as much disappointed as he was that he didn't get the prize. But that is the nature of awards; I've gone through it myself. Many people came and shook my hand, some even said 'thank you'. One gentleman, obviously someone who mattered, gave me a clue to why I had been made the chairperson. When he congratulated me on the choice, I said it was the best book, that was all. 'We wanted someone who could see it that way,' he said.

What I felt most uncomfortable with was the sense of entitlement; that, because Rushdie had come home, he deserved a reward. Of course I may be wrong, it is possible that he thought his was the best book. Or perhaps he assumed that having got such major prizes, why would this one evade him? Whatever his reasons, he wrote an article in *The New York Times* in which he spoke of me disparagingly, and called me 'a stony-faced judge'. I was, still am, too small a person to be able to respond to him, either verbally, or in writing. But if I could have, I would have reminded him of Lincoln's response to a man who called him two-faced. 'If I had two faces, would I have chosen this one?' Lincoln asked. I would have asked, 'If I could have had any other kind of face, do you think I would have chosen this stony face? I was born with it.' Rushdie also referred to me as Banquo's ghost at Macbeth's table, which, for some reason, I didn't mind at all. It was a pleasure, indeed an honour, to be one of Shakespeare's characters, even if it was only a ghost! But this allusion made it clear that I had spoiled his fun, I had been a party pooper by not giving him the prize. As if it was mine alone to give!

I had another experience of a fracas, a very small one, with another Big Author. No, I am wrong in saying it was a fracas *with* this author. He, Sir Vidia Naipaul, did not know me at all. The contretemps happened at a festival, one of the most ambitious ones held in India. It was to be a coming together of Indian writers in all the languages, of writers who lived in India, as well as Indian writers who lived abroad. This festival was held in the most picturesque locale of an old fort in Neemrana, renovated and converted into a heritage hotel. The location and the friends I met were the best things about the festival. The proceedings were a total washout. I don't remember a single meaningful statement made by anyone in all the three days.

In an account of his time in a German internment camp during the Second World War, P.G. Wodehouse has a story of how a fellow internee, bored with the constant talk of food in the camp, once followed Wodehouse and a Roman Catholic priest as they were walking together, hoping to hear conversation that would give him some 'mental and spiritual uplift'. What he got, instead, was a discussion of the respective merits of two kinds of sausages! I was reminded of this on the second day in Neemrana when Prof. U.R. Ananthamurthy greeted me at the lunch table with a beaming 'good food today, there's *masuru anna*' (rice and curds), his plate raised in a kind of salute.

Looking back, I wonder whether this was the most genuine and meaningful statement I heard in all the days of this festival in Delhi and Neemrana. No, there was one delegate who said in exasperation during a heated argument, 'We do not have any information about one another.' He was right. All of us live in isolated islands of our own language literatures, having no idea of what is being written in the other languages. A few prominent names are known to some, but that is all. And right from the beginning, there was an air of hostility in the place, hostility between the *bhasha* writers and the English writers. I don't know where it began, but it was most obvious in a magazine feature on the festival, in which the *bhasha* writers condemned the English writers and abused them in a very uncivilised manner; they called them traitors, prostitutes, pimps and many other colourful names. One writer even suggested that English writers stop writing their own stuff and, instead, translate the works of the *bhasha* writers into English. I thought this was more insulting than the name-calling. Incredible that a writer should say this! I would have imagined that a writer would know that one is a writer, or a translator, not by design, but by talent and inclination.

There were angry exchanges during the sessions, many spurts of temper. I cannot really blame the *bhasha* writers. The entire festival centred round Naipaul; he, with his recently acquired Nobel Prize, was its showpiece. Naipaul's comment on the inaugural day that the Indian language writers did not have a readership and his gratuitous advice, that they should write better to get more readers (I swear he said this), seemed to cast a shadow on the entire conference, leaving the *bhasha* writers on the defensive. Naipaul also told us that every penny he had earned had been through writing. As if, the rest of us, whatever language we wrote in, would not have loved to make a living by writing! I thought of my father and how he had struggled all his life to find enough time to write, in spite of a full-time job, and how, not having a job was a luxury he could not afford, since he had a family to support. I thought of how, when I was on the point of taking up a job to cope with our money problems, my husband gave up his academic post, instead, and went into private practice, telling me, 'You concentrate on your writing, I'll earn the money.' I thought of men who worked full time and wrote in the little time they could snatch in a day, I thought of some of the women writers I knew, who juggled with a full-time job, with the needs of their family *and* with writing. In fact, all Indian writers need another means of earning money; living only by writing was, no, still is, a luxury, never a viable possibility.

When one looked at the titles given to the sessions, it became even clearer that this festival was a kind of toast raised to the success of English writing in the world. For example, some of the titles of the sessions were: A Way in the World, Midnight's Children, In an Antique Land, The Circle of Reason and so on. The issues to be discussed in these sessions were equally significant pointers to the perspective of the festival: Who is an Indian writer?, Ideas of home, Versions of India, Translating India, Exile, The Diaspora, Exoticising, etc., etc. All these are issues more relevant, or, perhaps, *only* relevant to writers who live abroad; or, more correctly, relevant to academicians and critics who work on the writing of such writers. Writers themselves rarely, or almost never, concern themselves with such abstract issues. Apart from this, some of the English writers had their agents with them, men who strutted about like gods. Whereas, even the giants among the *bhasha* writers, those who were idolised in their own languages, were given short shrift.

I remember the rage of a writer, who was almost a god in his own language, when he was forced to stop reading a story because of the time factor. These writers were not used to such treatment. It was not a good atmosphere. I, who in some ways straddled both the worlds, the *bhasha* as well as the English world, could see how wrong things were. But I could also see that the *bhasha* writers, in their eagerness to condemn English writers, took it for granted that all English writers were published abroad, that they all made a lot of money, that they all wrote for the Western reader and so on. They took no account of the many Indian writers who lived in India, had Indian publishers, Indian readers, and who in no way made the kind of money that those who were published abroad did. This wilful blindness made me angry. 'Read us,' I pleaded in a piece I wrote in response to the article in which the *bhasha* writers had been vitriolic about English writers. 'Read us and then talk.' I don't think that those who spoke so strongly against English writers had read us. They knew the famous and celebrated writers; they did not know about those of us who were living and writing in India and rarely came into the news.

The last day of the sessions in Neemrana was a bad finale to a bad festival. The final session was open to the media who had come from Delhi in full force. The session had one more of the inane titles which had marked this festival, about writing and history or something like that. I, who was the first to speak, referred to the total absence of women's voices in the past, and of their gradual emergence, and of how feminism had made a great difference. Nayantara Sahgal, who spoke after me, brought in colonialism which was a part of our history. Even as she was speaking, she was rudely interrupted in the middle of a sentence by Naipaul who asked, in a kind of put-on exasperation, how long did he have to listen to such rubbish, and how colonialism was long over and feminism was banal and so on. It was a shocking exhibition of rudeness and arrogance. There was silence after he was done, until the chairperson asked Nayantara to continue. She, a gracious lady, who looked gentle but was very strong, obviously refused. The session then went on in its usual dull path.

When the media was allowed to ask questions, most of the questions were addressed to Naipaul and Vikram Seth, I think, and perhaps to one or two others. Naipaul's outburst seemed to have been buried by an unspoken agreement. Until a woman journalist asked me how I felt about feminism being called banal. Later, I thought of all the things I could have said, but I am afraid I am what we Indians call a tubelight: I get the right and the most cutting responses hours later, usually in the middle of the night, sometimes even days later. At the moment, however, a friend told me I didn't do too badly, because I gave a kind of shrugging-off reply, saying that someone who had no idea about what women's lives were like, would obviously find feminism banal. So do I find the idea of the anguish of exile boring, I said.

This incident made headlines the next morning. My husband rang me up to ask me what it was all about. A storm in a teacup, I told him. Later, when Naipaul came to know that Nayantara, who had set him off on his diatribe, was Pandit Nehru's niece, he apologised to her. As for me …? I thought of Emily Dickinson's 'I'm nobody! Who are you?/ Are you nobody, too?' Undoubtedly, compared to the great authors I have just written about, I was a nobody. (Though I consider all writers to be colleagues, members of a fraternity.) Naipaul certainly was not a nobody. He was an eminent author, a Nobel Prize winner. And Rushdie was a celebrated, world-famous author, known not only for his writing (his *Midnight's Children* was revolutionary), but for the way he had been hunted after *Satanic Verses* and for his courage in refusing to retract.

And, therefore, even to speak of these two incidents as a fracas is wrong; it was more like shadow boxing. But I saw how the result of fame is always a big ego, which does no one any good. Celebrityhood, fame and the media searchlight are deadly for any artist, specially for the artist's work. I think of how women writers of earlier times – Jane Austen, the Brontë sisters, Mrs Gaskell – concealed their identities.

There is a marvellous story in Mrs Gaskell's *The Life of Charlotte Brontë*, of Charlotte and Anne Brontë bravely going to London to meet their publisher to correct the rumour that *Jane Eyre*, *Wuthering Heights* and *The Tenant of Wildfell Hall* were all written by the same person. They could not allow this wrong fact to pass uncontested. So they went, two intrepid women, they stayed in the only inn they knew of in London, and went to the publisher, Smith and Elder's office the next morning. They had not told Mr Smith, the publisher, they were coming. And Mr Smith knew them only collectively as the Bells; he did not know the Bells were women, he had always written to them as if they were men. His astonishment on seeing these two women, dressed in shabby, old-fashioned clothes, can be imagined. Once he realised these two women were Currer and Acton Bell (the third, Ellis Bell, was at home in Haworth, she was dying), he was eager to entertain them, he wanted to have a party for them with other literary figures attending. But they resolutely refused. They shrank from meeting anyone, they didn't want to go out in public. Jane Austen was happy to be read, she made a list of the people in her circle who had read her novels, adding their impressions of it. But at no time did she want to be known in public as an author. She was described as 'A Lady' for her first published novel, *Sense and Sensibility*, and 'The Author of *Sense and Sensibility*', for the next. It was such a different world. The writing mattered, not the persona (or the good looks) of the author.

In general, today, there is a pressure on writers to look good, to present themselves in the best possible way, to promote their own books. I am glad I began writing at a time when writers didn't have to work at selling their own books. I still believe that my job is to write and it is for the publisher to do the selling. But it doesn't seem to work this way any longer. With the huge number of books being published, obviously there is so much competition that authors need to walk the extra mile, or miles, if their books are to be noticed. And reviews, which were, I thought, the best way of making books known, are getting fewer and far more selective. Yes,

I am truly glad I am coming close to the end of my innings. It's not a world for shirking from publicity, for wanting anonymity, for being low-key. The literary world is now like the rest of the world, greased by publicity and running on money. Even in India, things were changing very fast, and another revolution in English writing in India was waiting in the wings, waiting for its cue to enter.

Being Part of a Community

You're part of a community, the community of writers, the community of storytellers that stretches back through time to the beginning of human society.

Margaret Atwood, 'Nine Beginnings', *Curious Pursuits*

I RECENTLY ATTENDED A poetry ... what do I call it? A reading? A performance? No, I will call it a poetry event, which is, hopefully, a comprehensive word. Two Kannada writers, one a poet, and the other a short story writer and novelist, read out Kannada poetry starting with a poet, Pampa, who lived in the tenth century (much before Chaucer), down to poets of the present times. They spoke of the context of the poetry, briefly explained the poem, occasionally referred to the critical reception of the time to the poetry, they told us stories about poets, about the clashes between different poets, both ideological and personal. I could not understand all of the poetry, specially the early poetry written in old Kannada. But I was amazed and awed by the picture of a literature which I had not known existed, I responded with joy to the poetry I could understand. And above all, I could feel the passion of these two writers, Pratibha Nandakumar and Vivek

Shanbhag, for what they were reading and talking about. This was not poetry that came out of books; this was something that had touched them, and their lives.

The same evening, I watched a programme on TV, a Marathi programme which presented the music from three of the Marathi *sangeet nataks* (musical dramas) of the last century: *Swayamvar, Samshay Kallol* and *Maan Apamaan*. I had heard some of this music in my childhood; an uncle passionately loved this music (actually, he loved all music), and he often sang or hummed the lines to himself. Besides, I had heard these songs on the radio, later through tapes and then CDs. The music that I listened to that evening was wonderful, all the more because it was music laced with nostalgia – a heady combination. The glass of wine I was drinking as I watched, could not give me the high that this music did. Both these programmes filled me with a kind of elation.

One question I had asked myself when I began writing this book was: why am I writing this? Why am I, who have always been very private and reserved, opening up my life to the world? There was no single answer to this question, but there have been many happy consequences of the writing itself. One very pleasantly unexpected result has been that I have relived my life as I wrote – both the joyful moments and the troubled ones. And, as always happens, to write about something is to attain a greater clarity about it. This apart, it has been a great delight to write about books, about writers, to quote some of their beautiful words – a kind of sharing I have not been able to do through writing so far. And I have realised, again a happy and unexpected thought, that I have very few serious regrets. Perhaps it was because I had no ambitions when young, and so I could not, I did not, disappoint myself. (Though I now know that I would never have been able to live a life of unthinking acceptance of anything.) Of course, there are some regrets. At one time, I greatly regretted the fact that I was not able to make much money through my writing. Apart from the fact that I would have felt good to bear my share of providing for the family, there is no doubt that work which earns money is more valued. Of course, this regret was acute at a time when the children were young and we needed money for their education, to give them small treats. Now they are on their own, our needs have shrunk and our wants are slowly getting extinguished. And, therefore, the fact that I am not able to earn much money does not seem to matter anymore. I have also stopped agonising over the fact that I have been supported (financially) by my husband all our married life. Formerly, when I heard young working women say that they did not like to ask their husbands for money, my own state of economic dependence used to be rubbed into me. I often tried to comfort myself with the thought that artists always, or almost always, need support or patronage. And does it matter if the support and patronage comes from a spouse? Well, this was a specious argument, and therefore this line of comfort didn't always work.

However, it truly does not seem to matter anymore that I have received very few awards and prizes. I am often introduced as an 'award-winning writer'; sometimes they say, 'She has won many awards.' I have to blink when I hear these words. Many awards? Where was I when they came to me? How come I don't know about them? I have received just one major award: the Sahitya Akademi award. (Two translations of my novels have won the Sahitya Akademi translation award, but the credit for that has to go to the translators.) And recently I was given the Soi Sanmaan, an award given by a literary women's group in Bengal. An award that matters to me because it was given to me by Mahashweta Devi and Nabaneeta Dev Sen, two writers I admire. And, oh yes, I have the Padma Shri. An unknown journalist rang me up from Delhi to tell me, in Kannada, 'Do you know you've got the Padma Shri?' I was in bed then with a recurring fever, and possibly, for that reason, I was unable to respond to his words with any excitement. I only asked, 'Have I?' 'Watch the TV,' he said, equally terse, and put down the phone. My husband came to ask me whose phone it was. 'I've got the Padma Shri,' I said, in a matter-of-fact tone. His pleasure told me it mattered. And I realised I should be pleased too, though I secretly wished they had given me the Padma Bhushan. After so many years of writing, of writing about people whose lives had rarely been written about (at least in English), I thought it was not too much to expect!

My grumpiness, however, didn't last long. Pleasure surfaced when I was in the Rashtrapati Bhavan for the award ceremony. It was not the solemn ceremony, nor the pomp, nor the VIP crowd that gave me a good feeling. It was the fact that it was a national award, even if given to me, as my son pointed out, by a President who had no stature at all. Even more, I was among people whose work had brought them this honour. People whose work mattered to the country. It felt good to be one among them. So there it is, these are all the awards and prizes I have received. And therefore, at times, when I have to listen to someone speaking of my 'many awards', I am sorely tempted to get up and say, 'No, I do not have many awards.' But that would be rude. I know that it matters to the organisers to have an award-winning writer as their guest. For me to announce that I am no such thing, would be to bring their event down a notch. And so I remain silent.

On the other hand, I have never lacked publishers. All my books have been accepted by publishers. Yes, there have been rejections abroad, but I know these rejections have little to do with the quality of my novels; they come out of the fact that the novels do not fit into the publisher's idea of what an Indian novel should be. (My agent always writes to tell me that the rejection is invariably accompanied by the words, 'We think this is a very good novel, but …' Oh yes, the *but* …). In fact, the truth is that I know I have been very privileged because I have written what I want, the way I want. I have been able to go my own way, uncaring of literary trends and market forces. I have had the freedom to write what I want; I can imagine no greater luxury for a writer than this.

But I do have two small regrets, both of which no longer matter very much. After a short stay in New York of just three days, I felt I would have loved to stay in New York for a slightly longer time, and experience its magic at first hand. To go about the city, visit museums, galleries, see plays, walk around in Central Park, eat in all the little places, which look so enticing from outside. But this, I know, will never happen. Perhaps it is good not to realise a dream; the reality may be, will be, completely and disappointingly different from the dream. The other desire I have had for years (after reading *A Room With a View*?) is to go and live in Italy, in Tuscany, for some days. Not in a hotel, but in a house, with family, perhaps, or friends. With younger people who would do all the hard work while I sat and read, was driven around, ate food which I had not cooked myself and drank the beautiful wine of the region. This too remains a dream.

The regret which is real, and which matters, is that even today there is no platform available to me, no place where I can write about my ideas and thoughts about literature, about what is happening in the country. I have no contacts anywhere, and absolutely none in the world of journalism; there is no journalist I know to whom I can send a piece and ask — can you use this? I have been approached by a great many journalists for various reasons. But I have never been able to use this little contact for my purposes. I quickly forget names and faces, never store them 'just in case …' There are times when I am deeply disturbed about things happening in the country and it is then that I wish I could write about it and get it published, somewhere, anywhere. I wish at times I could review a book, and be able to write the kind of review I think we need in IWE (well, I could certainly try). I would be grateful for a little space for these things. But it is not there. There was a time when I was able to have my pieces accepted and published. Not anymore. Perhaps it is my age that has pushed me out of the magic circle, made me invisible. A magazine in Delhi did give me an opportunity for a few years to write about books and literature. I loved it. I wrote about Daphne du Maurier, about Steinbeck, about Priestley and Virginia Woolf and so many other writers I had loved and enjoyed. I wrote not only about novels and novelists, but also about poets and poetry. It was wonderful while it lasted. But the staffer who had interacted with me quit her job and I was left high and dry. And, therefore, the thought that perhaps I am writing this book to talk about the books I have read, the books I have loved, that I am using this space to talk about writers, to quote some of their wonderful lines. A celebration of words, of language, of writers' ideas. The thought pleases me.

Reading was a passion as I have said earlier, perhaps more than once, one that began when I was still a child in short frocks. I was often chided, specially when the examination results came, and was told that reading was a waste of time. Time well wasted, I now think. I couldn't have wasted it better. And look at how faithful reading has been! It has stayed with me through all the years since then. If I believed in the Day of Judgement – and it is possible that, having begun life in a Roman Catholic school, the belief is there, lurking somewhere within me – and if I am asked by whoever is supposed to ask the question (I can't go so far as to believe in a bearded wise old man), 'What have you done with your life?' I will say, 'I have read, I have read many books, I have read many good books, some great books.' And if the voice then asks, 'And …?' I will add in a small voice, 'I have written.'

Yes, I have written, but it is so minute a part of all that has been written, merely a microdot, that I would be reluctant to speak of my writing. Recently, I watched in fascination, as a young and successful writer was ushered on stage and presented to the audience as the author who has sold more books than any other writer, as the writer who earns more money than most writers. All this was said with such a flourish, one could almost hear the trumpets. And I wondered at the composure with which the author listened to these words, the calmness with which she took in the applause; I marvelled at her aplomb. Such enormous self-confidence can only come, I thought then, and still think, with success, through earning large sums of money. And, perhaps, let me add, because the author has not read much, has not read the greats, she has no idea of her place in the world of literature.

When Hemingway was asked, in an interview for the *Paris Review Interviews*, 'Who are your literary forebears, those you have learned the most from?', he began listing them: Mark Twain, Flaubert, Stendhal, Turgenev, John Donne, Andrew Marvell, 'the good Kipling', and many more. And added, 'It would take a day to remember all the people who have been an influence on my life and work. Then it would sound as though I were claiming an erudition I did not possess.' And he finally said, a very simple and direct answer, 'I am telling you because you asked me.'

If I were to try to give an answer to the question Hemingway was asked, I would think of Emily Brontë's *Wuthering Heights*, of Jane Austen's *Persuasion* and *Emma*, and yes, *Pride and Prejudice*, too. I would speak of Elizabeth Gaskell's *North and South*, of Dickens' *Bleak House* and *Our Mutual Friend*, of George Eliot's *Mill on the Floss* and *Middlemarch*, of Forster's *Howard's End*, of Thornton Wilder's *The Bridge of San Luis Rey*, of Tagore's stories, of Tolstoy's *War and Peace*, of Solzhenitsyn's *Cancer Ward* and *One Day in the Life of Ivan Denisovich*, of Atwood's *Cat's Eye*, of Marilynne Robinson's *Gilead* and *Home*, of Elizabeth Bowen's *Friends and Relations*, of Anne Tyler's *Saint Maybe* and *Dinner at the Homesick Restaurant*, of Shakespeare and John Donne, of Virginia Woolf and Simone de Beauvoir, of Shaw and Ibsen and Arthur Miller and Tennessee Williams …

There I go a-listing again. It is a futile exercise, because there is no end to the books I have loved, books which have been a great part of my life. But it would not stop at that. Hemingway counted painters among his influences as well – Tintoretto, Hieronymus Bosch, Brueghel, Goya, Cezanne, Van Gogh, Gauguin. I would have to add so much more, apart from the painters: the stories and myths I have heard in my childhood, the music, the songs and poems I've fervently responded to, the beliefs and the faith which run in my blood – they are all part of it. There is a song sung by the great M.S. Subbulakshmi, one which speaks of the gopis and Krishna frolicking in Brindavan, and then asks, 'Was it a dream?' What a wonderful thought that the entire story of Krishna, which is so much a part of us even today, was a dream we dreamed.

To go back – undoubtedly, it is the curious mixture of influences, both Indian and Western, that have made me the writer I am. In time, I also began to understand that there was no getting away from the fact that I was a part of Indian writing in English. The very nomenclature embraced me into its fold, because I was Indian and I wrote in English. However much I had distanced myself from the literature when I began writing, I had been a part of it and I had travelled along with it, from the time of the Big Three (R.K. Narayan, Mulk Raj Anand and Raja Rao, the Holy Trinity of IWE). I was with the literature when these writers flagged and when, for a while, there seemed to be no one to take their places.

Then came Rushdie, and soon a host of Indian writers flooded the scene and Indian writing was recognised the world over. After which, came IWE's Crowning Glory, the Booker for Arundhati Roy and later for Kiran Desai and Aravind Adiga. Yes, and the Pulitzer for Jhumpa Lahiri. Indian writing in English became the toast of the literary world and the bane of the *bhasha* literatures in India. For, the great hostility to English writing and English writers continued, in fact it got worse – they should not write in a foreign language, they cannot write of Indian culture in an alien language, they write for money, for fame, they are traitors, slaves of the English and so on and on *ad infinitum*. As Vijay Nambisan, a poet, put it in his inimitable style in his book *Language as an Ethic*, 'In standard-fare Hindi films, the villain is easily stereotyped. He smokes and drinks and wears "smart" clothes. In *bhasha* circles, the villain writes in English.' Ha! Spot-on Nevertheless, whatever the carpers said, it was a wonderful time for English writers in India.

But ... but .. but ...

Someone, sometime, somewhere called me curmudgeonly. I wish people would consult their dictionaries when they use a word not often, or not commonly used. Curmudgeon is mainly used in connection with miserliness and I am sure that whoever used that word for me did not intend that meaning. I think the right word would be crotchety. At my age, I have every right to be crotchety. With so many dreams, both personal and national, unfulfilled, so many illusions fallen by the wayside, why wouldn't I be crotchety? Yes, I could see faults in this much-feted writing. One of the problems about fault-finding, specially if you are not a great beneficiary of the boom, is that you will be called jealous. I remember the Marathi/English writer Gauri Deshpande wrote a piece on *The God of Small Things*, beginning with, 'I know I will be called jealous for saying these things, but I will say them nevertheless.' 'Crabs in a bucket,' a publisher once called those who did not bow in reverence to the writing which was so much valued outside the country. But, like Gauri Deshpande, I will say what I want to, never mind if I am called jealous, or a crab in a bucket.

I have no quarrel with any particular book or author, but I have to say that I find it very strange that a literature should be judged outside the country of its origin. Why, even Naipaul, with whom I have nothing in common, said (critically, I think) that IWE must be one of the few literatures, if not the only one, which is so valued. An Indian book, which is appreciated in London or New York, which gets good reviews in these places, becomes, *only* on this account, a book of much greater significance than any book published only in India. The 'published abroad' tag gets the book quick reviews, longer reviews, and therefore the stamp of being a significant book. It is not generally understood that Indian books published in the West have to conform to a certain idea the publishers have of what an Indian book should be like (I am speaking only of fiction), of whether Western readers can easily enter the book and, therefore, whether it will sell and sell enough. Literary agents know these things, they often get a great deal of the book rewritten.

Of course, there are writers whose writing is acceptable both in India and outside and there are writers who have made themselves so known in the West that I am sure agents don't dare to make them re-write. And, books published in India do not reach the Western reader at all. Which means that you have to be published abroad to be read by readers outside India. This is how it is; one cannot quarrel with facts. But what makes me, well, crotchety, is that even Indians, when they speak of IWE (and not to praise it, mind), only speak of those authors who, having been published in the West, are more known. Lists of Indian writers often begin and end with those who are known outside India – and this, because they have been published outside India. It has become a vicious circle. An intellectual like Ramachandra Guha, the historian, a man whose views and courage I much admire, once said, 'A Kannada or a Bengali writer has a connection to his (*sic*) people which an English writer simply does not. Most Indian writers who are acclaimed abroad have no impact on society.'

A strange statement to make, because he moves from the general

'English writer' to a qualified, 'Indian writers who are acclaimed abroad'. What then about English writers *not* acclaimed abroad? Do they have an impact on their society? And is it *because* they are not acclaimed abroad? The questions are rhetorical. The answer is clear: whether the writer's work has an impact or not, does not, or should not depend on the language. It is a fact that literature in any language is limited to readers who know the language. Nor should the impact depend on where the books are published. A good book can rise above all these matters and speak directly and clearly to its readers. Even more recently, a young writer who has earned a good name for himself, both as a novelist and a non-fiction writer, spoke of India having in the last three decades produced many excellent writers in English, such as Rushdie, Ghosh and Roy. And then added that none of them 'could credit India alone for their success. They all came to India via the West, via its publishing deals and prizes.' This writer, Aatish Taseer, then goes on to say, 'India left to its own devices throws up a very different kind of writer, a man such as Chetan Bhagat.'

Astonishing! I was aghast when I read this, I wanted to reply to it. But this appeared in *The New York Times* and I would be a fool to think that *The New York Times* would give me space. (Oh, the importance of having a platform!) Bhagat, for the ignorant (though I don't think there is anyone in India who does not know who or what Bhagat is), is an immensely popular writer whose books sell more than most books in India do. In effect, if you are published in India, you must be a Bhagat-like writer. Both this statement and Guha's make a whole lot of writers invisible. Writers like Kiran Nagarkar, Githa Hariharan, Allan Sealy, Upamanyu Chatterjee, K.R. Usha, Anita Nair, Anjum Hasan, and so many other younger writers as well. And older writers, too, like me! (Yes, I am very much an interested party. Perhaps I can therefore validly be called a crab in a bucket. So be it!) All, or many of us, have produced a body of work which has been published in India, read by Indian readers, studied in colleges and universities, and some of us have been translated both into foreign and Indian languages. To dismiss a whole group of such writers screams aloud for an explanation. The kind of generalisations that are made in these two statements are unfortunate. I dislike generalisations, anyway.

To my own surprise, I have been a staunch crusader for Indian writing in English. Not because of the language, but because I believe in the right of the writer to write in any language she wants, to write of the themes she wants to write about. I must admit that at times it is hard to respond to statements that condemn English writing, specially those that come from the *bhasha* writers, because political correctness puts English writers on the wrong side. They, rather we, cannot say anything negative about writers in the *bhashas*. There has been one man, P. Lal, who took English-bashers head-on, who even brought out a whole book of responses by Indian English poets to a statement that Indians should not write poetry in English. One of the finest responses in this book is that of A.K. Ramanujan: 'If they can (write poetry in English) they will.' As simple as that! This comes close to P. Lal's response to the problem imposed on Indian English writers who are published abroad, the problem of constantly having to prove they are Indian, or that their writing is, which Meenakshi Mukherjee called 'the anxiety of Indianness'. 'If we look after the honesty of our feelings and the skill of our craft,' P. Lal said, 'the Indianness will look after itself.' Touché!

Yes, there have been defenders of Indian writing in English. I have had my say often as well, though not much notice has been taken of what I said. (Am I moaning *yet again*?) But my defence of IWE did not mean that I could not see the flaws in Indian English writing. I was living in the house and I could therefore see all the flaws: the cracks and leaks in the ceiling, the uneven plastering, the window and door frames being set a little askew, the uneven floor and so on. Anita Desai once said, a long time ago, 'There is too little of writing in English.' And what little there was, was heavily weighed down by literary fiction.

> 'Unless the novel, particularly the so-called literary novel, can reach the hearts and minds of ordinary people, reading will increasingly become a minority interest.'

The words of P.D. James. A little biased, perhaps, but I can understand her. She has been labelled a genre writer, a crime writer, which means that, though her novels are of an excellent literary quality, they have never been recognised as good literature, or been in the reckoning for any major literary prize. Which is a shame, for some of her works are excellent novels, *Innocent Blood*, for example, or *Original Sin*. To go back to James' statement, I think that reading *is* and has always been a minority interest. Yet, a literature becomes meaningful only when it has books for all kinds of readers. In fact, a literature is kept alive by good books, for great books come but rarely; it is good books that keep readers hooked to reading.

I think of all the writers who kept me alive as a reader: Graham Greene, J.B. Priestley, Wodehouse, Daphne du Maurier, Somerset Maugham, A.J. Cronin, Georgette Heyer, Rumer Godden and so many others. And the crime writers – Agatha Christie, Ngaio Marsh, Dorothy Sayers, in recent times Sue Grafton and many, many others. None of them Booker Prize or Nobel Prize material, perhaps (except Greene, maybe, and it is a mystery why he was not more awarded), but I have found many of the Booker Prize books unreadable. Whereas, the real gems were the ones I found on my own. Anne Tyler, for example, and Anita Brookner. I discovered them long before they became well known and much before they got their share of literary acclaim. *Disturbances in the Field*, by Lynne Schwartz, was a book I had never heard of, by an author I had never read. But there it was, an excellent book, one I go back to again and again. *The Bird Artist* by Howard Norman – another delightful surprise. Ann Patchett's *Bel Canto* which, when I first read it, almost made me swoon in delight. I hadn't heard of it then, though it is more known now. *The Bridge of San Luis Rey* by Thornton Wilder, which has been my companion for decades. Carol Shields' *The Stone Diaries*, which took me to her *Small Ceremonies,* such excellent novels, both of them. Mrs Gaskell's *Cranford*, a gently humorous book that led me into the world of this writer whom I had somehow missed out on. John Gunther's *Death Be Not Proud,* which I'd found in my grandfather's bookcase in Pune and read as a girl.

There's poetry too. Though I gave up on poetry in my later years, I discovered Robert Browning's *My Last Duchess* when my friend, Amrita Bhalla, quoted it to me, the entire poem, without a pause. What a poem! So much unsaid in it, the way the poet gradually reveals the craftiness of the Duke, the tremendous cruelty concealed under a seeming uxoriousness. However, as far as Indian books are concerned, the Booker became the touchstone for Indian writing after three Indians won it. All other books became invisible. Amit Chaudhuri, a writer who cannot be called a crab because he has been published and recognised in the West, recently wrote about the gargantuan shadow of the Booker which falls over IWE. The Booker-winning books became the acme of Indian writing.

I once had a dream. I dreamt of a time when Indian publishers would have the money, and therefore writers from outside would come to Indian publishers and would then be told: your book is not exotic enough, it is not English or American enough, it is not accessible to our readers, you need to rewrite, make it more accessible to them, if you could just remove this chapter, after all our readers wouldn't be interested in American history ... Oh well, only a dream. But there are some changes that I wished for which did happen. Yes, Indian publishers were suddenly able to give writers the kind of money writers in India had never dreamt of. This, because the number of readers in English, in India, went up by leaps and bounds. And this happened because of the belief of most Indian parents in India that English education was good for their children, it happened because of liberalisation, because of globalisation. And it led to more readers for English. And another result – English writing became more democratic. Those who, a generation earlier, would not have written in English, now did. Besides, many young people began earning more money than the earlier generations, and they had a great desire for something that took them away, even if only for a while, from their stressful jobs. Therefore, there were more English writers and readers among the young. I consider it very good for a literature when there is a lot of writing happening. It is only then that a literature thrives. Many good books, and possibly one or two great books, may emerge out of the plenty. Besides, young writers are exploring more genres: crime, romance, mythology. The bestseller phenomenon has now entered India. Who would have believed that mythology-based books would become bestsellers? I think of my story on Amba and how much it travelled, being rejected by many before it found a place in a corner of the women's page of a newspaper. Now, even non-fiction, the step-child of the literary world, has become popular; in fact, more popular than fiction. Non-fiction books are on bestseller lists. The books of Amartya Sen, William Dalrymple, Ramachandra Guha are grabbed by publishers and read by avid readers. Things had changed, changes which were all very wonderful.

But ... but ... but ...

There I go, being a curmudgeon all over again. Sorry, being crotchety yet again. *What's your problem now*, I can imagine being asked in exasperation? The answer is simple. It is language. What alarms me about this success is the way language is being devalued. It is fine that young writers, at least the successful ones we most hear of, do not want to write literary fiction. It is even fine when they speak with contempt of the earlier generation of Indian English writers who wrote literary fiction. I can understand a generation looking at an earlier generation critically; it is a part of breaking free of the past, it is a part of moving on. I have done it myself. But you need to know the tradition you are breaking away from, you should have read the books you don't want your books to be like. Which, as I can guess from what these writers say, is not the case. However, what really troubles me is that they speak of good language with contempt. They openly say that they write a language their readers easily understand. Who, one of them asked, understands the high-flown language the earlier writers wrote?

What I don't understand or appreciate is that these young writers seem to think that language has to be dumbed down, because, presumably, readers are dumb. It shows a contempt for readers which is unforgivable. How else, but by constantly challenging itself, has the human race got to where it is now? To take the easiest way out is not part of our survival kit. Do we give up on language, one of the greatest gifts given to, no, earned by humankind? A gift which we have, through the millenniums, made into something which is the means of connecting with other humans, the means of telling millions of human stories, the means of articulating complex and complicated emotions and ideas, of expressing an immense number of human experiences?

Without language we would not have known as much as we do now, because to name a thing, to express a feeling, is to know of its existence. 'God called the dry land earth and the gathering of the waters he called the sea.' So says the Bible. Which shows, Tony says to Madhu in *Small Remedies*, that naming things is part of the act of creation. To show a contempt for good language seems to me almost blasphemous.

I sometimes wonder whether this supposed scorn comes out of an inability to write better language. I think of my father's and grandfather's letters to my mother, letters, which she carefully preserved and which are still with me. These letters are written in such chaste English that I have to marvel, because both my father and grandfather were village-educated, they started learning English at a much later stage (yes, strangely, both of them wrote to my mother in English). Perhaps we need to say it aloud, that books do not have to be badly written to be popular. I remember a review of a popular book in which the reviewer, a writer himself, and one whose own language, even when he speaks, is impeccable, said that the sales of the book validated it! I despaired, I thought it was all over for good writing. But I cannot give up on my belief that all writers need to respect both language and the craft. P.G. Wodehouse seems to be a light-weight writer, but reading his book *Performing Flea* (that's what he called himself. There never was, and never will be, a writer more genuinely modest), I was amazed to discover the immense trouble he took over his writing, the amount of time he took to write one particular passage, a passage that is so hilarious it should never be read in public. Seeing you laughing hysterically for no apparent reason, people will wonder about your sanity. Impossible to imagine that Wodehouse had to work so hard to get this effect, that he was nervous, wondering whether it would work. The language he uses is always right for his purposes; Gowers would approve of him.

Though I am glad that IWE now has many more genres, that literary fiction is not the only genre being written, I find this competition between the genres futile. There is room for all kinds of books, there are all kinds of readers for different books. I found *The Da Vinci Code* an appallingly badly written book, yet millions loved it, as the sales figures showed. Many readers find Paulo Coelho and Alexander McCall Smith profound and uplifting, but I must confess I find their attempts to be profound both banal and depressing. F.R. Leavis, a man who showed such exquisite taste in calling Jane Austen a great writer, despises J.B. Priestley. But I adore Priestley's *The Good Companions*, which has given me more pleasure than I can ever say. When my first copy of the book, which was a second-hand book, anyway, turned up its toes and prepared to die, the pages sadly parting from one another, I got another copy from my son in the USA. Another second-hand copy, but my library was incomplete without it. Such a rousing, rollicking, jolly book with such wonderful, almost Dickensian, characters. Who can ever forget Inigo Jollifant? Or the entirely enchanting Susie Dean? And just look at the chapter heading: 'Inigo Jollifant quotes Shakespeare and departs into the night'. That's amazingly wonderfully tantalising. Exactly what a novel should do to a reader. Never mind what Mr Leavis thinks, this book has brought me much joy.

Yes, there is room for all kinds of books, room for all kinds of writers. But Indian writing in English is a strange creature, with many avatars, and has been plagued from the very beginning by a divisiveness, by an either/or understanding, the categories changing in course of time, but the differences remaining. Differences between writers in the *bhashas* and writers in English. Between writers published abroad and writers published in India. Between writers who had made it in the West and those who were known only at home. Now it is the younger popular writers set against the earlier generation of literary fiction writers. It is the bestsellers against literary fiction. Thinking of these things, I have to wonder whether Margaret Atwood's words about the existence of a community of writers, words which seem to me so profound, have any truth in them. In fact, her words remind me of the Buddha's words to his father. The story, apocryphal, perhaps, but a beautiful one, goes like this:

The Buddha's father found him at the city gates, begging bowl in hand, and asked him, obviously in consternation, what he was doing.

'This,' the Buddha said, 'is the custom of my race.'

'What race is that?' the father wanted to know.

'The race of the Buddhas,' he replied. 'I am one of them and what they do, I do.'

This statement of the Buddha, as well as Atwood's words, gave me, perhaps, an exalted idea of writing and writers, but one I truly believe in. There are connections, connections that you suddenly become aware of when you hear the words of a writer from another country perhaps, in another language, maybe, which eerily echo your own words and thoughts. When I read Eudora Welty's words, 'I just think of myself as writing about human beings, and I happen to live in a region, as do we all, so I write about what I know …', I want to stand up and shout out to her across the years, across the barriers that divide the living from the dead, 'How extraordinary. I've said that too.'

I remember how, in Australia, after the early touristy-treatment, when we were finally able to meet writers, I felt a sudden sense of kinship, of being among people we could talk with. We spoke the same language, we understood one another in a way only those who are professionally bonded do. I have seen this sense of cohesiveness from the glimpses I had, in my childhood, of the world of Kannada literature. Of course, there were schisms, rifts, antagonism, animosities. Writers were divided by ideologies, by personal feelings, and there was, and still is, the big divide of caste. In Dharwad, even as children, we knew that there were groups among writers, that our father, who was an agnostic and a rational thinker, had nothing to do with. I am sure they were equally hostile to him. But that did not prevent my father from being an admirer of the poet, Bendre, who belonged to the other group.

Some years back, a feud, an ideological one, between two major Kannada writers, spilled over on to a daily newspaper, which carried an entire page of readers' letters; so strong was the feeling about these two points of view. Yet, there was something in the response to the feud which spelt out that the literature mattered to readers. And that, in spite of all the slanging among Kannada writers, there was, and still is, an idea of a Kannada literary world to which all of them belonged.

IWE is an entirely different animal. Writers are dispersed not only through the country, but through the world. 'Do you know Anita Desai?' I was asked more than once when I went abroad. No, I didn't. How would I know her? Where would I meet her? We live in two entirely different worlds, and it's not just that she lives abroad and I live in India, and our paths never cross. IWE did not have the kind of *sammelans*, the meetings, that the *bhasha* literatures had. 'English literature is like a family in which one half of the family is not talking to the other half' – I read these words somewhere, I have forgotten where, but they seem to me to say exactly what ails IWE. There is a lordly indifference to other writers. We are just not interested in the writing of others, we scarcely read one another. Zadie Smith's wonderful essay on *Middlemarch* ('Middlemarch and Everybody') is to me an excellent example of how a contemporary writer can revisit an earlier writer and forge a connection to her tradition, enriching, not just a reader's understanding of the earlier writer, but her own writing as well. Smith has written just such an excellent essay on E.M. Forster too. I doubt whether any writer in India, English writer, I mean, has done this kind of thing.

Literary festivals do provide an opportunity for, both, English and *bhasha* writers, to meet and mingle. Perhaps many writers have benefited from them. My own experience has not been a very happy one, though I would blame myself for this, for not being the outgoing type, for being unable to talk to strangers and becoming friendly with them. And I find panel discussions, which are the meat of festivals, excruciatingly boring. Perhaps my dislike for literary festivals comes from my first experience, which was not a happy one. The organiser asked me to travel by train, because, I was told, there could be a fog during that season, and planes would have trouble landing or taking off. Were all writers travelling by train, I asked. (There were some writers from outside India on the list.) Or did the fog specially appear when my plane was to land and take off? I politely declined the invitation, prestigious though the literary festival was. I wrote to the organisers that I had stopped travelling by train because of age and health problems. I then got a letter saying that there had been a mistake. Someone had blundered, as Tennyson had so famously said about the charge of the Light Brigade. And, of course, I would be given air fare. Well …!

Today, I find that festivals outsource the management of it and the people conducting the festival have no clue about writers, books or anything literary. I remember once, just as I was getting on to the stage for an interview during a festival, an officious, in-charge of that session, man, said, 'Remember, Shashi, only twenty minutes!' I don't know what made me more angry, his addressing me by my name (I'm older than your mother, man, I wanted to say. Have young people forgotten how to address an older person?), or his warning about the time. Was I an idiot not to know how much time we had? My interviewer, a veteran of such do's, saw my face and gently led me away, saying, 'Forget him. He doesn't matter.'

Perhaps I'm being unrealistic, perhaps I'm forgetting that we live in an age where the book has become a product and writing, a profession like any other. The other day, a writer-friend told me that she was asked by a younger writer, 'Can I intern with you?' Intern as a writer? Isn't writing a wholly individualistic, almost solipsistic profession? The idea of writers as prophets, as intellectual leaders, also has no place in the world today. Writers have long abdicated that role. They are too busy promoting themselves and their books to become the voice of a society. 'Just for a handful of silver he left us, just for a riband to stick in his coat': Robert Browning's words in *The Lost Leader*, referring to Wordsworth who had abandoned the liberal cause and accepted a government position and a pension. In IWE, the anxiety of Indianness has been replaced by the anxiety for success, for fame and for money.

Then something happened which seemed to bring writers belonging to all languages together. Well, some of them, at least. And for some time, at least.

The BJP government, which came to power with promises of development and progress, seemed to embolden certain fringe Hindutva elements who went on a spree, trying to impose a dubious idea of 'an ancient Indian culture' on the country, ignoring our long and glorious history of multiculturalism, of many religions living together. These culture-defenders decided what was right and what was wrong, they made their pronouncements on what could be done and what could not be done. But even worse was to come. Three men, two of them rationalists who were intent on eradicating superstition, and one of them a scholar, were killed.

The scholar, Prof. Kalburgi, was shot dead in his own home by a man who came on a motorcycle, rang the bell, and shot the Professor when he came out to greet a supposed visitor. (Most strangely, the day I am writing this is an anniversary of his death and the murderers have not yet been traced.) Prof. Kalburgi had been threatened before for writing something about Basaveshwara, the man who broke away from Hinduism because of its caste system and the inequality that it created. He had unearthed some facts about Basaveshwara, which the custodians of Basaveshwara did not like. At that time, the Professor had retracted from what he had written, but he had not stopped his research.

When I saw the news of his killing on TV, I was shocked. I had met him earlier, when he had been the Vice Chancellor of the Kannada University at Hampi. My sister and I had contacted him in connection with our desire to give our father's manuscripts to the university. He had been courteous enough to come home to discuss this. I met him again later at the meeting of the newly constituted General Council of the Sahitya Akademi to which I had been nominated as a member. Prof. Kalburgi was a member as well. He was a soft-spoken, gentle man. That such a man had been shot, and in Dharwad, which had always seemed to me the most civilised of towns, was hard to believe. I expected the Akademi to say something about his death, to put out a statement, perhaps, condemning the killing, expressing their grief at the loss of a writer, a writer who was a part of their organisation. Nothing happened. The silence made me uneasy and I wondered whether there was a reason for it. I then heard from a friend that the Akademi had held a condolence meeting in Bangalore, during which no mention had been made of the fact that he had been murdered; they spoke of his death as if it was a natural one. I could not believe this. I was haunted by an uneasiness I could not pin down.

Then something else happened. A Muslim man was killed on the suspicion that he had eaten beef. To my great surprise, and even greater pleasure, two writers, yes, writers, Nayantara Sahgal and Uday Prakash, stood up to protest against these happenings and as a protest returned the awards the Sahitya Akademi had given them. Now my uneasiness congealed into a resolve: I could not be a part of an institution which did not stand up for the writers it was supposed to represent. The Akademi, I thought, had failed writers.

I made up my mind to resign from the Akademi. I spoke about it to my friend Githa Hariharan, who convinced me to release my resignation letter on the internet at the same time as I wrote to the Akademi. She also warned me, 'The media will descend on you.' I was confident very few would bother about my action. I was not a newsworthy writer, I would not attract any attention. But a journalist, one of the first to call me after my resignation letter appeared on the internet, said the same thing. 'Do you think you can cope?' she asked, very gently and kindly.

But responding to the media, and answering their questions, was no problem. I was saying what I believed in, these were things I wanted to say, things which I had written about, so it was all right. Coping with constantly ringing phones and continuous rings at the door, journalists asking for a 'byte', in fact, the disruption of our routine, was a nuisance. But it was in furtherance of something that mattered. And all the journalists I met, as well as the TV crews, many of whom I had met earlier in the course of my public engagements in the city, were friendly. What I hated were the cameras and the bright lights. The camera does all the wrong things to me; I squirm, I make faces, I lose my composure and know that I am not at my best. And the lights hurt my eyes; I had been suffering from a dry eye problem for years, part of a larger syndrome, of which photo phobia is a part. But I knew this media attention was short-lived. The media and the public both have very short attention spans.

The most wonderful thing was what followed; it was a tremendous surprise, not only to me, but to a great many people. Writer after writer joined the protest, they resigned from their positions, they returned their awards. Others followed with supporting statements; artists, scientists, film-makers, social scientists, teachers and many more writers joined the protest. Suddenly, for the first time after Anna Hazare's anti-corruption movement, which had fizzled out so badly, there was a national movement, which came out of an idea of what kind of a country India should be. I was elated that writers had spoken out. Writers throughout the country, writers in all the languages. It gave me hope. In fact, ironically, it took me back to the first meeting of the Sahitya Akademi's General Council, where I had seen writers from all parts of the country, writers in so many different languages, gathered in one room. There was something about the sight that had both pleased and heartened me. Now I felt the same way as more and more writers joined the protest. It was very pleasing to see many younger writers among them.

But things soon got complicated. Another group of writers appeared on the scene, writers who were on the side of the government. Which was all right, because there are bound to be differing opinions and convictions. What was not so all right was that this group indulged in name-calling. The writers who had joined the protest were called sheep, they were called traitors, anti-national, intellectual mercenaries, political stooges, a mafia and many other words of abuse. The protest was belittled, it was trivialised by being called 'award wapsi'. The word 'intellectual', became an ugly word, as ugly as 'secular' and 'liberal'. Ministers said that the protest had been done at the behest of the opposition parties to influence the Bihar elections. (If only writers had so much power!) It is a sad day when a government shows that it disrespects its writers, its artists and scholars. A sad day when the government takes the lead in vilifying its creative people. No country can call itself a civilised country if writers, artists, scholars and thinkers are treated with contempt.

I read a conversation between President Obama and the writer Marilynne Robinson, a one-to-one serious conversation about various matters, and I thought that, with this conversation, President Obama had shown his respect, not only for this writer, but for all writers, for all thinkers. Things have changed now, with President Trump at the helm. In fact, all over the world, the rightist/leftist division has never been sharper or clearer. Perhaps the USA is closer to the post-Second World War McCarthy years, when Senator Joseph McCarthy initiated an interrogation of all Americans, who, at some time, had had contact with Communists, or had been party members. The question asked of them was, 'Are you, or have you ever been, a member of the Communist party?' Nobody was exempt from questioning.

The entertainment industry was especially targeted, as were writers, for artists are often mavericks, people with independent views. Charlie Chaplin, Danny Kaye, Dashiell Hammett, Elia Kazan, Arthur Miller, Lillian Hellman were some of those brought in for questioning. Arthur Miller refused to answer. Miller has spoken of how the chairman of the (very clumsily named) House Un-American Activities Committee sent him a message that, if Miller's wife would have a photograph with him, shaking his hand, 'he would call off the whole thing'. Arthur Miller's wife, as most people know, was Marilyn Monroe! People were encouraged to inform on colleagues and friends, which would make their own punishment lighter. Lillian Hellman's often-quoted response was, 'To hurt innocent people whom I knew many years ago in order to save myself, is to me inhuman, indecent and dishonourable. I cannot and will not cut my conscience to fit this year's fashion.' Writers and actors under suspicion were blacklisted, which meant they could not get work anywhere. There is a story of Samuel Goldwyn, film producer, exclaiming, 'How'm I gonna do decent pictures when all my good writers are in jail?' Perhaps we too need to think of how, unless people stand up for themselves, for their convictions and for their friends, it is easy to suppress any kind of dissent.

If the writers' protest gave some of us a sense of euphoria, it did not last very long. Things cooled down. As they should. Shri Krishna in the Gita speaks of the sword going back into the scabbard when the need to fight is over. And, after all, the protest was not meant to shake the government, but to remind it of the citizen's right to freedom of speech and expression. I am curious to know how things will play out. (Though, even as I write, a journalist, Gauri Lankesh, was murdered, shot in front of her house in Bangalore, by motorcyclists who sped away. Exactly what happened in Prof. Kalburgi's murder.)

'The only way to keep ourselves free is to speak, not to let ourselves be silenced, either by pernicious laws or by mob screaming.' Sara Paretsky's (the American crime writer) words. In India, we see a great deal of mob screaming. A Tamil writer Perumal Murugan, driven to desperation by the hostility with which his writings were received by his community, dramatically declared himself dead as a writer. But the law ruled in his favour, it told him to live and go back to writing. Between the writers' mass protest and Murugan's 'death', there are two truths: that we need to speak up and fight for our rights and that there is always hope. Indira Gandhi's Emergency seemed to have successfully silenced her detractors and critics. But she was very soon voted out of power. My one hope is that we never have to announce the death of 'L.I.Bertie, son of T.Ruth and D'Ocracy' ever again.

The Requisite Ending

There is one thing missing, of course, from personal life writing: that requisite ending. Tick without the tock.
Penelope Lively, Dancing Fish and Ammonites

THERE IS ALWAYS A sense of sadness in coming to the end of a book. Something that had occupied almost your entire life for months, for years, something around which you built your daily life, will soon no longer be with you. It is like letting go of a loved child; there is a feeling of emptiness. Sometimes it seems to me that writing is very much like parenting. A person becomes a parent in one single magic moment when a child is born. Most parents are full of happiness, but I remember how inadequate I felt to be responsible for the little life, which had just come into the world. What did I know about how to take care of this fragile little creature who, it seemed, depended entirely on me? A writer, too, gets into writing wholly untaught, totally untrained (except those who go to creative writing classes, I presume), completely ignorant of how writing is done. You learn as you go along, the same way parents do. And, like with parenting, a lifetime is not enough to know all about writing, to have the confidence of complete knowledge. There's always the nagging thought – I could have done better. And, like it is with new parents, life is rarely dull for a writer. Troubled, maybe, but not dull. Just as each day is a new day when you have children, each story/novel/poem/play is something a writer feels she has never done before.

However, for a writer, sending a book out into the world does not have the same finality that sending a child out has. There is the anticipation of another book waiting for you. I know that there are people who are waiting to take me into their world, into their lives, asking me to tell their stories. And so it begins all over again, another book, some more years of absorption in writing, again a sense of being out of this everyday world. The emptiness, the blankness, that insinuates itself between books does not last long.

I have always wondered at the interest the world has in 'writer's block'. For some reason, it is a phenomenon that fascinates the world, the world which is interested in literature and writers, that is. The question, 'Have you experienced writer's block?' or, 'How do you deal with writer's block?' is often asked of writers during interviews. It is as if the gunshot with which Hemingway killed himself continues to resonate in the world of literature. Perhaps people think of it as a condition writers sometimes suffer from, a condition that can be cured the way a cardiac surgeon deals with an arterial block, bypassing the blocked artery and letting the blood flow through a new passage. But a writer's block is not like that. It needs, not a surgeon, but a physician – Time. I know that if for some reason I cannot write for a while, I just have to wait and, in time, it will come back to me. Most writers get back into writing after a while. If they don't, it just means they are written out. Or, perhaps, they have become too famous. Fame is the dreaded enemy of an artist. Virginia Woolf put her finger on it when she said in *A Room of One's Own*:

'Now I think Shakespeare was very happy in this, that there was no impediment of fame, but his genius flowed out of him ...'

'Impediment of fame' – the right words, the right understanding of what fame does to an artist. Writers need to be invisible. I know that I often eavesdrop on other people's conversations (what on earth are they talking about?), on other people's lives. I used to be ashamed of my inordinate interest in people, until I realised that all writers are interested in people. Which is a dignified way of putting it. Writers can also be called nosey parkers, peeping Toms, looking into lighted rooms from the dark outside. Writers, I sometimes think, are also ghosts who inhabit other people's bodies. And for all this they need to be anonymous, to be invisible. To be known, to be famous, takes away the ability to be anonymous. Truly, writers can be destroyed by the false gods of fame and success. Both are lethal and can put an end to creativity, unless the writer has an immense inner strength, which helps her to ignore fame and allows her to go back to her inner resources, rather than keep looking to the world for applause and admiration.

I am not afraid of writer's block, not now, at this time of my life. Okay, I admit I'm touching wood as I write these words. And no, I am not superstitious (or maybe I am, just a little bit!), I believe in being careful. I also believe that the world is for the young, that it is better to move aside before one is shoved aside. Besides, I have always lived with pauses, both short and long, in my writing life because of health problems and family concerns. Now, my fears are different. What I fear are the depredations of age. Old age is treacherous. Martin Amis, in his review of John Updike's last book, *My Father's Tears and Other Stories*, in the *New York Book Review*, speaking of the 'portrait of the artist as an old man', says that the artist 'loses energy as he ages'. And adds that, 'age waters him down'. I am, as I said earlier, always suspicious of generalisations, but I agree with Amis that there is what he calls 'an inner dwindling' which comes with age. What remains, according to him, is 'the habit of writing', words that to me have the sound of a funeral knell. To write out of sheer habit is worse, much worse, than not being able to write at all.

Yes, writing can become a habit, for, after all, a writer has been doing it almost all her adult life. But it can become something more than a habit; it can become an addiction, hard to give up, even when you know you should stop, because of age. It's like an alcoholic trying to stop drinking, or a smoker to stop smoking. 'Just one glass more', 'Just one more cigarette', addicts tell themselves. Or 'I'll give up tomorrow', or 'next month', or 'next year'. And so on and on it goes; the time to give up never comes. For writers it is the same, except that the inability to stop writing may also be accompanied by the loss of that sharp self-critical faculty, an invariable ally of creativity in a good writer. No good writer is in love with everything she writes. She knows, on reading and re-reading, what needs to be rewritten, revised, what needs to be struck out. 'Mawkish', Keats called his early poetry; but he also said, 'I shall be among the English poets after my death.' This combination of self-confidence and self-criticism seems to get diluted in old age; it is like you lose your taste buds, you are no longer able to discriminate, it is like diminished vision, it is like the loss of hearing in old age. Truly, old age is treacherous.

At times, when I am confronted by a fear of losing the ability to see my own writing with an objective critical eye, I comfort myself with the thought that there is a reliable filter called the publisher. I am confident that the publisher will reject bad work. I often tell young hopefuls, who imagine that a word from a known writer will help them, that a publisher will not publish even her/his own mother's work, if she/he is not sure it will sell. A publisher has to make money, because publishing is a business, and therefore the publisher will never compromise on saleability. But what if the author is a big name whose name alone will sell the book? Well, we just have to look at what was done to Harper Lee very recently. Her 'accidentally discovered' manuscript was carefully presented as a new novel and the world went into a tizzy at the thought of reading another novel by the brilliant writer who had stopped at one novel. The literary world was full of surmises and anticipation. When it was finally revealed that this was only an earlier draft of *To Kill a Mockingbird*, they still tried to make it seem something more than what it really was. But it was, undeniably, only a draft that was, perhaps, rejected by the publisher. And there is always a reason for rejecting, for asking for rewriting; this thought should have flashed a warning. But no, the book was hyped enormously and came out to great expectations. Finally, readers, who had no vested interests, rejected the book as just a bad one. *Go Set a Watchman* was a disaster. One bookstore even offered to buy back the books from readers who felt cheated. It was not just the readers, it was clear that Harper Lee herself had also been exploited, perhaps her age making it impossible for her to exercise her literary judgement and take the right decision about something written decades back. Perhaps she didn't even know what was going on. Her statement, that she was 'humbled and amazed' that her book was being published after so many years, makes me deeply suspicious. No author worth her salt would speak of being 'humbled' by publication.

There's also Agatha Christie, whose marketability made publishers republish her books under different titles after her death, misleading loyal readers into thinking it to be a book they had not read. This apart, there are books she wrote when she was too old to know what she was doing. So one guesses from the quality of the writing, from the rambling, the repetitiveness; she became almost a parody of her own earlier self. It often seemed that no editor had touched the book, possibly because to edit it would have meant that there would be nothing left of her original writing. When P.D. James, a writer I much admire, wrote a sequel to *Pride and Prejudice*, a book I have long loved, I was eager to read it. But *Pemberley* was an embarrassment, hard to read without squirming, and hard to forgive the author and the publisher for. Surely, the publisher should have known how bad it was? However, P.D. James was a name that sold and Jane Austen, of course, had become famous, what with all the serials and films based on her novels, with macho sexy Darcys jumping into ponds to reveal their rippling muscles. The combination of James and Austen should have worked; it most emphatically didn't. I am curious to know what James thought of her own work in *Pemberley*. Such a fine, elegant writer, had she reached the stage where she could no longer see the flaws in her own work? Can age be so cruel?

However, very few writers have to worry about their undeserving works being published, for only some have the kind of name that makes this exercise profitable for publishers. I am grateful that some of my early work has been lost, though there are still many early stories, which embarrass me. This may sound meretricious, but I am thankful that I am not a big name, not big enough to tempt a publisher into publishing whatever I have written. Even just a decade or two ago, I could never have imagined that I would be grateful not to be successful. Well, *very* successful, or *very* famous. (Though the carpers could say, what choice did you have, anyway? I admit it. None.)

Though I have to admit that for years I carried a burden of hurt, feeling that my writing had not got its due. I still think that, to a small extent, the diminishing lens through which my writing has been viewed (women's writing, writing about women) has ensured that my writing has remained outside the mainstream. My husband, who has been an observer of the literary world for decades, says that he has yet to meet a writer who thinks she/he has got their due. He says that all writers think of themselves as being underrated. Perhaps he's right. Actually, this phenomenon goes back a long way. We, the moaners, are indeed in very exalted company. In the prologue to his play *Malavikagnimitram,* Kalidasa defends himself against possible criticism by saying, 'Only the ignorant follow the opinions of others.' In other words, please disregard the words of critics! Another Sanskrit dramatist, Bhavabhuti, obviously comforting himself, or trying to comfort himself about the disinterest in, or the indifference to his work, in his play *Malati Madhavam,* loftily wrote, throwing a challenge to Time: 'The earth is vast, time is endless, someone will be born who will understand me.' Truly, every writer's hope, every writer's dream.

Coming closer to our time, there was Saul Bellow, who, I read somewhere, called himself 'a born slightee'. I almost cried out in astonishment when I read this. I knew I was often slighted, I could produce umpteen concrete examples of being slighted. But Saul Bellow? Of course, this must have been before he got the Nobel Prize. Nevertheless, I loved the phrase 'born slightee', I immediately thought, 'Me too!', convinced as I was that my life was full of slights.

There was that mother of all slights (though, calling it the grandmother of all slights may be more appropriate), which spoke of me as a 'Grandmother who writes in an old-fashioned way'. There have been many more comments and omissions, some hurting, like a book on IWE, which did not even mention my name – and this when I already had written three novels and innumerable short stories. The book, a Sahitya Akademi publication, was put before us during a Sahitya Akademi meeting. Nissim Ezekiel, who was chairing the meeting, picked it up during the coffee break, swiftly scanned it and then turned to me, his eyebrows shooting up in surprise. 'You are not here,' he said. No, I was not, God knows why. There was a magazine feature about IWE women writers, which mentioned anyone and everyone who was a woman and wrote in English, but ignored me completely. Why do you care about these things, I am often asked. Because it is my work which is being ignored, my work which is being slighted.

Today, though I can laugh at many of the things that disturbed me once, I know that self-pity is always dangerously close to the surface. Why not? All artists put their entire being into their work. And the world, most of the time, receives it so casually, often with such disinterest, that I wonder what makes most artists go on. 'Look,' we want to cry out, 'listen to me,' we say, 'I've put all of myself into this story, this novel, this poem, this film, this painting, this piece of music, this sculpture, this dance. Let me have the dignity of your serious attention.'

I'm afraid I have to quote Virginia Woolf yet again:

> '... it is the nature of the artist to mind excessively what is said about him. Literature is strewn with the wreckage of men who have minded beyond reason the opinion of others.'

I don't agree with her. I think that most artists, in spite of everything, go back to their work after hurts and slights, they start all over again, everything else forgotten. Colm Tóibín's *The Master* and David Lodge's *Author, Author,* both books on Henry James, highlight James' disastrous play, *Guy Domville*, which, along with its author, was booed off the stage. A terrible, unforgettable disaster. James was, understandably, devastated. And yet he went back to writing novels, and wrote three books, which Graham Greene considers 'three poetic masterpieces': *The Wings of the Dove, The Ambassadors* and *The Golden Bowl*. And there is Keats, who was believed, as Byron wrote, 'to have died at Rome of the *Quarterly Review*'. And, Byron added, 'I know by experience that a savage review is Hemlock to a suckling author.' But Keats died, not of the review, but of TB. My father, in his memoirs, thanks all his enemies, because, he says, they made him determined to go on. I can bring in my own experience of a review which damned my book, saying, I could not write, I could not write English, I did not know how to write a novel, my metaphors were bad, my characters dead and so on and on. It was like having my skin stripped off me, leaving me bleeding all over. When I could think of it with greater composure, I wondered why the reviewer took the trouble to read a book which was so little rewarding; it puzzled me. (Unless, of course, the reviewer found pleasure in condemning me, pleasure in humiliating me.) Equally puzzling is the fact that another review spoke of the same book as deserving the Booker! In any case, I went back to my next book, after a short period of grieving and raging.

'Don't moan.' I often think of the friend who said these words to me. She was right. But there was an even more salutary lesson waiting for me, which I learnt when I read the crime writer Sara Paretsky's *Writing in an Age of Silence*. I was amazed to read her statement that her parents, 'highly educated and highly literate', while ready to borrow money for her brother's education, told her that, if she wanted a college education, it would be at her own expense. I was stunned. Paretsky lives in the USA, which we consider far ahead of us in all things, she lives in a time after mine. And yet her parents denied her higher education, which they were willing to give their son. Whereas, my parents, who had very severely limited means, made no difference between their daughters and their son. My sister and I had the same opportunities as our brother; we were free to study what we wanted to, within their financial means, of course. It was never easy for them; as I grew up, I saw their problems. But there was no question – it was a level playing field for the three of us. My father held on to his job until my sister completed her MBBS and her internship. When she started earning money, he gave up his job and with great relief, I am sure, gave himself up wholly to writing.

I realised, when I thought of these things, that I was privileged. Privileged in this and in many other ways. There are the families I was born into. My father's was a family of scholars and teachers. (My father used to say that the family consisted of either geniuses or lunatics!) One of his uncles was a great Sanskrit scholar. When he died, all his books were given to my father, then only a boy of fourteen, and he read the entire Mahabharata in Sanskrit soon after. He also wrote a long poem on Lokmanya Tilak after Tilak died – in Sanskrit! During one of his last interviews before he died, I remember my father saying, 'I am an intellectual.' He was not bragging, he was merely stating a fact. My father's father was known to be a remarkable teacher. I remember him, on his visit to our house, reading all day, the book held so close to his face that his nose must have been touching it, because his eyes were very bad. But he read. I remember my father reading late at night outside the house (Bangalore was so safe then), reading by the light of a dim bulb above the front door.

My mother's family was equally remarkable. Her father came to Pune from his village, his three younger brothers in tow, for education. He was successful in his mission, and how! He became one of the most successful lawyers in Pune, one brother worked in the police department, another did his LLM and was in time the Dewan of the tiny State of Sawantwadi. And the youngest went to England, completed his FRCS and came back to join the Maharaja of Baroda as the Maharaja's Chief Medical Officer. I was fascinated to read in Maharani Gayatri Devi's autobiography, that she was helped in her affair with the Maharaja of Jaipur by my mother's uncle. (Gayatri Devi's mother was the daughter of the Maharaja of Baroda.)

My grandfather was a great believer in educating girls. Pune at the time was buzzing with ideas of social reform, in which the education of girls was a major factor. This was the era of great reformers like Jyotiba and Savitribai Phule, Mahadev and Ramabai Ranade, Gopal Krishna Gokhale, Lokmanya Tilak, Maharshi Karve and so on. There already were, in my mother's time (the second decade of the twentieth century), two schools for girls in Pune. Huzur Pagah, the second girls' school to be founded in the city, is where all the girls of my mother's family went. (The name of the school indicated that the building had originally been the Peshwa's stables, which gave the boys a chance to make clucking, horse-encouraging noises, or trotting sounds, when the girls went past.) Some of the eminent students of this school were Irawati Karve, Kamal Ranadive, the scientist, who worked in the field of cancer research, and if I'm not mistaken, the great jurist B.R. Ambedkar's second wife, Mai Ambedkar, neé Sharada Kabir, was also from this school.

It was my grandfather's greatest pleasure when he came home in the evening after work, to see all the children, boys as well as girls, sitting at the little desks he had got made for them, their heads bent studiously over their books. 'Not only that,' my uncle once told me, with an indignation laced with pride in my grandfather, 'he engaged tutors for us and after a whole day of school we had to come home and sit with our tutors.' (This uncle went on to become the Chief Justice of the Supreme Court of India. Remarkably, his son, Dhananjay, is now a Judge of the Supreme Court, as well.) Of course, not everyone in the family agreed with my grandfather's views. There was opposition from one of his brothers and from the older women to the girls going to school. The girls had to sneak out of the back door, their footwear in their hands, to avoid their uncle, who, if he saw them, would let loose a volley of foul words on them. (People were less finicky then, about their speech; even women were good at using abusive words.) My aunt told me this. They also often had to go to school on empty stomachs, because, like in all orthodox households, no one could eat until the family priest had performed the daily puja. They used to beg one of the aunts, the kindest one, to keep some leftovers of the night, bits of *bajri bhakris*, for them. My mother told me this. In spite of this, my mother completed her graduation, the first female in the family to do so. My grandfather was so delighted that he brought home a garland and garlanded her – this became a legend in the family.

And there is my husband's family. Rural, conservative, very orthodox they may have been, but I was lucky my husband had an open, scientific mind, that he was proud of my intelligence and supported all my efforts to find my work in life. The time came when our need of money meant that either I had to take up a job, or he had to quit his academic job and get into practice. He did not hesitate. 'I'll give up my job and earn enough money for the children's education and to build a house for ourselves; you go on writing,' he said. At the time he had just got a prestigious fellowship to go to the USA, but he did not think twice about giving it up. I think of my mother-in-law, a shaven widow, who, when she heard that I had got three medals in my journalism course, went off to forage in her ancient tin trunk and came back with five rupees, which she gave us, saying, 'Go out and have coffee.' If this is not being privileged, what is?

When I entered the world of IWE, I began a journey which was not planned, I was travelling on a road which was not mapped, a road with no signposts. I had set out with absolutely no idea of any destination in my mind. I wanted to say some things, I wanted to write, hopefully to be published, and later, even less hopefully, to earn some money, enough for my dignity and self-respect and for the dignity of my work. I got so much more than I ever thought I would; I have met a number of very interesting people I would never have met otherwise. People it was a privilege to meet, like Dr Paul Love, a man whose like I have never seen, and his team at

SCILET in Madurai. And there was P. Lal, who, although recovering from an illness at the time, quoted Keats' *Ode to a Nightingale* during a visit, and spoke of the poem with such love and erudition that I have never forgotten it. I made friends through whom I was able to live, what I can only call, the life of the intellect, however pompous it sounds, something I thought I had lost when I got married, had children and became a householder. I have been able to talk with these friends about everything on the earth, from books and writers to politics, religion and the worsening environment, from the Babri Masjid and the Ram Mandir in Ayodhya (do we need another temple? Or another masjid?), to Donald Trump's latest *faux pas*, from language to literary gossip and, of course, husbands and children.

My friend Laeeq Futehally used to say, tongue-in-cheek, 'Someone should record our conversations.' She liked to read my novels in the manuscript stage, she was the only one apart from my husband and my editor to do so. 'When am I going to get your masterpiece?' she would prod me. Recently, I came across one of her old letters to me, and I found myself chuckling as I read it. What a sense of humour! And yet my eyes were wet as well. I miss her enormously. There was also Anupama Niranjana, who became my window to the Kannada literary world. She was one of the few people at the time with whom I could talk about feminism. She is one of those rare people I know, who, when she got cancer, called it by its name. No euphemisms. I miss her too, a woman with a large heart and great courage.

Today, I have younger friends who take me out of my preoccupation about age. Friends who are with me in the ups and downs of writing and being published, who have been with me in my sorrow. Younger friends, yes, but I think, yet again as I once did, that the mind has no age. I have often thought that if my dining table could talk (most of my chatting with women friends has been at the dining table), what stories it would tell, of both serious matters and trifles, what jokes it would recount, how much laughter it would speak of!

To my own surprise, very late in life, I formed an online group where people could talk about books, about writers and anything else connected to literature. And other things too. I had often rued the fact that only those books which were talked about, or which were on bestseller lists, were read by most people, while there were so many books outside this charmed circle that could give a reader greater pleasure, perhaps. I kept talking about forming some kind of a group to converse about all kinds of books. However, my philosophy of 'I'll do it tomorrow, not today' meant it kept getting postponed. Meenakshi Mukherjee, when I told her about my idea, was very happy. Do it, she said. And then, unexpectedly, she died. I thought I had to do it now in Meenakshi's memory. I made a list of people I knew who would be interested and wrote to them. I had no idea how to form a group, I wrote to each person individually. But my friend Poile Sengupta's daughter, Anasuya, offered to form a Google group and she did. I was warned, 'It won't last long.' I didn't mind. What had I to lose?

It has been nearly ten years now and it is still alive. It has become a lively group. I am proud of this group of readers, writers, translators, editors, teachers, even philanthropists. We can call ourselves international, perhaps, because we have members from Canada, from England from France. Most of us are women (we do have a single man among us, whose presence and ideas are invaluable), women whose thoughts and ideas illuminate my life. We talk, no, we write, not just of literature, but of many things, of women's plight, of politics, of democracy, of freedom and the minority fringe, we talk of life and death and of 'cabbages and kings'. It is something I am very pleased about.

My writing has taken me all over the world, something I never expected. I have travelled a great deal, in the country and outside, on invitations. I have seen some wonderful cities, brought back memories of places and people which have stayed with me. Apart from these journeys, I have made other unexpectedly delightful cross-country forays. John Steinbeck's *Cannery Row* took me from California back to India, to the twelfth-century poet Bilhana and his beautiful poem, with which Steinbeck's book ends. I read the Sanskrit poem decades later, in a translation by Barbara Stoler Miller as *Fantasies of a Love-Thief*. I found great pleasure in reading the lines in the Upanishad that speak of the vastness of the spaces of the heart, which can contain heaven and earth and much else, lines that are so eerily echoed in Emily Dickinson's 'The brain is wider than the sky'. And amazingly, Emily's words are, in turn, close to those of an obscure unlettered Marathi woman, the saint-poet Bahinabai: 'The mind is so small/ as tiny as a poppy seed/ The mind is so large/ the sky cannot hold it.'

Eliot's *The Waste Land* led me to the Upanishads, to the story of Prajapati, who instructed his children with three syllables, Da, Da and Da, which his children rightly interpreted as *Damyata* (have control), *Datta* (give) and *Dayadhvam* (be compassionate). This passage gave me the amazing idea of gods, demons and men all being the children of Prajapati. A mind-boggling thought. I read Michael Frayn's *Headlong*, which took me to Bruegel's paintings and Joyce Carol Oates' reference to Albrecht Dürer in her *American Appetites*, sent me in search of his paintings. And, strangely, an American crime writer, Michael Connelly, gave me an introduction to Hieronymus Bosch's terrible world of sinners and punishment. Donna Tartt's book, *The Goldfinch*, let me into the beauty of Fabritius' painting of the goldfinch (such a still, composed, perfect beauty), and I am still in search of a painting I saw in a museum (which one, I wonder) of a little passage with an open door which Gopal remembers in *A Matter of Time*. The kind of light I remember seeing in that painting makes me think that perhaps it was a Vermeer.

I have listened to music with great pleasure and I have written about music and musicians with equal pleasure. Music continues to haunt me. The image of a performance, the main performer and the support artists grouped together on a stage, communicating with one another throughout the performance through gestures and smiles, stays with me; it is a picture that says much to me about art, about togetherness, about joy in the art. I am sorry that I cannot write another novel with a musician as the main character. Even if a musician-character comes to me, I think it most unlikely that I will be able to write a novel, considering the limited time I now have. But who knows?

Above all, I have lived my life among books, something that I think I always wanted, even when I did not know what I wanted. As a writer, I have done work, which has given me great happiness. Even today, I go to my table in the morning with the eagerness of a girl going to meet her lover. This, in spite of the fact that I now know that literature is a queer animal, full of contradictions, often self-contradictory. You work as hard at it as you do at any other profession; your working day ends, not according to the clock, but when you are tired, or when there's something else you just have to do, or when you have run out of steam. Yet, you are never sure that you will earn any money through this book, and if you do, how much you will earn. You never know, after months, at times after years of working, whether you have produced a dud, or a masterpiece. You have no idea whether a publisher will accept your book, or, if she/he doesn't, why it was rejected.

Even after so many years, no, decades, in the writing business, I know nothing about how reviews work: why some books are reviewed quickly and at length, why others take months to be reviewed, if at all. I have no idea why editors give books for reviews to the people they do, and how someone who has never read anything but that one book by an author, can make pronouncements on the author's work with authority. All that I know is that I write because I have to, that something drives me into writing what I write. And while I'm writing, the book is the most important thing in the world as far as I am concerned. After it is published, I feel distanced from it; it is no longer mine the way it was when I was writing it. It is out in the world and becomes one of many and I have no idea what place it will find in the ocean of literature.

A writer at times asks questions of herself, questions which are difficult to answer: why am I doing this, isolating myself from everyone and from all other things, writing something nobody has asked for, something nobody may want to read? Why do I spend my time, my life, working on something the world does not really need? I don't have the answers, but I know that I envy people whose work makes a direct impact. I envy my husband when he comes home after a day's work, knowing that he has helped some people in the course of the day, made a diagnosis which helps the physician/surgeon to treat the patient. I envy him because he has earned some money at the end of the day. On occasions, when I put down my pen in the evening, I have nothing to show of my day's work, sometimes not even a few pages, or, sometimes, pages which are so unsatisfactory that I have to trash them and begin all over again. As for money, well, the less said the better. Knowing all this, it is heartbreaking when I meet writers, both young and old, who are struggling, hoping that the novel they are writing is the one that publishers and the world are waiting for. They are willing to give up their jobs and devote themselves to writing. They come to me, hoping I can give them an open sesame to the publishing and the literary world. I can't. I can only tell them, or try to tell them, that you can't put the weight of your entire life on writing. It can't take the pressure. Keep your job, hold on to it.

Thankfully, the one big question that is rarely asked of writers is: what is the purpose of literature? Of what use is writing? A question that leaves most writers tongue-tied, hesitant. No one has been able to say with a finality that ends all questions, with a certainty that comes from within, what writing is for. The question is easily answered when it concerns genres other than fiction. Non-fiction, for example, provides knowledge, information, analysis. What does fiction do? Naipaul once called fiction 'made-up stories about made-up people'. The word 'stories' itself makes the genre seem purposeless, or with no serious purpose, for what are stories for, except perhaps to amuse or entertain for a short while and to be forgotten in the next moment? In fact, fiction with a purpose becomes bad fiction. Does anyone today remember Marilyn French's *The Women's Room*? A novel in which every page screamed out its purpose of propagating feminism. As a novel, it was terrible. Embarrassing, even to a feminist sympathiser; all the men were bad, all the women victims. It was almost like the novels that came out in the Soviet era, novels written to acclaim communism and, hopefully, to win a Stalin or a Lenin Prize. When the USSR disintegrated, these unreadable novels were, I am sure, pulped as they deserved to be. And yet to say that writing has no purpose at all is to bring back the ghost of the old argument of 'art for art's sake'. An idea vehemently rejected by different people for different reasons and so hard to support, specially in a country like ours, in which fiction is ideally supposed to be used as a tool for social reform.

'Fiction can provide a form of truth': the words of Sara Paretsky. But how does one know what the truth is? It is a question that has no answer. A classic story in our mythology is that of Raja

Harishchandra, a man who was an embodiment of truth and is therefore called Satya Harishchandra. However, when I read the story some years back, I discovered to my astonishment that the idea of truth in it is very different from the way we see truth today. In Harishchandra's story, truth means honouring one's word. It seems to me that what fiction can do is to give a reader the many nuances, the many different shades and the complexity of life. It leaves a reader, not with answers, but questions over which the reader will need to ponder, to try and find her own answers.

'Writers bear witness to an age': Toni Morrison's words, which, like much of her writing, have a Biblical ring to them. And which carry a hint of the truth. Yes, fiction does give us a picture of an age, an era; it gives us a picture of the times, of people's lives, of their preoccupations, their moral struggles. 'When I wrote *Doctor Zhivago*,' Boris Pasternak said in an interview, 'I had the feeling of an immense debt towards my contemporaries. It was an attempt to pay it … it seemed to me that it was my duty to make a statement about our epoch.' But in the course of making a statement about an epoch, he also wrote a wonderful novel. Like Alexander Solzhenitsyn, who also wrote about his epoch in *Cancer Ward*, in *The First Circle* and in *One Day in the Life of Ivan Denisovich* – all amazing books. If these novels had been bad, what they were trying to say would have reached nowhere, no one. As far as I am concerned, if I were to think of the unimaginable, of a life without books, a world without literature, I would see a world without meaning. A world in which we would have no understanding of what this life is about, because it is literature that gives us glimpses of some meaning in the chaos in the midst of which we live. But no individual writer, however good, or however great, can play any kind of a meaningful role. Only a community of writers can spell out the ethos of an age, only together can they present an entire picture, cover the whole canvas, only a community of writers can make an impact, however small, on society.

Sadly, this kind of a community is what IWE lacks. We are too divided. But the brief interlude of togetherness, when writers came together to protest, gives me some hope that we will never go back to being helpless, voiceless, impotent. Hope that the greater the peril, the more humans will learn to look into themselves for their innate strength. And hope, after all, is what all humans need. I remember the lines in Eliot's *Little Gidding*:

'And all shall be well and
All manner of thing shall be well.'

I had loved the words when I first read them, they had filled me with happiness and excitement; they seemed like both a prayer and a benediction. And it seemed like a miracle, an omen, when I read that the words had first been uttered by a woman, a mystic, a theologian, an anchorite of the twelfth century, Lady Julian of Norwich, words which had come to her in a dream, spoken to her by Jesus. Had Eliot taken them from her? It doesn't matter. The Sanskrit shloka, which begins with *Sarvepi sukhinah santu* (may everyone be happy), and ends with *ma kascit dukhabhag bhavet* (may no one know sorrow), expresses almost the same thing, but as a hope not an assertion. Writers make it possible for words, for ideas, never to die.

When I look back at the many years of my life, I realise I have been privileged in this as well, in being granted the gift of the love of beauty, something which has made my life richer and fuller. It is this love of beauty, which made me love the colours in my first book, *Pedro Picks Coffee in Brazil*, made me love and remember the paintings I so often pored over in the *The World's Greatest Books*. Love of beauty which made me, later, respond to the paintings of Rembrandt, Vermeer, Goya, El Greco, Gainsborough and so many others, some of the originals of which I have been fortunate enough to see in museums abroad. It is love of beauty which has made me drown myself in the magic of words, of language, of books. (Look at the words 'tick without the tock'. So beautifully evocative.)

I was a teenager when I read Elizabeth Bowen's *Friends and Relations*. I read it, having no clue to its writer, to the context of the book, ignorant of the English society it was located in. But something in me responded to the book and it stayed with me; the book is still with me. Today I know it is a beautiful novel, intense, with a spare and austere beauty. It is love of beauty which made me lose myself in the amazing beauty of music. The music of Bhimsen Joshi, of Ashwini Bhide Deshpande and many others, has given me an entry into another world. Love of beauty has added the excitement to my life which, to an outsider, it may seem to utterly lack.

'Some people are born to make art,' a character in Ann Patchett's *Bel Canto* says, 'and others are born to appreciate it. Not everyone can be an artist. There have to be those who witness the art, who love and appreciate what they have been privileged to see.' I have been specially privileged because I have been both an artist and a lover of art. I am always amazed at the opinion that art is something separate from life, that it has nothing to do with real life, that it is merely a spare-time passing interest, of no real importance. Auden's *Musée des Beaux Arts*, one of my favourite poems, brilliantly shows the tangential but strong connection between life and art, the first lines, 'About suffering they were never wrong,/ The Old Masters: how well they understood/ Its human position …' spelling out the prescience and the omniscience of art.

My entire life has been lived by my faith that it is art and a moral core in us that have given human life its greatest value. In fact, I believe that it is in art that humans find moral values. People who destroy works of art are paving the way to a dreadful nihilism, a loss of all values. Whether it is the destruction of the Bamiyan Buddhas, or the vandalising of an M.F. Husain painting, whether it is the banning of a book, a play or a film, or the burning of books, it is a sin committed against human creativity, which is the flame that illuminates life.

As I come closer to the 'requisite ending', I find some satisfaction in thinking that I have brought, or at least tried to bring, women's lives centre stage. I have told their stories, which most male narrators would not have thought worth telling. I have tried to destroy the stereotypes of women, and written of them as human beings. I have seen changes in women's lives, in the way they are regarded, though the changes are not as radical as they should have been; it has always been one step forward and two steps backward. Change, however, there is. Feminism, which in its first wave, during the sixties and seventies of the last century, was ridiculed, belittled and ignored, seems to have got a fresh lease of life today; it is more confident, more positive, often better accepted.

I think of a poem of Amrita Pritam (quoted to me, again, by my dear friend Amrita Bhalla), which speaks of a game in which a woman could pick up one of two chits. Each time she picked up the one that said *suno* (listen), never the one that said *kaho* (speak). I think that things have changed and that a woman picks up the *kaho* chit as often as she does the *suno* one. But to speak is not enough. There has to be a listener to make the communication complete. And this is the change that has now happened: the world, which was deaf to women's voices, has now begun listening to them – to some extent. Like the recent movement of '#Metoo', in which women suddenly began speaking out about the sexual harassment they had to endure, and the world sat up and took note. And therefore, perhaps, there is now hope that men will no longer take liberties with women who are in their power. Or with any woman, for that matter. And if they do, the woman will no longer be silent, but she will speak out. I think of the statement, 'My daughter is Jyoti Singh', with a sense of awe.

Yet, I have to admit that there seems to be some kind of a backlash against the increasing awareness that women now have about their real place in the world. Strangely, despite this, I still have hope, because women are no longer as complicit in their own suppression as they were once. I see hope too, not only in women Directors and CEOs, but in the girls I have seen on rural roads in Tamil Nadu, in Kerala, in a village near Bangalore, confidently cycling to school. I saw hope in a group of schoolgirls in Konkan, Maharashtra, waiting for the boat to take them across the river to school. These girls wore headscarves, but the faces under those headscarves were bright, eager and smiling, like the faces of children should be.

As I said, there is sadness in coming to the end of a book. Yet there is relief, too, because I can now do all the things I have put off, thinking, I'll do it when I finish this book. I'll take time off and do nothing for a few days; I can now read all the books I have put away lest I be tempted. But there is also the happiness of feeling something new stir in me, something which has been waiting patiently until I finish with the book I am working on. And there's the fear of having to look at the pile of blank pages, knowing that I have to fill them, that I have to go through the struggle of writing a book all over again.

At this moment, however, I am not sure of anything, I have no idea whether I will write one more novel, or whether it is over for me. For the massive, almost unimaginably cruel blow that I received, even as I was completing this book, a bereavement that has laid me and my family truly low, so that I feel I can never rise again, makes me think I will never be able to write any more. If that is how it is going to be, I am willing to accept it. So be it.

I said that IWE and I have travelled together all these decades. Perhaps I should have said that I have been a small part of the story of IWE, for IWE will continue even after I have gone. Not being a seer, I have no idea which way IWE will go, what it will become. A more mature literature? A more self-confident one, standing on its own feet, depending only on the response of its readers? A literature which will be recognised as being relevant to the lives of the people it talks about? Whichever road it takes, there is too little time left to me to expect to see any of this. It does not matter. This journey has been a wonderful one. At times, I feel as if I have lived in a constant state of open-mouthed wonder about the world, at finding myself where I am: a part of the community of writers, part of a long chain of story-tellers, connected to all those who threw a magic ring round people with the words 'once upon a time'. This is something I cherish as the greatest gift given to me in this life.

www.ingramcontent.com/pod-product-compliance
Lightning Source LLC
LaVergne TN
LVHW010307070526
838199LV00065B/5470